VMware vSphere™ 4 Administration
Instant Reference

VMware vSphere™ 4 Administration
Instant Reference

Scott Lowe

Jason W. McCarty

Matthew K. Johnson

Wiley Publishing, Inc.

Acquisitions Editor: Agatha Kim
Development Editor: Candace English
Technical Editor: Tom Howarth
Production Editor: Dassi Zeidel
Copy Editor: Liz Welch
Editorial Manager: Pete Gaughan
Production Manager: Tim Tate
Vice President and Executive Group Publisher: Richard Swadley
Vice President and Publisher: Neil Edde
Book Designer and Compositor: Happenstance Type-O-Rama, Maureen Forys
Proofreader: Rebecca Rider
Indexer: Robert Swanson
Project Coordinator, Cover: Lynsey Stanford
Cover Designer: Ryan Sneed
Cover Image: iStockPhoto

Library of Congress Cataloging-in-Publication Data

Lowe, Scott, 1970–
  VMware vSphere 4 administration instant reference / Scott Lowe, Jase McCarty, Matthew K. Johnson. — 1st ed.
      p. cm.
   ISBN 978-0-470-52072-7 (pbk.)
   1. VMware. 2. Virtual computer systems. I. McCarty, Jason W. II. Johnson, Matthew K., 1974– III. Title.
   QA76.9.V5L6735 2010
   005.4'3--dc22
                                                    2009043716

Dear Reader,

Thank you for choosing *VMware vSphere 4 Administration Instant Reference*. This book is part of a family of premium-quality Sybex books, all of which are written by outstanding authors who combine practical experience with a gift for teaching.

Sybex was founded in 1976. More than 30 years later, we're still committed to producing consistently exceptional books. With each of our titles, we're working hard to set a new standard for the industry. From the paper we print on, to the authors we work with, our goal is to bring you the best books available.

I hope you see all that reflected in these pages. I'd be very interested to hear your comments and get your feedback on how we're doing. Feel free to let me know what you think about this or any other Sybex book by sending me an email at nedde@wiley.com. If you think you've found a technical error in this book, please visit http://sybex.custhelp.com. Customer feedback is critical to our efforts at Sybex.

Best regards,

Neil Edde
Vice President and Publisher
Sybex, an Imprint of Wiley

I dedicate this book to my Lord and Savior, who renews my strength (Isaiah 40:13). Moving from one book directly into a second book has been a real challenge, and only in the Lord did I find the strength to finish. I also dedicate this book to my kids, who weren't happy about the fact that I started writing a second book so quickly after finishing up the first. Thank you for your patience and understanding! Finally, I dedicate this book to my wife Crystal, who continues to be a constant source of inspiration and joy.

—Scott

To my family, who has made me the person I am today.

—Jason

Acknowledgments

Where to start? I'll start with Jase McCarty and Matthew Johnson, who were gracious enough to allow me to join them in writing this book. Guys, it has been great working with you on this book, and I hope that we have the opportunity to do so again in the future.

I'd also like to thank all the fine folks from Wiley, who continue to be a tremendous pleasure to work with. I would ask the same question I asked with my first book—"Who's ready for another one?"—but I'm not sure that I'm ready for a third book just yet. Don't worry, Agatha—when I'm ready for another book, I'll be sure to let you know.

A big thank you goes to Tom Howarth and Rick Scherer, the technical editors, for helping me provide the most technically accurate writing possible. Kudos to Tom—who is British—for remembering not to constantly remind me that it's *virtualisation*, not *virtualization*!

Finally, I'd like to thank all the hardworking members of the VMware community. There is such a tremendous community of forum participants, bloggers, and Twitter users (Twitterers?) who are constantly sharing useful information. Thanks to such people as Eric Siebert, Steve Beaver, Ken Cline, Scott Herold, Duncan Epping, Ed Haletky, Eric Sloof, Mike Laverick, Jason Boche, and Rich Brambley. I know that I have benefited on more than one occasion from their willingness to share what they've learned. To all of you—and the many, many more that I didn't name—thank you.

—Scott Lowe

I would like to thank Sybex for the opportunity to be a member of this project. I was honored to be asked to be a part of it. I would like to thank Matthew Johnson for being my wingman from the beginning of this project. He and I have been in lockstep on the direction of this book, and I thank him for his contributions. I would like to thank Tom Howarth for his technical skills, and this book benefited from his years of experience working as a technical editor. Tom brought a seasoned and objective approach to ensuring content was accurate as well as complete. I would like to thank Scott Lowe for becoming a part

x   Acknowledgments

of this project. His expertise and aggressive input made a significant impact on the completion of this book. I would like to thank Agatha Kim and Candace English for their guidance, tremendous effort, and behind-the-scenes work. Without them we would certainly not have succeeded. Agatha is a seasoned acquisitions editor who kept the tempo and pace of this project on track. Candace is an exceptional developmental editor who acted as my glue when my content did not seem to fit just right. Finally, I have to finish by giving thanks to my wife Toni and my children, Emma, Ethan, and Parker. They have been my best source of strength throughout my professional career and my personal life. I would not have been able to achieve the goals, for myself or my family, without their continued support and love.

—Jason W. McCarty

Even at a young age I demonstrated an uncanny ability to be able to take any process or system and find ways to make that system work more efficiently, to streamline it and leave it better than when I first came across it. From the very humble days when I worked at a pizza place, I made improvements in how to make and prepare food. And throughout my professional life I have always remained true to that ability from my time working in finance, redesigning Excel and Access databases, to my time working in IT, finding better ways to accomplish tasks. Process improvement is the one task where I am at my best. And throughout all the challenges it has always been my loving mother who has encouraged and guided my passions in life. To her I dedicate this book and say thank you for all your support and love.

I would also like to take a moment to say thank you to Dan Liptak, Steve Beaver, Sonny Noto, Randy Jones, Patricia Jones, and Cheryl Eagan—each person contributed to helping me get here. Lastly I would like to thank my fellow authors, Jase and Scott, for contributing so much of their personal time to this project.

—Matthew Johnson

About the Authors

Scott Lowe

Scott Lowe is an author, consultant, and blogger who focuses on virtualization, storage, and other enterprise technologies. As the national technical lead for the virtualization practice at ePlus Technology, Scott has been involved in planning, designing, deploying, and troubleshooting VMware virtualization environments for a range of companies both large and small. He also provides technical leadership and training for the entire virtualization practice at a national level. Scott has provided virtualization expertise to companies such as BB&T, NetApp, PPD, Progress Energy, and more.

Scott's experience also extends into a number of other technologies, such as storage area networks (SANs), directory services, and Ethernet/IP networking. His list of industry certifications and accreditations include titles from VMware, Microsoft, and NetApp, among others. In addition, Scott was awarded a VMware vExpert award for his role in the VMware community, one of only 300 people worldwide to have been recognized by VMware for their contributions.

As an author, Scott has contributed to numerous online magazines focused on VMware and related virtualization technologies. He is regularly quoted as a virtualization expert in virtualization news stories. This is his second published book. His first book, *Mastering VMware vSphere 4*, also by Sybex, was published in August 2009.

Scott is perhaps most well known for his acclaimed virtualization blog at http://blog.scottlowe.org. VMware, Microsoft, and other virtualization industry leaders regularly refer to content on his site. It is here that Scott shares his love of technology and virtualization with his readers through a wide selection of technical articles.

Jason W. McCarty

Jason McCarty (VCP2/3/4, VMware vExpert 2009) is currently a senior systems engineer with an ASP component of Equifax Inc., in Baton Rouge, LA. As the team lead and virtualization architect, Jason is responsible for managing a datacenter that delivers loan-origination software to banks, credit unions, and other lending institutions across North America. Jason's education includes a master's of science in engineering technology, a bachelor's of science in electronic engineering technology, and an associate's degree in computer information technology, all of which have contributed to his technical and business success. Jason's background spans approximately 20 years, with technical experience in a wide variety of platforms, and business experience in areas including finance, insurance, academia, and military operations. In addition to his technical and business experience, Jason has taught technology courses as an adjunct instructor at Tulane University College in New Orleans, LA, for three years and at the University of Phoenix in New Orleans, LA, and Baton Rouge, LA for five years. Jason is active in the VMware Community Forums, and has obtained the rank of Virtuoso. He has presented on various topics through the years and maintains a technical blog on his website at http://jasemccarty.com.

Matthew Johnson

Matthew Johnson (VCP, CCNA, MCSA) is currently a systems engineer for one of the largest hospitals in the country, managing their virtualization infrastructure. He is tasked with ensuring the hospital's disaster recovery efforts are effective for virtualization as well as setting up, maintaining, and upgrading VMware virtualization. With five years of virtualization experience working for Fortune 100 and other large corporations, Matthew brings a wealth of knowledge to this book. He has documented a working V2P process, is a moderator and contributor on the VMware forums, holds his VCP certification, and has been a featured speaker at VMworld(s) and other virtualization events. He has an undergraduate degree in finance and is currently pursuing his MBA while continuing to work full time with virtualization.

Contents

Introduction

For those of us who have been working in the virtualization industry since its earliest days, it's hard to imagine what datacenters were like without virtualization. Still there are many organizations that have yet to adopt virtualization within their datacenter. With the release of VMware vSphere 4, VMware's flagship enterprise-class virtualization solution, VMware aims to change that reality.

However, even though virtualization has many benefits—not the least of which include reducing your hardware footprint, enabling faster server provisioning, and simplifying disaster recovery—some people feel that virtualization also has a steep learning curve. IT professionals who want to become more familiar with virtualization need to learn about terms like VMotion, Storage VMotion, VMware Fault Tolerance, and VMkernel interfaces. All these new terms and new technologies can seem confusing to someone not familiar with how all the pieces fit together.

In addition, virtualization sometimes forces IT professionals to think differently about how to solve old challenges. The "traditional" way of doing things often isn't the best way of handling something after you've virtualized your datacenter.

This book is intended to help address these concerns. For administrators who might be new to virtualization, this book explains how virtualization works, what the components are, and how these components fit together—while doing so in a hands-on, how-to approach. We believe this approach will help new vSphere administrators come up to speed quickly.

For more experienced administrators, such as those familiar with previous versions of VMware's virtualization product suite but not VMware vSphere 4, this book will fill in the gaps through the step-by-step review of vSphere's features and functionality.

While this book isn't an in-depth, highly technical view of VMware vSphere—that's what you'll find in *Mastering VMware vSphere 4*, also from Sybex—it is a comprehensive reference guide for finding information quickly, just when you need it. We hope that it will earn its place on your reference bookshelf as a book to which you can return when you need a little extra guidance on how something works or how to perform a task within VMware vSphere.

What Is Covered in This Book

This book is written as a blend of explanatory text and "cookbook-style" recipes that are intended to help administrators become more familiar with installing, configuring, managing, and monitoring a virtual environment using the VMware vSphere product suite. We start by introducing the vSphere product suite and all of its great features. After introducing all the bells and whistles, this book details how to install the product, including considerations and steps you should take to upgrade to VMware vSphere from VMware Infrastructure 3 (VI3). After showing you how to install vSphere, we move on to configuring VMware vSphere to meet your specific needs. This includes configuring VMware vSphere's extensive networking and storage functionality. Next, the book moves into virtual machine creation and management, importing and exporting virtual machines, security, and finally monitoring and resource management.

You can read this book from cover to cover to gain an understanding of the vSphere product suite in preparation for a new virtual environment, but you might find it more useful as a reference work to which you can refer when you're stuck and can't remember exactly how something works. If you're an IT professional who is new to virtualization with VMware vSphere, this book is intended to help you hit the ground running.

Here is a glance at what's in each chapter:

Chapter 1: Introduction to vSphere   Chapter 1 takes a look at the features of VMware vSphere 4. This includes vSphere's "legacy" features—those features that were also present in earlier versions of VMware's enterprise virtualization products—as well as the new features specific to VMware vSphere 4. This feature overview should provide you with some idea of how VMware vSphere can address business problems.

Chapter 2: Installing and Configuring ESX and ESXi   VMware ESX and VMware ESXi are the foundation of the vSphere product suite, and Chapter 2 provides information on how to install and configure both VMware ESX and VMware ESXi.

Chapter 3: Installing and Configuring vCenter Server   Many of the advanced features within the VMware vSphere product suite are only present when you also have vCenter Server, the management server for VMware ESX/ESXi. Chapter 3 describes how to install and configure vCenter Server to manage your ESX/ESXi hosts and your virtual machines.

Chapter 4: Understanding Licensing   VMware vSphere 4 uses an entirely new licensing mechanism. This new licensing mechanism, how to assign and manage licenses, and how to review current license usage are all covered in Chapter 4.

Chapter 5: Upgrading from VI3 to vSphere   Perhaps you already use VMware Infrastructure 3 but are looking to upgrade to VMware vSphere 4. This chapter provides information on the upgrade process, which tasks should come first, and the various methods for upgrading the different components.

Chapter 6: Creating and Managing Virtual Networking   Chapter 6 provides information and procedures for creating and configuring VMware vSphere's virtual networking features. This includes vNetwork Standard Switches as well as the new vNetwork Distributed Switches.

Chapter 7: Configuring and Managing Storage   Storage is an essential part of every virtualization implementation, so Chapter 7 covers the different types of storage that are supported by VMware vSphere 4 and how to configure each of them.

Chapter 8: High Availability and Business Continuity   Chapter 8 discusses the different ways that administrators can configure VMware vSphere to provide high availability for virtual machines. Features like VMware High Availability, VM failure monitoring, and VMware Fault Tolerance are all included in the discussion.

Chapter 9: Managing Virtual Machines   Managing virtual machines is a pretty broad topic, but Chapter 9 attempts to cover it by discussing the most frequently performed tasks. Tasks such as creating virtual machines, adding or removing hardware from virtual machines, managing virtual machine power state, and managing virtual hardware versions are all covered in this chapter.

Chapter 10: Importing and Exporting Virtual Machines   Creating new virtual machines sometimes means converting physical systems to virtual machines. This type of migration, a physical-to-virtual migration, is one of a couple of different types of imports discussed in Chapter 10. This chapter also provides information on how to export VMs out of VMware vSphere for use with other VMware virtualization products.

Chapter 11: Configuring Security Chapter 11 covers security-related aspects of VMware vSphere, such as role-based access controls and how to harden VMware ESX and ESXi.

Chapter 12: Managing Resources and Performance Chapter 12 covers the important topics of resource management and performance, two areas that are closely related. This chapter discusses how to allocate resources, how to modify resource allocation behaviors, and how to identify performance concerns related to resource allocation.

Appendix A: Fundamentals of the Command-Line Interface To help build your proficiency with command-line tasks, this appendix focuses on navigating through the Service Console command line and performing management, configuration, and troubleshooting tasks.

Who Should Buy This Book

This book is for IT professionals looking to strengthen their knowledge of constructing and managing a virtual infrastructure on VMware vSphere 4. Although the book can be helpful for those new to IT, we assume the target reader has the following:

- A basic understanding of networking architecture
- Experience working in a Microsoft Windows environment
- Experience managing DNS and DHCP
- A basic understanding of how virtualization differs from traditional physical infrastructures
- A basic understanding of hardware and software components in standard x86 and x64 computing

How to Contact the Authors

We welcome feedback from you about this book or about books you'd like to see from us in the future. You can reach Scott Lowe by writing to scott.lowe@scottlowe.org or by visiting his blog at http://blog.scottlowe.org; Jason by emailing jase@jasemccarty.com or by visiting his blog at http://www.jasemccarty.com; and Matthew by writing juchespam@yahoo.com.

PART I

Building a VMware vSphere Environment

IN THIS PART ❯

1

Introduction to vSphere

IN THIS CHAPTER, YOU WILL LEARN TO:

V Sphere is here! Administrators who have been around for a while may think of the new product as the fourth generation, or simply VMware Infrastructure 4. However, the name vSphere better aligns the new product with the direction that virtualization is taking, and this version of VMware introduces many new and promising features. Not since the introduction of VMware Infrastructure 3 (VI3) has there been this much excitement surrounding new features that promise to continue to revolutionize the infrastructure of the modern and evolving datacenter. The most sought-after three features—VMotion, Distributed Resource Scheduler (DRS), High Availability (HA)—have been improved and are better than ever. And of course a new version wouldn't be complete without additional new features—VMware has worked hard to make this release even bigger than the VI3 release.

Understand the Legacy Features of vSphere

Welcome to the legacy features of vSphere. Why devote an entire section to them? Because they serve as the foundation that brings tremendous flexibility to managing an x86 environment. One of the best is vMotion, which offers the ability to relocate a running virtual machine or server from one physical location to another without any downtime. Another legacy feature is Dynamic Resource Scheduler, which you use to make sure that your servers are getting all the resources they deserve. Finally, with High Availability you'll never have to rush into the office to address bad hardware. There are other legacy features, but we'll cover only the best!

VMotion

The last major version release of VMotion was VI3, released in 2006. VMotion remains one of the most powerful features of virtualization today. With VI3, you can perform work on underlying hosts during business hours rather than having to wait until the wee hours of the morning or weekends to upgrade BIOSs or firmware or do something as simple as add more memory to a host. VMotion requires that each underlying host have a CPU that uses the same instruction set, because, after all, moving a running virtual machine (VM) from one physical host to another physical host without any downtime is a phenomenal feat. VMware runs on top of the Virtual Machine File System (VMFS); Windows still runs on New Technology File System (NTFS), but the underlying file system is VMFS3. VMFS3 allows for multiple access, and that is how one host can pass a running VM to another host without downtime or interruptions. It is important to realize that even momentary downtime can be critical for applications and databases. Zero downtime when moving a VM from one host to another physical host is crucial.

Unfortunately, there is no way to move from Intel to AMD, or vice versa. In the past there were even issues going from an older Intel CPU to a newer Intel CPU.

VMware has several years of experience mastering virtualization while the competitors are playing catch-up. Furthermore, VMware has explored many approaches to virtualization and has seen firsthand where some approaches fall short and where some excel.

One downside to VMotion is that the technology does require shared storage, but the virtual machine files do not move from that shared storage during the logical transition. If, for example, you have to change the virtual machine's physical location, you must first power down the VM and then "migrate" it from one logical unit number (LUN) or hard drive to another LUN or hard drive.

Another possible downside to VMotion is that traditional Intrusion Detection Systems (IDS) and Intrusion Prevention Systems (IPS) may not work as originally designed. Part of the reason for this is that the traffic of VMs that are communicating with one another inside a host never leaves the host and therefore cannot be inspected. Virtual appliances are being developed to address this concern as they have the ability to run side by side VMs.

Since uptime is important, VMware developed Storage VMotion so that the physical location of a running VM can be changed, again without any downtime and without losing any transactional information. Obviously Storage VMotion is very exciting because one of the reasons that virtualization is the hottest technology in IT today is the flexibility it brings to the datacenter (compared to running servers the old-fashioned way in a physical environment).

There are other ways to leverage the technology. Virtual machines can be moved on the fly from shared storage to local storage if you need to perform maintenance on shared storage or if LUNs have to be moved to other hosts. Imagine moving a physical server by simply clicking on a new rack in your datacenter and then clicking OK; the move then takes place without any downtime or sweat on your part—wouldn't that ability be useful for a variety of needs and tasks every day?

VMware Cluster

A VMware cluster allows you to pool the resources of several physical hosts and create logical and physical boundaries within a virtual infrastructure or datacenter. Some organizations may want to create several clusters in their vCenter (formerly VMware Virtual Center) based on functionality—for example, a demilitarized zone (DMZ) cluster or an application cluster. You may want to create a VMware cluster based on the type of LUNs, their speed, maybe their size, or the type of appliance they represent—for example, EMC DMX versus Left Hand Networks. Networking teams may not always want to present all networks to all hosts in the cluster. By creating pools of resources, you can manage these assets and work may be performed on individual clusters rather than the entire infrastructure.

What kind of resources are pooled? CPU, memory, networking bandwidth, storage, and physical hosts are all shared by the VMs that are defined on the specific cluster. A good rule of thumb is to have sufficient capacity to run extra VMs in the event that one or more ESX hosts go down. For example, a cluster with three hosts that runs at 50 percent of resources on each host could probably handle one host failure; the remaining two hosts would then take on 25 percent of the load from the failed host and the cluster would be running at 75 percent of resources. In this scenario, a second host failure would overwhelm the remaining host and some virtual machines would not be able to start on the last host. Obviously, you should plan for extra capacity when designing clusters if failover is important.

Distributed Resource Scheduler

Another feature introduced with VI3 is DRS, which helps you load-balance workloads across a VMware cluster. Advanced algorithms constantly analyze the cluster environment and even use VMotion to move a running server or VM from one host to another without any downtime. You can specify that DRS perform these actions automatically. Say, for instance, that a VM needs more CPU or memory and the host it is running on lacks those resources. With the automatic settings you specify, DRS will use VMotion to move the VM to another host that has more resources available. DRS can be set to automatically make needed adjustments any time of the day or night or to issue recommendations instead. Two circumstances that often trigger such events are when an Active Directory server is used a lot in the morning for logins and when backups are run. A DRS-enabled cluster shares all the CPU and memory bandwidth as one unified unit for the VMs to use.

DRS is extremely important because in the past VMware administrators had to do their best to analyze the needs of their VMs, often without a lot of quantitative information. DRS changed the way the virtualization game was played and revolutionized the datacenter; you can load VMs onto a cluster and the technology will sort out all the variables in real time and make necessary adjustments. DRS is easy to use, and many administrators boast about how many VMotions their environments have completed since inception.

For example, let's say an admin virtualizes a Microsoft Exchange server, a SQL Server, an Active Directory server, and a couple of heavily used application servers and puts all of them on one host in a cluster. The week before, another admin virtualized several older NT servers that were very lightweight; because those servers didn't use very much CPU, memory, network, or disk input/output (I/O), the admin put those servers on another host. At this point, the two hosts are off balance based on their workloads: one host has too little to do because its servers have low utilization, and the other host is getting killed with heavily used applications. Before DRS, a third admin would have to look at all the servers running on these two hosts and determine how to distribute the VMs evenly across the hosts. On average, administrators would have to use a bit of ingenuity—along with trial and error—to figure out how to balance the needs of each server with the underlying hardware. DRS analyzes these needs and moves VMs when they need more resources so that you can attend to other, more pressing issues.

High Availability

When CIOs and management types begin learning about virtualization, one of their most common fears is "putting all their eggs in one basket." "If all our servers are on one host, what happens if that host fails?" This is a smart question to ask, and one that VMware prepared for when they revealed The HA, or High Availability, feature of VI3. A virtual infrastructure is controlled by vCenter, which is aware of all the hosts that are in its control and all the VMs that are on those hosts. Each host has a "heartbeat," and if that heartbeat is lost, vCenter believes the host is down and tasks other hosts with restarting the VMs that were affected. VMware recommends a strategy referred to as N+1. This simply means that your cluster should include enough hosts (N) so that if one fails there is enough capacity to restart the VMs on the other host(s). Shared storage among the hosts is a requirement of HA. When a host fails and HA starts, there is a small window of downtime, roughly the same amount that you might expect from a reboot. If the organization has alerting software, a page or email message might be sent indicating a problem, but at other times, this happens so quickly that no alerts are triggered. The goal of virtualization is to keep the uptime of production servers high: hosts can go down, but if servers keep running, you can address the challenge during business hours.

NOTE VMotion is not utilized in a High Availability scenario.

VMware vCenter Converter

If your organization is new to virtualization, VMware vCenter Converter is handy. It's a plug-in to vCenter in the Enterprise version, but there is also a free stand-alone download that lets you convert physical servers into the virtual infrastructure without downtime—thanks to a technology that enables incremental changes to be captured during the physical to virtual (P2V) conversion process. This application works extremely well, and you can use it to convert a single server or multiple servers, move a VM from a workstation or another virtual infrastructure, resize hard drives, or work with partitions. Organizations are choosing virtualization because they have the flexibility to convert already-built working servers, or if the need exists, rebuild a server from a known good build. Both Windows and Linux servers can be virtualized, and there is interoperability with other third-party formats, such as Norton Ghost, Acronis, and Windows Virtual PC (a feature of Windows 7).

VMware vCenter Update Manager

A second plug-in that has proved to be invaluable is VMware vCenter Update Manager. This feature allows for a baseline creation that represents a security standard. A baseline, for example, would be one host or virtual machine that has been configured to be the golden image; it has all the right patches and all other hosts or VMs should have this level of configuration. You can then apply this baseline to all hosts or select Microsoft and Linux virtual machines, and the technology will remediate updates and apply them to the infrastructure, thus saving you valuable time. The technology will automatically place one host in a cluster in maintenance mode, migrate the VMs to another host, update the host, reboot, exit maintenance mode, and move to the next host to continue the process. You can remediate one host at a time to achieve a fine level of control in environments or organizations that have high visibility or special needs, or you can remediate an entire cluster and sit back to watch it happen.

Another outstanding feature of VMware vCenter Update Manager is its ability to patch offline virtual machines. Obviously not possible with physical servers, this feature offers a level of security compliance far superior to datacenters without virtual infrastructure.

Although this may not sound like a breakthrough in technology, in the old days administrators would have to go to the VMware site; download several patches with long, cryptic names; copy the patches to each host; clear off the virtual machines; open the command line; run an even more cryptic command to work with each file on each ESX host; reboot—and do the same thing over on each and every host. Now with the click of a mouse, VMware vCenter Update Manager does all these steps quickly and efficiently. Furthermore, since a baseline is utilized, each host receives the exact same build. No longer will you need to worry whether you applied every patch to every host; the technology handles this task for you.

VMware Capacity Planner

A third plug-in we'll look at is VMware Capacity Planner. When tasked with virtualizing a physical datacenter, this tool enables you to gather quantitative data from physical servers to better understand which servers are the best candidates for virtualization. Of course, the underlying premise of virtualizing is that on average, most physical servers use significantly less than 10 percent of the resources available on a server; it only makes sense to take a handful of those servers and place them on a host to achieve better utilization of the company's hardware. VMware Capacity Planner analyzes over time how much CPU, memory, disk I/O, and network bandwidth a server uses, and how much it isn't using. As any tenured VMware administrator will attest, VMs need less CPU and less memory than their physical counterparts. Capacity Planner is the quantitative friend in the virtualization journey.

VMware Consolidated Backup

A virtual infrastructure would not be complete without a backup solution, and so VMware introduced its Consolidated Backup feature back in 2006. The traditional approach to backing up virtual machines (agent-based backups) utilizes a lot of system resources from a host; Consolidated Backup relieves that unnecessary pressure by providing a centralized and agent-free process to back up virtual machines. A separate physical server or servers that have access to the shared storage will pull the data through their own network instead of pulling the data through the ESX host, thereby reducing the load on the ESX/ESXi servers and allowing the host to provide its resources for performance instead of backups.

NOTE   ESXi hosts are both bare-metal enterprise-class hypervisors that function as hosts for virtual machines.

In earlier releases the backup tool did not enjoyed widespread adoption. Backing up was done mostly via the command line, and several physical servers were required to back up the virtual infrastructure. In addition, the backup tool wasn't terribly easy to use for file-level restores. However, VMware Consolidated Backup can be integrated with backup tools and technologies that already exist as part of your organization's datacenter. Full and incremental file level backups are much easier to perform in this release.

vSphere Client

One of many areas where VMware excels over its competitors is management features. There are several ways to interact with a VMware infrastructure, chief among them vSphere Client. (The other methods, vSphere Web Access and VMware Service Console [vSphere's command-line interface], are discussed in upcoming sections.) You can use vSphere Client to connect directly to vCenter or directly to a host; however, we recommend that you use vCenter as the central administrative unit for the infrastructure. vSphere Client is installed on a Windows machine and with it you can do the following:

- Configure vCenter
- Create virtual machines
- Monitor, manage, and adjust settings for hosts, VMs, and vCenter

vSphere Client is not a tool for end users; it's intended for VMware administrators only. As tools go, this is a great one. The user interface is intuitive and the features are easy to navigate. You can open up your favorite browser, enter the server name of vCenter or any ESX hostname, and download the client.

VMware Service Console

The command-line interface, or VMware Service Console, is an interface used to configure, manage, and monitor an ESX host from a granular level. The Service Console is in essence the first virtual machine on an ESX, and it serves as a communication device between the administrator and the hypervisor. ESXi uses a similar command line called the vSphere Command-Line Interface. For all intents and purposes it performs all the same functions that the Service Console does. An interesting recent development is that PowerShell is starting to be used to configure and manage the infrastructure as well, and this will open up many powerful opportunities for scripting.

> **NOTE** A hypervisor is a high speed scheduler. It hands out resources (CPU, memory, network, disk) to the virtual machines asking for them, very quickly.

vSphere Web Access

The final interface is the vSphere Web Access; this access method allows for basic VM management and configuration and is often given to end users that need access to their respective virtual machines but not beyond their sphere of influence. This method is useful because there is a limit on how many vCenter clients can connect to vCenter without impacting performance.

Understand the New Features of vSphere

The list of new features is a lot longer than what we will introduce here, but the following sections detail some of the most exciting ones.

64 Bit

First and foremost, ESX has gone to 64-bit technology for both the Service Console and the VMkernel. Because of this, an ESX host can now handle greater workloads: 64 logical CPUs and 320 VMs per host, with a total of up to 512 virtual CPUs per host and 1TB of host memory. The difference between 32 and 64 bit is that with 64 bit you can achieve higher consolidation ratios (VMs per host) and a better return on investment (ROI) on your hardware. Most likely, only the largest organizations will approach those top ends, but either way, the infrastructure just became more robust.

The downside is that many organizations will have no choice but to purchase new hardware for their infrastructure. With prior versions of VMware, organizations had the option of virtualizing some of their newer servers, and then turning around and using that hardware as their next ESX host. This is still a possibility; however, since 64-bit servers are relatively new compared to their 32-bit counterparts, the 64-bit variety has not yet saturated datacenters to the same degree.

Distributed Power Management

Distributed Power Management (DPM) is the ability of the system to identify when there is enough extra capacity to either automatically shut down hosts or make recommendations to reduce power consumption (think holidays, evenings, and weekends!).

You don't have to be "green" to appreciate this feature. Studies by many industry analysts are available that point out how fast energy costs have gone up in the past few years, and those costs now account for a significant portion of operating costs. The ability to reduce unneeded capacity during the course of a fiscal year can add up to a bigger bonus at year-end. And as any business student will point out, cutting costs adds directly to the bottom line.

VMware states on their website that power and cooling costs can be cut by up to 20 percent in the datacenter during low utilization time periods. How this works is simple: the technology utilizes Distributed Resource Scheduler (DRS) to accomplish the task. During a weekend or holiday, vCenter recognizes extra CPU capacity in a cluster and uses DRS to migrate VMs off a designated ESX host. Once all systems are off the host, that host can be powered off or put in standby mode to conserve energy and lower costs. If the need for capacity starts to increase, that host will be powered back up and VMs will migrate back onto it to take advantage of all cluster resources.

Enhanced VMotion Compatibility

Although VMotion is not new to vSphere, there is a new feature called Enhanced VMotion Compatibility (EVC) that will add more flexibility when you are configuring VMotion between the same chip manufacturer. As noted earlier, VMotion is not always compatible between older and newer CPU generations. However, the EVC feature allows the hypervisor to mask or hide certain differences (CPU instruction sets) so that compatibility between generations is more relaxed—and this works for both Intel and AMD.

Enhanced Storage VMotion

vSphere includes a new feature called Enhanced Storage VMotion (ESV) that works across iSCSI, Fibre Channel, and Network File System (NFS). ESV can also be used to:

- Convert from thick disk formats to thin virtual disk formats during a move.
- Reduce CPU and memory usage of the host.
- Provide a more efficient block copy method from prior versions.

NOTE   A thin disk is presented to a VM as the total size, but it only consumes what is needed by the server, thus saving disk resources.

Storage VMotions are faster, take fewer resources to perform, and have fewer problems completing tasks compared to the earlier version.

Why is ESV important? Storage area network (SAN) storage is expensive and administrators often face a need to dole out small amounts of resources—in this case shared storage—while at the same time not running out of disk space inside the operating system. ESV addresses both sides of the equation. Now you can overprovision storage space by using thin disks. ESV allows you to convert the disk without downtime to the thin format and then use the overprovision feature. If most of your organization's VMs have free space on their hard drives, you can reclaim valuable shared storage with these two technologies.

As you can imagine, this new feature requires additional viewpoints into the datastores so that overprovisioning will not hurt your infrastructure. To that point VMware has introduced several new events and alerting within vCenter to address this new need.

Enhanced High Availability

While VMware High Availability is not a new feature, vSphere adds many enhancements to make it better, smarter, and more efficient than ever before. As we noted earlier, HA is a feature that guards against hardware failure in a VMware cluster. If the hardware goes down, vCenter recognizes this and restarts VMs on the remaining hosts in that cluster.

What has been enhanced in this version? vSphere High Availability now guards against operating system failures as well as hardware failures, and it does so through heartbeats detected via VMware tools. As an added benefit, if DRS is also enabled on a cluster, vCenter will restart VMs, choosing which host to restart a VM based on its resource needs. In the older version, VMs were simply thrown at the remaining hosts and restarted without taking resource needs into consideration; clearly we are moving forward.

vCenter does a much better job of positively detecting high availability events rather than false positives because vCenter monitors the heartbeats of multiple VMs on each ESX host (versus just the Service Console in the older version). One of many reasons administrators will love this feature is because it singlehandedly eliminates the need for them to rush into the office at night, during holidays, or any other time hardware has an issue; because everything keeps running, the problem most likely can be dealt with during regular business hours or at the next convenient opportunity.

Another major reason VMware High Availability will be one of your favorite features is because this technology rivals physical clustering—all it takes to set up High Availability is a single mouse click and all your VMs and applications in that cluster will be protected. There's no complicated process of setting up duplicates of hardware—it's ready to go on the spot!

Virtual Machine Scalability

Virtual machine scalability has been increased. There's now eight-way virtual symmetric multiprocessing (SMP) for even more demanding workloads; 256GB of RAM can be assigned to VMs; and more support is available for hot-pluggable devices such as memory and virtual CPUs. All this is accomplished with new virtual hardware, which diminishes downtime for compliant guest operating systems. If a VM is running low on hard drive space, you will be able to "extend" the hard drives on a running VM instead of having to shut down the VM and use other tools to extend the hard drive.

However, the caveat is that the operating system must support these features (hot add memory or hard drives). You will also have the ability to virtualize bigger or more important systems, and organizations will do this to get the added flexibility for their most important applications. The organization I work for is now virtualizing Microsoft Exchange because we like how easy it is to be able to recover VMs as opposed to recovering a physical Microsoft Exchange server. The flexibility to add hard drive space or memory with only a few clicks of a mouse, fault tolerance, and HA clusters—all of these reasons are driving organizations to virtualize more and more of their physical infrastructure.

vCenter Improvements

The management platform has been significantly expanded in vSphere:

- Licensing is no longer done via a licensing server; it is all included in a 25-character license key.

- Performance charts have been revised so that you can view all metrics in the same window.

- Enhancements have been made to alarms and notifications, including storage awareness enhancements.

- A resource usage statistics feature has been introduced for VMs, and at the resource pool layer, think chargeback for utilized resources! (For example, if your organization charges for servers or resources used, this feature will help you out.)

- The new vSphere Management Assistant functions as a VM and includes software that you can use via the command line to run scripts and agents against ESX and ESXi hosts.

The licensing change is a special gift from VMware since the old licensing server in version 3 was sometimes challenging. Usually after it was working everything went well, but many administrators, myself included, pulled out some of their hair during that first install.

The ability to see all four main metrics—memory, CPU, disk I/O, and network utilization—in the same window in performance graphs may not sound worthy of mention; however, due to the nature of virtualization, troubleshooting is greatly simplified when an administrator can see them all at the same time. You can quickly assess what is and is not happening on a virtual machine or ESX host. When viewing these four metrics, for example, you can see that the issue is an isolated memory issue, or that CPU is out of whack and the network is not doing anything. And since these graphs can be viewed at different time intervals, you can pinpoint when the problem started.

Fault Tolerance

Fault tolerance is one of vSphere's exciting new features, and it promises both zero downtime and zero data loss from hardware-based failures. The technology is able to accomplish this task using the playback feature that was perfected in VMware Workstation (a desktop virtualization product). A second VM on a different host has every action from the original VM replicated, so setup and maintenance are easier compared to a physical cluster. If hardware on one host fails, the other VM takes over on the spot—there's no need for HA (to restart a VM on another host) because the VM is already running live on a separate host. Additionally, the technology is savvy enough to spawn another fault-tolerant VM after an event like this, so the redundancy can be maintained after a failure automatically.

This is not a feature that you will want to use for all VMs, however, because it will require twice the amount of hardware. For example, if an organization wants to provide fault tolerance for all its existing virtual infrastructure, it will need to acquire twice the hardware to match what it currently runs on. Obviously this technology should be reserved for your most important servers.

vNetwork Distributed Switch

VMware has created vNetwork Distributed Switch (DVS) so that you can set up networking once and then everything else becomes plug and play. DVS essentially spans multiple ESX hosts so there is less need to set up each and every host with identical virtual networking. This would be similar to downloading a configuration file for a new router—downloading it, running, and saving the changes instead of reconfiguring settings every time. There will also be support for third-party virtual switches, the ability to track VMs as they migrate around a cluster, and better support for private virtual local area networks (VLANs) into existing networking environments.

The goal of this feature (and host profiles, discussed next) is to eliminate extra work and to make ESX hosts more like devices and less like operating systems. You can simply plug in a device and associate it in vCenter with a cluster; then all the settings that need to be specified are done automatically. Under those conditions, you could add and subtract additional CPU and memory (do you even need to think of it as a host at that point?) anywhere in the infrastructure.

Host Profiles

Host profiles are similar in notion to a template or a golden image used to consistently replicate new desktops or virtual machines. Prior to this new feature, you either rebuilt each host from scratch or used some kind of automated build process and then did your best to create consistency across all hosts. Host profiles greatly reduce configuration management by allowing you to build a golden image once and then "plug it" into any new hosts, thus ensuring standards across the infrastructure.

Every organization and administrator chooses how they want to configure their hosts. Some manually build each one; some use scripting to create exact copies. These approaches all have their merits. However, host profiles will allow an administrator to create a golden image and then apply those settings to any new or replaced ESX hosts.

vCenter Linked Mode

vCenter Linked Mode creates a simplified approach to management in large environments by allowing you to use a single interface for multiple vCenter servers. If there is more than one vCenter server in your environment, they can be interconnected in a mode that allows you to share management roles across the infrastructure, licensing, and other related tasks. This yields a further reduction in workloads associated with setting up the same configurations on multiple vCenter servers.

Virtual Disk Thin Provisioning

In the storage realm there is a new feature called *virtual disk thin provisioning*. SAN storage is more expensive than hard drive space; therefore, administrators are careful to properly provision each new VM with the right amount of GBs on their drives. Virtual disk thin provisioning allows you to overprovision valuable shared storage while at the same time allowing the VM to grow into its allocated hard drives. This technology would not be complete without the underlying reporting and notifications that ensure proper maintenance of the storage occurs, and that is well taken care of on the management side in vCenter Server. This feature will reduce the need for SAN storage, thus helping keep costs low and under control.

Take a moment to imagine a virtual infrastructure that has, say, 255 virtual machines in version 3.5, update 2. If on average each VM has between 1 and 5GB of unused space on just the C drive, that means between 255GB and 1.2TB of SAN storage is unused. If each VM has two hard drives, that could mean almost 2TB of space could be reclaimed if this feature is utilized; now that is valuable.

VMkernel Protection

The new VMkernel Protection technology helps protect the hypervisor by ensuring that the integrity of the VMkernel is not compromised and/or changed by either common attacks or software loaded on the host. The VMkernel modules are now digitally signed and validated during each reboot so that nothing is overwritten, and they use memory integrity for protection from buffer overflow. When you combine this technology with VMware VMsafe (which is used to protect VMs by including an Application Programming Interface (API) for third-party developers to create security products), you'll see that security has been enhanced yet again.

VMkernel Protection is somewhat similar to what Microsoft did to try to eliminate the "Blue Screen of Death": they created digitally signed device drivers. Before this, third-party vendors created all sorts of software that interacted with Windows operating systems, and sometimes that software was coded well and played nicely; other times it bluescreened the operating system. Microsoft did not have control over outside companies, so they did the next best thing by introducing digitally signed drivers. In a similar manner, VMkernel Protection ensures that the kernel is not modified; VMware can thus ensure that their platform is stable and will most likely remain that way.

VMware vShield Zones

VMware vShield Zones is a virtual appliance that acts as a firewall. It can be enabled to monitor, log, block, and allow inter-virtual machine traffic within an ESX host or between hosts in a cluster without having to direct traffic externally through physical devices like routers or switches. If you need to isolate, bridge, or firewall VMs between multiple zones, you can do so with vShield Zones. Successful and denied activities can be logged, graphed, and analyzed.

VMware Data Recovery

vCenter now comes with an easy-to-use plug-in that allows for disk-based de-duplication of all your virtual machines. This technology runs on a VM in either ESX or ESXi and allows you to restore individual files or entire VM images. A wizard-driven interface is used to configure and schedule backup jobs, and multiple restore points can be easily selected for specific points-in-time copies or restores. The technology uses de-duplication to significantly reduce the size of backups while allowing for multiple incremental changes; it even supports the Volume Shadow Copy service to enable backup of Microsoft applications.

NOTE   De-duplication is the process of identifying redundant pieces of data and essentially compressing it to save space.

This feature is a huge win for any business, whether it is big or small, as it will have the ability to back up applications and/or servers with relative ease as well as restore those applications and servers using intuitive wizards.

2

Installing and Configuring ESX and ESXi

IN THIS CHAPTER, YOU WILL LEARN TO:

▶ **PREPARE FOR INSTALLATION (Pages 22–26)**
- Identify Hardware Requirements (Page 23)
- Partitioning and Sizing (Page 25)

▶ **INSTALL ESX AND ESXI IN GRAPHICAL MODE (Pages 26–47)**
- Install the ESX GUI (Page 26)
- Install the ESXi GUI (Page 38)

▶ **INSTALL ESX TEXT MODE (Pages 47–51)**
- Navigate Text Mode (Page 47)

▶ **PERFORM A SCRIPTED INSTALLATION USING A USB DEVICE (Pages 51–55)**
- Identify the USB Device (Page 53)
- Format the USB Key (Page 54)

▶ **POSTINSTALLATION CONFIGURATIONS (Pages 55–68)**
- Configure Network Time Protocol (Page 55)
- Configure the Firewall (Page 57)
- Configure the Service Console (Page 58)
- Configure Active Directory Authentication (Page 64)

They say that when you build a house, one of the most important steps in that process is building the foundation, since everything will depend on its integrity. When deploying a virtual infrastructure, the underlying installation and its configuration is equally important. And while it is very easy to just follow the default parameters, this will not necessarily keep your hosts running error free.

One of the things you can and should do is set up extra partitions to store the logs, rather than storing the logs inside the default parameters. In this way if there are issues and the logs fill up, you won't have a host get effected because of that situation.

In this chapter, we are going to cover the most common approaches to deploying ESX and ESXi and some extra caveats that will help you manage your infrastructure and especially your growth down the road.

Prepare for Installation

The release of vSphere signals that the 32-bit era is nearing its "virtual" end. vSphere is only available in 64 bit, and while 64-bit hardware has been available for a while, most likely at least some organizations will run a mix of ESX 3.*x* and vSphere until all their hardware has been upgraded so that it's capable of running vSphere. VMware is fully aware of this; the new version is capable of running and managing older versions as well as vSphere—in other words, a mix of the two. Furthermore, Virtual Infrastructure 3 (VI3) is nowhere near the end of its life.

Small environments tend to keep it simple by deploying each host through the Graphical User Interface (GUI). There is no real problem with this—a host can be completely installed in 20 to 30 minutes by someone who knows what they're doing. Scripted installations can be carried out; just create a ks.cfg file and put it on a CD or at another location (such as FTP or HTTP).

There is a downside to manual installations: as the number of hosts that are to be manually installed increases, the likelihood of a consistent build across those hosts decreases. Focus on how important it is to have consistency across your builds, and implement a suitable deployment methodology.

With the release of VMware vSphere, the requirements of hosts capable of running ESX have changed; VMware ESX and ESXi version 3.*x* can run on either 32-bit or 64-bit hardware, while VMware ESX and ESXi version 4.0 now require 64-bit hardware.

Identify Hardware Requirements

When planning to install VMware ESX or ESXi version 4.0, it is important to know what hardware is required. The following lists are current as of the time of this writing. For the most up-to-date information, refer to the VMware website at the following URL:

www.VMware.com/go/hcl

Processor Types   The following 64-bit processor types are acceptable:

- 64-bit x86 CPUs

- All AMD Opterons

- All Intel XEON 3000/3200, 3100/3300, 5100/5300, 5200/5400, 7100/7300, 7200/7400

- All Intel Nehalems

RAM   You need 2 GB of RAM, at a minimum.

Network Adapters   Follow these guidelines for network adapters:

- For best performance, select adapters with dedicated Gigabit Ethernet cards for VMs, such as Intel PRO/1000 adapters or better.

- For security purposes, keep the Service Console on its own network interface card (NIC) (or teamed NICs for redundancy).

- The more NICs you have on a virtual switch, the better the performance and the more redundancy there is in case of failures.

- Broadcom NetXtreme 570x Gigabit controllers are acceptable.

- Intel PRO/1000 adapters are acceptable.

Adapters and Controllers   The following Fibre Channel adapter, SCSI adapter, or internal RAID controllers are suitable:

- Use only Fibre Channel HBA cards as outlined in the Hardware Compatibility Guide.

- Basic SCSI controllers are Adaptec Ultra160 and Ultra320, LSI Logic's Fusion-MPT, and most NCR/Symbios controllers.

- RAID adapters supported include Dell PERC (Adaptec RAID and LSI MegaRAID), HP Smart Array, and IBM (Adaptec) ServeRAID controllers.

Installation and Storage Factors   Consider the following hardware requirement for installation and storage:

- You will need a SCSI disk, Fibre Channel LUN, or RAID LUN with unpartitioned space. In a minimum configuration, the disk or RAID is shared between the Service Console and the virtual machines.

- For hardware iSCSI, you will need a disk attached to an iSCSI controller, such as the QLogic QLA405x. Software iSCSI is not supported for booting or installing ESX.

- You will need serial-attached SCSI (SAS).

- For Serial ATA (SATA), you will need a disk connected through supported SAS controllers or supported onboard SATA controllers. Only SATA disk drives connected behind supported SAS controllers or supported onboard SATA controllers are supported in ESX hosts.

- Supported SAS controllers include LSI1068E (LSISAS3442E), LSI 1068 (SAS 5), IBM ServeRAID 8k SAS controller, Smart Array P400/256MB controller, and the Dell PERC 5.0.1 controller.

- Supported onboard SATA controllers include Intel ICH9, NVIDIA MCP55, and ServerWorks HT1000.

SATA Drives   When installing ESX on SATA drives, consider the following:

- Ensure that your SATA drives are connected through supported SAS controllers or supported onboard SATA controllers.

- Do not use SATA disks to create Virtual Machine File System (VMFS) datastores shared across multiple ESX hosts.

ESX supports installing and booting on either an ATA drive or ATA RAID, but make sure that your specific drive controller is included in the supported hardware. IDE drives are supported for ESX installation and VMFS creation.

Partitioning and Sizing

Consider the default size for partitions during the install; to avoid troubleshooting and installation or upgrade issues later, do yourself a favor and at least double (if not more) the size of all the defaults. After all, local hard drive space is usually abundant enough and planning ahead will save you aggravation in the future.

Also, consider adding a /var and a /var/log partition; if an ESX host has issues and begins to rapidly create logs of the event, the root of the drive will not fill up if you have these two additional partitions. Without them, the root may run out of space due to excessive logging and cause even more problems.

A Bit About Cloud Computing

Imagine for a moment you needed more capacity in a VMware cluster. You could install an additional ESX and configure it to have the same setup as all the other ESX hosts in that cluster. But even if you script the build and everything is automated, the process can still take a few hours. Now imagine you have Host Profiles set up and working alongside of vNetwork Distributed Switching. You can take a host from one cluster that is underutilized, remove it, and place it into the other cluster that needs resources. You just apply the host profile and the switching, and the cluster then has more resources.

You could have spare hardware to put in place. Or you could perform a physical-to-virtual (P2V) conversion and then commandeer that hardware and install ESXi on it.

The two primary aspects of cloud computing you must consider are

- How easy is it to add additional capacity and resources to the cloud?

- How easy is it to move applications or servers to and from different clouds?

Virtualization is moving toward a device-like host that is as simple as possible to plug into the virtual infrastructure so that additional power (CPU, memory, network, storage) can be added with minimal effort.

Install ESX and ESXi in Graphical Mode

The GUI is probably the most widely used method for installation. Administrators from novice to expert will use this method to get a host up quickly and easily. There isn't anything terribly tricky or complex to master with this method.

Install the ESX GUI

As with any technology, there are things you must consider before sitting down and performing your workload. VMware has put together a list of prerequisites that you should be aware of before traveling down the virtualization highway. Take a moment to become familiar with this list. That way, you can avoid frustration down the road if something doesn't work the way you expect it to.

For a production environment, the most important thing is to make sure all hardware is on the Hardware Compatibility Guide before you purchase it. Check specific pieces of hardware like NICs and SAS and SATA controllers. If problems occur during or after an installation, hardware compatibility is the last thing you want to deal with; however, it is often the first thing support will ask about. Additionally, check to make sure that the hardware clock (in BIOS) is set to UTC. If you're planning to build multiple ESX hosts, document the settings in BIOS for the CPU and ensure they are the same on all hosts. If the settings in BIOS are not the same on all hosts, they may prevent the ability to VMotion virtual machines; with documentation, you won't have to guess what is and is not enabled or disabled on other hosts.

If your hardware is 64 bit capable, also ensure that you turn this feature on in BIOS. This will allow your hosts to run both 32 bit and 64 bit and VMotion properly across the hosts.

TIP ▶ Be careful when upgrading firmware and BIOS. Some hosts may lose their settings in BIOS. It is a good idea after upgrading these software pieces to double-check and make sure the settings you have in place are still accurate and have not changed on their own.

Now that you have an understanding of hardware compatibility, let's begin the installation using the ESX GUI:

1. Insert the installation media into the CD drive and reboot the server.

The first screen to come up contains some useful installation options. On this screen you will have 30 seconds to make a choice,
but if you click the down arrow, the ticking clock will stop. An
installation using graphical mode or text mode is a no-brainer.
You also have the option to specify an installation using USB, to
use a scripted installation, or to boot from the first hard disk. If
you press F2, a script will appear near the bottom of the screen,
and you can add parameters for specific installation options.

2. Choose Install ESX In Graphical Mode (as shown in Figure 2.1)
and then press Enter.

Figure 2.1: Select Install ESX In Graphical Mode.

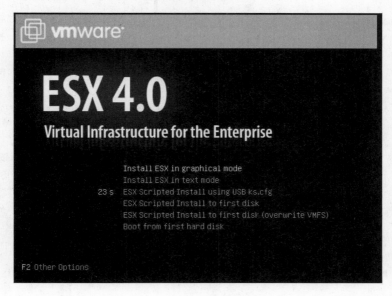

3. The Welcome To The ESX Installer screen is next; you'll see a
reminder to check the Hardware Compatibility Guide before proceeding. Click Next.

4. On the End User License Agreement (EULA) screen, in the
bottom-left corner check Accept The License Agreement, and
then click Next.

5. On the Select Keyboard screen, select your keyboard type and
then click Next.

NOTE Third-party software suites are available that integrate with vSphere. The caveat here is that if you are using a DVD to install, you must use that DVD device to install the custom drivers by removing the DVD, inserting the custom drivers DVD, and then replacing the installation DVD when finished. If you are using an ISO image, the custom drivers must also be on an ISO image. Unfortunately, if a USB device is the installation device, it *can not be removed* for this process. If you forget to install custom drivers at this stage, you can install them later, but only via the command line and vCenter Update Manager.

6. On the Custom Drivers screen, select Yes (to install custom drivers) or No (to continue without custom options), and then click Next.

   You'll see a small pop-up window (Figure 2.2) that is somewhat counterintuitive. Select Yes to continue the install without custom drivers. Selecting No means you want to return and install custom drivers.

Figure 2.2: This pop-up is rather counterintuitive.

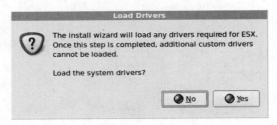

7. On the Loading Drivers screen, select No, and then click Next. When you see the Load Drivers pop-up, select Yes to continue the installation. When the drivers are finished loading, click Next.

   Licensing is covered in more detail in Chapter 4. However, if vCenter is used to centrally manage ESX hosts, it is not necessary to enter a serial number at this stage.

8. On the License screen, select Enter Your Serial Number Now and enter the number, or you can select Enter a Serial Number Later. (Note: Choosing the latter will put you into an evaluation mode). Then click Next.

9. On the Network Configuration screen, select your preferred NIC (this is your Service Console NIC), and then click Next.

NOTE   There are circumstances where administrators are required to know which physical NIC is which from inside the operating system—for example, when troubleshooting. This is not always easy to accomplish postinstallation. One strategy is to label the NICs at this stage by plugging one cable in at a time, labeling it, and repeating (look for the link light).

---

10. Select Set Automatically Using DHCP, or enter your IP address, subnet mask, default gateway, primary and secondary DNS, and your fully qualified hostname. In the bottom-left corner is a button to test your settings. Click it, and then click Next (see Figure 2.3).

Figure 2.3: Enter your network configuration information.

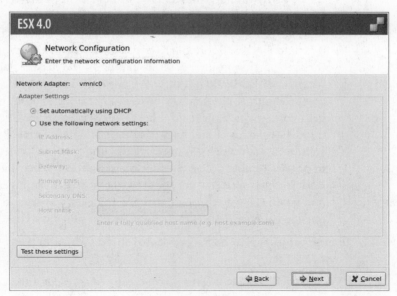

NOTE Be sure to add a DNS entry for each host. Also, when adding hosts to vCenter, always use the fully qualified domain name (FQDN); features like High Availability (HA) and vMotion depend on this information. If your environment does not have DNS, you will want to add a host file after installation.

This window contains the following options:

Standard Setup A standard setup fills in most of the questions with automatic defaults that will fit a majority of installations. In most cases the user can simply click Next to accept the choices. Standard Setup isn't a bad option; however, if you have a second hard drive, a need for custom partitioning, or other custom needs, this option won't be the best choice.

Advanced Setup Advanced setup is just what this sounds like; it allows for more customization of the installation parameters. This is the choice we will select.

Boot Loader Most installations will not add this extra complexity into the installation. This feature might be used if extra software arguments have to be passed to the kernel on every boot; if there is a need for a boot loader password (up to 30 characters); or, in some cases, on older hardware if Grand Unified Bootloader (GRUB) must be installed on the first partition of the disk instead of on the master boot record (MBR). If the Boot Loader option is unchecked, and you configure a password, a host will not boot without the password—which means if a host experiences an error in the middle of the night and tries to reboot, it will be unable to do so until some unlucky administrator either physically drives in or uses remote access to enter the password. When the Boot Loader option is not selected, the host will simply boot and go all the way through without any need for input from outside sources. This is the way most computer systems boot.

11. On the Setup Type screen, choose Advanced setup and then click Next.

Attached Storage This next screen will present a list of storage devices that could possibly contain production data or virtual machine storage areas that are not physically located on the host and could be shared with other hosts. There might even be running virtual machines on these remotely attached hard drives. Smart administrators disconnect shared storage devices during an installation to avoid this potential issue. Don't be that admin who formatted production volumes and then had to restore or rebuild those deleted virtual machines! Many administrators have wiped out VMFS storage LUNs during this stage of installation. As an extra check, make sure the size of the LUN matches expectations for the storage, and this will help you have a simple and straightforward installation.

Options to Address Attached Storage   There are many ways to address attached storage. One of the best ways to handle this is to make sure the host is powered off and to simply unplug the fiber to the remote storage, or whatever physically connects the storage to the host. Another option is to ask the SAN administrator to disable the port(s). The moral of the story is to be certain that when you go through the installation, there is no chance of deleting important storage.

12. On the ESX Storage Device screen, select where the ESX host will be installed and then click Next (refer to Figure 2.4).

Figure 2.4: ESX storage device

13. The Data Loss Warning pop-up opens; this is your last chance to make sure your shared storage is not connected. When you are ready, click OK.

When you're using more than one hard drive, you'll see an Optional Install On More Than A Single Hard Drive screen, which allows for three pivotal choices:

- Create New Datastore (On Same Hard Drive As ESX Installation)
- Create New Datastore (On Separate Hard Drive)
- Use Existing Datastore

If this is a single installation of ESX that will not use shared storage, consider the effect of trying to run multiple virtual machines on the same hard drive where ESX is installed. If there is more than just a couple of virtual machines, or if the virtual machines have a considerable amount of I/O, this strategy may result in sluggish virtual machines even if they have plenty of CPU and RAM; the bottleneck becomes the hard drive. A second or third hard drive on a separate channel will help minimize this effect and keep the virtual machines running at peak performance.

In this example, a second hard drive will be used to install the datastore for virtual machines. If there is only one hard drive, continue as normal as the option will be grayed out.

14. On the Datastore screen, deselect the Create On The Same Device As ESX check box. This will allow the grayed-out section to illuminate and you can now click the Select Device button (see Figure 2.5).

Notice in Figure 2.5 that the size of the hard drive is not visible. In this example the choice is obvious, but if there were more options to choose from, it would be advisable to scroll to the left and view the available sizes to help narrow the choices (see Figure 2.6).

15. Highlight the correct storage device and click OK.

Figure 2.5: You must specify a datastore.

Figure 2.6: Scroll to the left and view the available sizes.

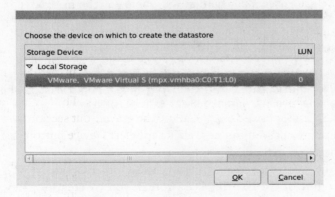

16. A window similar to the first pop up warning will pop up. On the
Data Loss Warning window, there is a potential to wipe out production data. Ensure this is the correct device and that you are not
selecting shared LUNs with production data, and then click OK.

The way that SAN administrators see LUNs and the way that vCenter and ESX see LUNs is not always the same (hexadecimal as opposed to decimal). Consider the example of a LUN named R003_DMZ_84_086a. A naming convention similar to the following will help not only the SAN team but also the administrators who manage the infrastructure:

R = Replicated storage

003 = Third LUN

84 = EMC DMX

086a = LUN device as seen by SAN administrators in hexadecimal format

Local storage, however, may not need such an elaborate naming convention.

Naming Convention for Datastores

Datastores are essentially hard drives where you can store anything from virtual machines to templates to ISO files. They should be carefully named so that your infrastructure is easy to navigate and has intuitive organization. The characteristics of the storage can be used to name the datastores; for example, which clusters the storage belongs to, if the datastores are replicated for disaster recovery, if the datastore is a 15,000 rpm drive for databases, or the hexadecimal/decimal name of the LUN (if it is on a SAN).

17. On the datastore screen, you can choose either Create New Datastore or Use Existing Datastore. If you are creating a new datastore, choose an appropriate naming convention and then click Next (see Figure 2.7).

The next step involves partitioning. Let's discuss this topic before moving on. The defaults for ESX partitions are as follows:

- Swap: 600MB
- /var/log: 2GB
- /: 5GB

Figure 2.7: Decide on an appropriate naming convention.

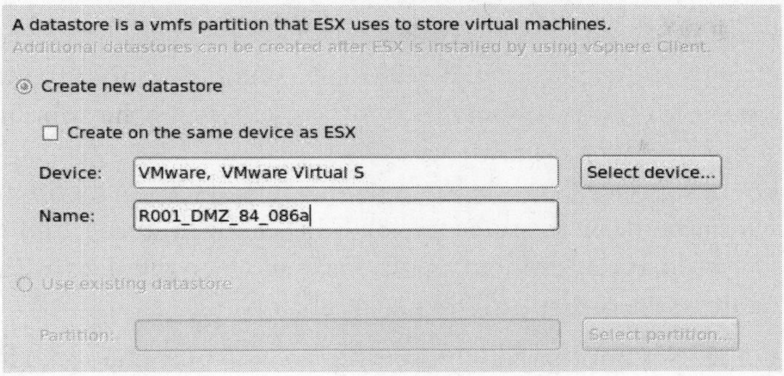

A datastore is a vmfs partition that ESX uses to store virtual machines.
Additional datastores can be created after ESX is installed by using vSphere Client.

◉ Create new datastore

☐ Create on the same device as ESX

Device: VMware, VMware Virtual S

Select device...

Name: R001_DMZ_84_086a

○ Use existing datastore

Partition:

Select partition...

Take note that these are minimums, meaning they are just large enough to do their job. Think about the minimum memory requirements for some operating systems; whenever possible, try to double these numbers for troubleshooting down the road.

The physical partitions are as follows:

/vmfs   This partition is required and is where future virtual machines are stored; in addition, the /vmfs/volumes partition contains the esxconsole.vmdk, /-root, and the swap partitions. For these all to fit on a single drive, you'll need to make the partition at least 8.5GB, but you'll need to make the partition much larger unless you use shared storage to allow for vMotion. Consider using this storage for templates, ISO files, and helper or test virtual machines. This partition can be installed on a separate device for performance reasons.

VMkcore   This partition is also required and is the first place VMware support will look if there are issues; core dumps are stored here.

/boot   Without this partition an ESX will not function. Boot files are located here, and this location must be the location where BIOS attempts to boot from.

However, the size of the /boot, VMkcore, and the /vmfs/volumes partition cannot be altered in the text or graphical-based installation; only in a scripted installation is this control relinquished to the administrator.

Here is what a sample partition table may look like:

```
Swap                 - 1600MB        -swap
/var/log             - 2000MB        -ext3
/                    - 10000MB       -ext3
```

```
/boot         - 1250MB
/home          - 512MB    -ext3
/tmp          - 2048MB    -ext3
/usr          - 1024MB    -ext3
/vmfs
```

18. On the Service Console Virtual Disk Image screen, highlight the mount point on the screen, click Edit, change the size, and click OK. Add any additional partitions, and when the sizes are adequate to the organization's needs, click Next.

19. On the Set Bootloader Options screen, you may choose to have a bootloader password. In most cases this is unnecessary; this option is used to make sure that no one can hijack the ESX during a reboot since they must enter a password first. If you're not using a password, simply click Next.

20. On the Time Zone Settings screen, choose your time zone and then click Next. Most locations can be found on the World Map that the installation media presents to you; also, you can click the Advanced button to open an additional menu for a finer level of selection.

21. A difference in time on a network can have disastrous consequences. The best approach is to designate a time device on the network that all other devices set their time to; for example, an Active Directory domain controller or the head router. But all devices, hosts, virtual machines, physical servers, and domain controllers should use the same time source.

    On the Date And Time screen, choose your date and time. Also, take a moment to specify a Network Time Protocol (NTP) server, and then synchronize (this will test whether the connection is working properly. You can choose either an internal NTP server or an external NTP server. Then click Next (see Figure 2.8).

22. For ESX, the minimum password length is six characters; for ESXi, it is eight characters (at the time of this writing). If you plan to use scripting installations in the future, and you need to have multiple accounts for administration, consider adding those accounts here. The reason is that the ks.cfg file generated from this installation will have those accounts and their passwords in an encrypted format—which is a good thing for a file that can be read in plain text.

Figure 2.8: Specify the time and an NTP source.

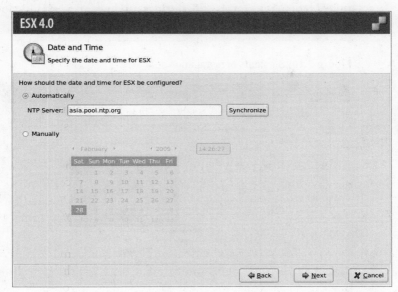

On the Set Administrator Password screen, enter your root password and make it secure (the password must be at least six characters). Add any other accounts used for administration and then click Next (see Figure 2.9).

Figure 2.9: Specify root and any other users.

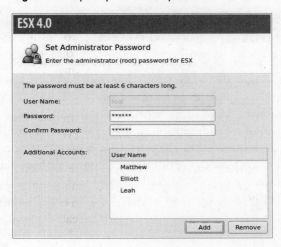

23. On the Summary Of Installation Settings screen (Figure 2.10), take a moment to review the settings, and when everything looks accurate, click Next.

Figure 2.10: Summary of installation options

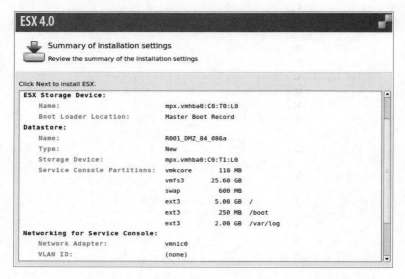

24. On the Installing ESX 4.0 screen, wait for status to read 100 percent complete and then click Next.

25. On the ESX 4.0 Installation Complete screen, click Finish.

Install the ESXi GUI

ESXi seems to be the direction VMware is taking in the future. Right now ESX is an operating system–like entity that must be maintained and configured, just like an operating system. Contrary to this, consider a device like a router. Most of the work involved with setting up a router involves the running configuration. In fact, the running configuration can be saved and uploaded to a replacement router (if the original goes bad or if the hardware dies) or can be loaded into another router for quick configuration. (During the install of ESXi that follows, compare the process to see how quick it is compared to its older and larger brother, ESX.)

The installation of ESXi is extremely fast and easy, which is why it is becoming more and more popular as a platform of choice. Part of the reason this installation is so fast is that system network and storage devices as well as the IP addressing (set to DHCP) are configured with defaults. In fact, you have to configure only one thing: which storage device to install on (which is different from partitioning).

> **NOTE**   Before installing, remember that ESXi has a hardware compatibility list similar to ESX. However, some administrators use ESXi to run on systems that don't support ESX. If centrally managing a test or development environment is not important, consider using the free version of ESXi as a cost-effective approach in the data center. VMware is just as free as other platforms.

And without further delay let's begin the installation of ESXi in a GUI.

1. Insert the installation media into the appropriate drive and reboot.

2. The first screen is very generic, as you can see in Figure 2.11. The choices are ESXi Installer or Boot From Local Disk. Highlight the first option and press Enter.

Figure 2.11: The initial ESXi installation screen

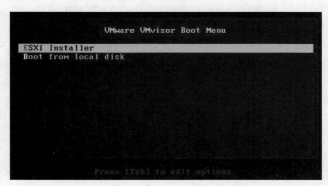

3. On the Welcome To The VMware ESXi 4.x.x Installation screen, you have an opportunity to repair a host gone bad. While there is a minimum of moving parts with ESXi, it is still possible that a setting or other misconfiguration could disrupt the host and keep

it from either functioning altogether or partially performing. In either case, the host can be booted up using the CD/DVD or the ISO file and then you can repair it. This feature is designed to be a helpful tool that is not dependent on being able to boot into the configuration. In this scenario, press R to repair your host.

You have the following choices (see Figure 2.12): (ESC) Cancel, (R) Repair, and (Enter) Install. Assuming this is an install and not a repair, press Enter to install.

Figure 2.12: ESXi install options

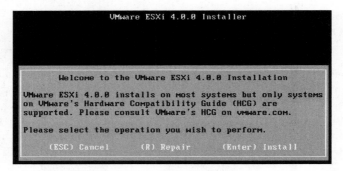

4. On the EULA screen, you can press Esc to not accept the agreement or press F11 to accept. Carefully read the agreement and when you are ready press F11.

5. The next screen tells you whether the storage device is empty. On the Select A Disk screen, you have two choices for hard drives (notice the GUI shows in this example that the storage is empty; verify this is true before proceeding). The size helps identify the different options. Select the hard drive space where the installation will reside and press Enter (see Figure 2.13).

6. On the Confirm Install screen, you have a chance to confirm your installation drive (Disk 0, Disk 1, etc.). Press F11 to install or press Backspace to go back and choose another option.

7. When you see the Installation Is Complete screen, remove your installation media and press Enter to reboot. The next screen will show the IP address and other system information (see Figure 2.14).

Figure 2.13: Selecting ESXi storage options

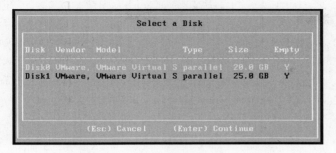

Figure 2.14: ESXi has rebooted.

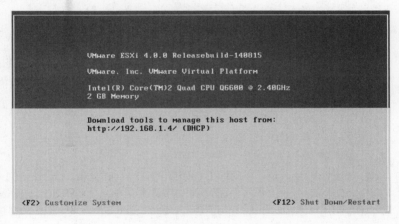

While the physical part of the installation is complete, there are still some tasks to complete before the ESXi host is ready to go into production.

Set Up DNS and Routing

This section assumes installation of this client has already taken place. If this is not the case, see the section "vSphere Client Installation for ESX or ESXi" toward the end of this chapter.

1. Start your vSphere Client, enter the IP, and enter **root** as your username, as shown in Figure 2.15. There is no password yet, so leave this field blank and click Enter.

Figure 2.15: vSphere Client login

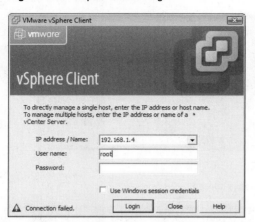

2. You may see a security warning about certificate warnings; click Ignore for now. You may also see a VMware Evaluation Notice; click OK for now.

3. In vSphere Client, select the Configuration tab; then in the Software section, click DNS and Routing, then choose ➢ Properties (in the top-right corner).

4. On the DNS and Routing Configuration tab, click the radio button Use The Following DNS Server Address. This will activate the previously grayed-out options (see Figure 2.16).

5. Enter the hostname, domain, and DNS addresses.

6. Click the Routing tab; verify that the correct default gateway exists and then click OK.

7. Add a new host (A) record to your DNS server.

   Hosts and vCenter find each other in the infrastructure by using Domain Name System (DNS) names to translate our names into IP addresses. The hosts you are building will most likely not be able to add their own IP addresses and names to your DNS records, so it is up to you to make a DNS entry for each ESX host. Also, when adding ESX hosts to vCenter, always use the fully qualified domain name (FQDN); features like HA and vMotion depend on this information to work properly. Here's an example of a FQDN: esx001@yourdomain.com.

Figure 2.16: DNS and Routing Configuration window, with the DNS Configuration tab selected

Change IP Address to Static from DHCP

Next we are going to change the IP address to Static from DHCP so that the IP address will always be the same. Let's begin:

1. With vSphere Client still open, click the Configuration tab, and then in the Hardware section, click Networking (see Figure 2.17).

Figure 2.17: Click Networking in the Hardware section.

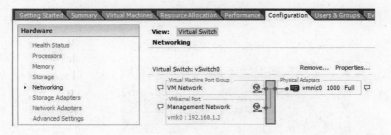

2. Next to Virtual Switch: vSwitch0, click Properties (this is not to be confused with Networking properties, which would allow enabling support for IPv6).

3. In the pop-up window, select Management Network (Figure 2.18), and then click Edit.

Figure 2.18: Selecting Management Network

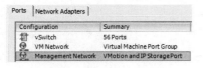

WARNING   This next step will disconnect vSphere Client from the host as the IP address will change.

---

4. As shown in Figure 2.19, choose the IP Settings tab and click the Use The Following IP Settings radio. Then enter the IP addressing information, click OK, and then click Close (see Figure 2.20).

Figure 2.19: The IP Settings tab

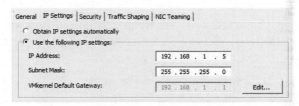

Figure 2.20: vSphere Client is disconnected.

5. Restart vSphere Client and log back in using the new static IP. If for some reason the new IP address was mistyped, it will show up on the console screen so that you won't have to guess what it is.

Change the ESXi Root Password

As mentioned earlier, the default root password is blank. When changing the password to something more secure, at the time of this writing an eight-character password is required. This is important to note as ESX requires only six characters. Additionally, the root password can be changed from either vSphere Client or directly from the host console. We'll outline each step in a moment. But first we'll set the root password from the console, and then by using the client.

First we will set the root password from the console. From the host console, press F2. The top choice allows the root password to be set or changed. Notice the right window provides basic information about each object on the left. Press Enter to select an option, and then change the password and press Enter to confirm (see Figure 2.21).

Figure 2.21: Changing the root password via the host console

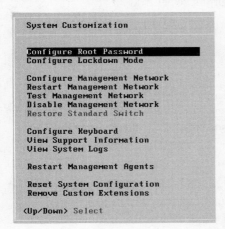

To set the root password from vSphere Client, click the Getting Started tab. In the middle of the screen, under Basic Tasks, click Change The Default Password, as shown in Figure 2.22. After you enter a password containing at least eight characters, the listing under Basic Tasks will disappear. This denotes a successful password change.

Figure 2.22: Changing the root password via vSphere Client

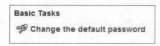

ESXi Licensing

Licensing can be entered via vCenter or through the host directly. Each step is outlined in this section.

To enter licensing on a stand-alone host:

1. Click the Configuration tab; under Software, click Licensed Features.

2. In the top-right corner, click Edit and then click the radio button "Assign a new license key to this host."

3. Click the Enter Key button and type your license key (including the dashes), and click OK twice.

To enter licensing using vCenter:

1. Start vSphere Client and log into vCenter.

2. Right-click on your datacenter and select Add Host.

3. Enter your fully qualified hostname, username, and password; click Next.

4. If you see a security alert, click Yes.

5. Review your host information and click Next.

6. Select a currently installed license or assign a new license key to this host; then click Next (see Figure 2.23) to move to the Lockdown Mode screen.

7. Lockdown mode is one of the features you are asked to config-ure during licensing; however, Lockdown mode is not explicitly part of licensing. This is a security feature that keeps remote access to root locked down to the console only. In other words, you will not be able to remote into your host directly with root if this is enabled; you would first need to remote in with a non-root account and then elevate your privileges. Therefore you should define other user accounts on the host before installing this fea-ture. Make your selection, then click Next twice, and then finally choose Finish.

Figure 2.23: Assigning licensing

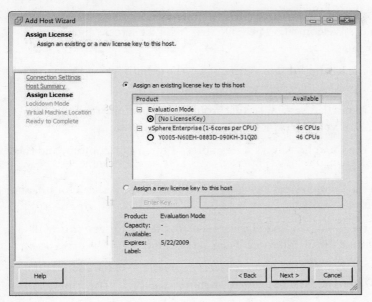

Install ESX Text Mode

Administrators choose text mode if the host has issues with a video controller, or if you are installing the OS remotely and graphics take up too much bandwidth.

Navigate Text Mode

In text mode, navigation around the screen must be done with the keyboard. Before going forward, let's outline two keystrokes that may help us on our way:

- < will get you back one screen at a time.

- ? will access the help function (though because the information is not always specific enough, it's not as useful as it could be).

Let's now perform a text installation of ESX:

1. Insert the installation media or ISO file and turn on the host server.

2. When the splash screen appears, select Install ESX In Text Mode and press Enter.

3. On the Welcome To The ESX Text Installer screen, click 1 to continue.

4. On the Keyboard screen, English is the default; press 1 to choose it, or press 2 to choose another version.

5. On the EULA screen, scroll through and carefully read the document, or you can type **accept** and then press Enter.

6. On the Custom Drivers screen, press 1 for yes or 2 for no, and then press Enter.

7. On the Load System Drivers screen, press 1 for yes or 2 for no, and then press Enter.

8. On the Going To Load Drivers screen, press 1 for yes; this will continue the installation. Then press Enter.

9. On the Enter Serial Number screen, press 2 to enter a serial number later and go into evaluation mode, and then press Enter.

   If you choose to enter the serial number now, press 1; then type the serial number (use your Cap Locks and include the dash), and press Enter.

10. On the COS Network Adapter screen, press 1 to keep the default settings, and then press Enter.

11. On the COS Network Settings screen, press 2 to select static IP addressing.

    Choosing Static will step you through each part of the IP scheme, starting with the IP address, and at the end of this module there is a review before you accept the settings. If the Static option is selected, skip ahead to step 14 (Disk Setup).

12. On the Enter The Hostname screen, use a fully qualified domain name, and then press Enter.

13. On the Current Network Config screen, you will see a breakdown of your choices. Press Enter to keep selections.

14. On the Disk Setup screen, press 1 for Basic (accepting the defaults) or 2 for Advanced.

15. If you choose Advanced, you will see a list of locations to install from. Choose the number to the left of the selection desired, and then press Enter (see Figure 2.24).

Figure 2.24: ESX storage device

```
ESX Storage Device----------------------------------------------------
   1) VMware,   VMware V... (mpx.vmhba0:C0:T0:L0)              20.48 GB
   2) VMware,   VMware V... (mpx.vmhba0:C0:T1:L0)              20.48 GB
[<number>: storage, '<': back, '?': help, '!': exit]
> 1_
```

16. On the Data Loss Warning screen, be certain there isn't any production shared storage connected to the ESX; if there is, disconnect it before proceeding to ensure that ESX doesn't wipe out production data. Then press 1 and Enter to proceed.

17. On the Specify A Datastore For ESX To Use screen, press 1 to create a datastore or 2 to use an existing datastore, and then press Enter.

18. On the Datastore screen, press 1 to create a new datastore on the same host as ESX is installed into, or press 2 to create a new datastore on the same ESX host but use a second storage device.

    If you press 2, specify the storage location by choosing the number to the left of the device desired. When you see a data loss warning, press 1 to proceed.

19. On the Volume Name screen, the option will default to Storage1. Press 1 if this is acceptable, or 2 to change it to another name. (Remember to choose a name that is descriptive and helpful for later management.) Then press Enter. (If you press 2, enter a descriptive name and press Enter.)

    Changing the partition size in text mode is easier to do than in GUI mode, and there are more options. We'll use text mode for step 20.

20. On the Service Console Virtual Disk Image screen, press 1 to keep the default settings, or press 2 to change them.

21. If you change the existing partitions, make sure you keep the partition type the same.

    a. If you press 2, then press 1 to create a new partition, and then press 2 to edit an existing partition.

    b. Pressing 2 will display a list of partitions to choose from (as you can see in Figure 2.25).

Figure 2.25: Choosing a partition to edit

```
Choose a partition to edit:
  1) swap     600 MB    (no mount point)
  2) ext3     2.00 GB   /var/log
  3) ext3     5.00 GB   /

  <) Back
  ?) Help
```

22. On the Boot Loader Options screen, press 2 if no kernel arguments need to be specified, and then press Enter.

23. On the Boot Loader Password screen, press 2 if no boot loader passwords will be provided, and then press Enter.

24. On the Timezone screen, press 2 to change the settings; you can then press Enter to scroll through the list. Press the number of the desired selection, then press Enter and confirm the selection by pressing 1 to keep your choice.

25. On the Time And Date Settings screen, press 1 to specify an NTP server, and then press Enter.

26. Type the NTP server address (as shown in Figure 2.26), and then press Enter. Once you specify a location, ESX automatically tries to confirm the connection.

Figure 2.26: Specifying an NTP

```
Time/Date Settings---------------------------------------
Time/Date (Automatic)
Specify the NTP server.

['<': back, '?': help]
> asia.pool.ntp.org
Attempting to contact server.
Time/Date Settings---------------------------------------

The system clock has been updated.  The current time is:
2009-03-29 15:32:11.005635

  1) Okay
  <) Back

> 1_
```

27. On the Administrator Password screen, enter the root password (the cursor will not move); then enter the root password a second time to confirm, and press Enter.

28. On the Review screen, if everything looks good press 1 to begin the installation, or press < to go back and change information. (See Figure 2.27.)

Figure 2.27: Installation review

```
Review-------------------------------------------------------------
  License:                        Evaluation Mode
  Keyboard:                       U.S. English
  Custom Drivers:                 (none)
  ESX Storage Device:
    Name:                         mpx.vmhba0:C0:T0:L0
    Boot Loader Location:         Master Boot Record
  Datastore:
    Name:                         testname
    Type:                         New
    Storage Device:               mpx.vmhba0:C0:T1:L0
    Service Console Partitions:   vmkcore      110 MB
                                  vmfs3      20.48 GB
                                  swap         600 MB
                                  ext3        5.00 GB  /
                                  ext3         250 MB  /boot
                                  ext3        2.00 GB  /var/log
  Networking for Service Console:
    Network Adapter:              vmnic0
    VLAN ID:                      (none)
    Network Settings:             Set automatically using DHCP
[1: start the install, <enter>: forward, '<': back, '!': cancel, '?': help]
> 1_
```

29. On the Reboot screen, the text version asks you to reboot the system, so press 1, and then press Enter.

Perform a Scripted Installation Using a USB Device

Scripted installations are an exciting way to build hosts in a fast and meaningful process. There are times when a fast build is necessary—think disaster recovery. Additionally, scripted installations ensure all builds are exactly the same. And most important, why spend unnecessary time doing something that can be accomplished while you relax and watch the process do what it is designed to do? A friend of mine says he does his best work while getting coffee (he scripts everything). The best approach is to create a master script, and then make copies of it for each ESX host in your inventory, customized with the IP address, hostname, and any other pertinent information needed. An added benefit of this strategy is increased knowledge of the moving parts encompassing an ESX host. An installation script is nothing more than a text file called `ks.cfg`; essentially it is an answer file.

A Sample *ks.cfg* Script

The following code is an example of a ks.cfg file. This file is used to perform a scripted installation; it is the answer key. This is only an example—you can add to or subtract from it—but it is a good starting point for a scripted installation.

```
accepteula
keyboard us
auth --enablemd5 --enableshadow
# Canonical drive names:
clearpart --drives=mpx.vmhba0:C0:T0:L0
# Uncomment to use first detected disk:
#clearpart --firstdisk
install cdrom
rootpw --iscrypted $1$RZG65IhM$geyOIiHJyKqeGqvioM8g.0
timezone --utc 'US/Eastern'
network --addvmportgroup=true --device=vmnic0
--bootproto=static --ip=192.168.1.31
--netmask=255.255.255.0 --gateway=192.168.1.251
--nameserver=192.168.1.15,192.168.1.1
--hostname=vsphere02.phoenix.com
part '/boot' --fstype=ext3 --size=250
--ondisk=mpx.vmhba0:C0:T0:L0
# Uncomment to use first detected disk:
#part '/boot' --fstype=ext3 --size=250 --onfirstdisk
part 'none' --fstype=vmkcore --size=110
--ondisk=mpx.vmhba0:C0:T0:L0
# Uncomment to use first detected disk:
#part 'none' --fstype=vmkcore --size=110 --onfirstdisk
part 'Storage1' --fstype=vmfs3 --size=8604
--grow --ondisk=mpx.vmhba0:C0:T0:L0
# Uncomment to use first detected disk:
#part 'Storage1' --fstype=vmfs3 --size=8604
--grow --onfirstdisk
virtualdisk 'esxconsole' --size=7604 --onvmfs='Storage1'
part 'swap' --fstype=swap --size=600
--onvirtualdisk='esxconsole'
part '/var/log' --fstype=ext3 --size=2000
--onvirtualdisk='esxconsole'
part '/' --fstype=ext3 --size=5000 --grow
--onvirtualdisk='esxconsole'
%post --interpreter=bash
```

When working with scripts, you should use a text editor that won't add any additional markups to the files. If you use WordPad, Notepad, or Microsoft Word to edit files, the script may no longer work and you'll spend time trying to hunt down a problem or failure that will be almost impossible to find. Everything will look exactly as it should to human eyes, but not from a file system perspective. What is odd is that these programs don't add errors every time; once in a while they work just fine. Find a program (on the internet, via a search engine of your choice) called Win32pad, install it, and use it. (When opening this application, be sure to change the format to Unix by selecting File ➤ Format ➤ Unix. Otherwise, Win32pad will default to DOS/Windows and files may stop working.) Another option is to modify all files via a session in Linux.

Where can you find an install script? There are two ways to acquire a script. First, a running ESX host has a copy of its configuration, called anacondo-ks.cfg, in the directory /root. A second option is to take a copy of what is in the anacondo-ks.cfg file, use a program similar to Win32pad, save the file as a Unix format, and then edit as necessary. A benefit of using a working copy of a ks.cfg file is that the root password will be encrypted.

Identify the USB Device

Unfortunately, there is no easy way to identify the USB device. Each piece of hardware has the potential to do this in a slightly different way. However, if you have several hosts that are all the same, identifying the USB device on the first one should tell you what it will be on subsequent hardware of the same make and model. In the following steps we will identify our USB device.

1. On an ESX host that is already installed, open a console session.

2. Without the USB device plugged in, issue this command:

   ```
   fdisk -l  (L as in lima)
   ```

3. Note the devices that are present. A screen shot may be helpful for the before-and-after comparison.

4. Plug in the USB key (in some cases the host may need to be rebooted) and reissue the following command:

   ```
   fdisk -l
   ```

USB devices often take the form of /dev/sda or /dev/sdb. Figure 2.28 shows a USB device before formatting.

Figure 2.28: Identifying the USB device

```
    Device Boot       Start          End      Blocks   Id  System
/dev/sdd1      *          1        32557    2051056    b  W95 FAT32
[root@vsphere02 ~]# _
```

Format the USB Key

Our next step will format the entire space on the USB key and then copy the ks.cfg file to the root of the partition. This assumes the ks.cfg file is already customized for the build it is to be used for. If that's not the case, open the file with Win32pad, make the necessary changes, and proceed.

1. From a console window under root, assuming the USB device is /dev/sdd1, enter the following commands (as shown in Figure 2.29):

   ```
   mkfs.ext3 /dev/sdd1
   cd /mnt/
   ```

Figure 2.29: Formatting the USB device

```
[root@vsphere02 ~]# mkfs.ext3 /dev/sdd1
mke2fs 1.39 (29-May-2006)
Filesystem label=
OS type: Linux
Block size=4096 (log=2)
Fragment size=4096 (log=2)
256512 inodes, 512764 blocks
25638 blocks (5.00%) reserved for the super user
First data block=0
Maximum filesystem blocks=528482304
16 block groups
32768 blocks per group, 32768 fragments per group
16032 inodes per group
Superblock backups stored on blocks:
        32768, 98304, 163840, 229376, 294912

Writing inode tables: done
Creating journal (8192 blocks): done
Writing superblocks and filesystem accounting information: done

This filesystem will be automatically checked every 25 mounts or
180 days, whichever comes first.  Use tune2fs -c or -i to override.
[root@vsphere02 ~]# _
```

2. Enter the following commands to create a directory where one didn't exist before:

```
mkdir usbdisk
cd /root
```

3. Enter the following commands to copy the file to the USB drive:

```
cp ks.cfg /mnt/usbdisk
unmount /mnt/usbdisk
```

The USB device is now formatted, has a copy of `ks.cfg` on it, and has been modified (prior to our copy) by an administrator to contain ESX host–specific information.

4. Insert the installation media and power on the host; the installation will boot from the CD/DVD and draw answers from the USB device.

5. On the splash screen, choose the option ESX Scripted Install Using USB ks.cfg and press Enter.

The process should take off; when complete, a prompt appears asking you to reboot.

Postinstallation Configurations

Time is very important in a virtualized environment. Next we will make sure that time is configured using NTP. All hosts should be pointed to the same device so that time will be consistent across the virtual infrastructure.

Configure Network Time Protocol

Whether you use Virtual Center or log into the host via vSphere Client, the process is nearly identical.

1. Select the Configuration tab.

2. Under Software, click Time Configuration. This screen will show the current date and time, whether the NTP client is running, and

which NTP servers are currently configured. If the date and time are wrong, go to the next step.

3. In the top right, click Properties. This window is the place to adjust the date and time. Or you can click Options in the lower right to configure the NTP daemon (see Figure 2.30).

Figure 2.30: Time configuration

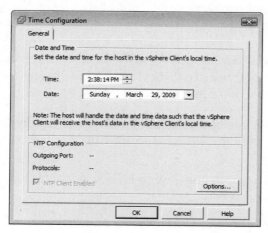

4. On the General tab, the service can be started, stopped, or restarted, or changed to start automatically, start and stop with the host, or start and stop manually (see Figure 2.31).

Figure 2.31: Setting an NTP server; virtual machines do not have the ability to keep time for themselves.

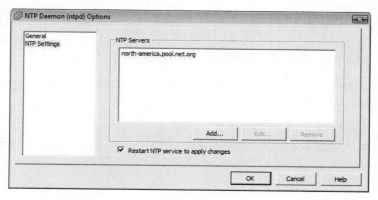

5. Click NTP Settings in the window on the left.

6. Click Add and enter the NTP server address; then select Restart NTP Service to apply changes and click OK.

7. As a further step in the process, make sure the firewall allows for NTP traffic.

Configure the Firewall

The firewall will need to be addressed one way or another. If you have monitoring software, you will need to open a port to allow the SNMP protocol through for monitoring. Some organizations may turn off the firewall or open other ports for other software applications. Here we outline how to find the firewall and configure it:

1. From vSphere Client, click the Configuration tab and under Software click "Security Profile".

2. This step varies a bit depending on whether you're using ESX or ESXi. But either host at this point will show what is running and allowed through the firewall.

   a. For ESX, click Properties in the top-right corner.

      The resulting window allows you to configure ports in the firewall. Simply check or uncheck a desired service or client to allow or disallow access through the firewall. The options button allows for fine-grain control of the highlighted service: Start, Stop, Restart, and so forth (see Figure 2.32).

Figure 2.32: ESX firewall properties

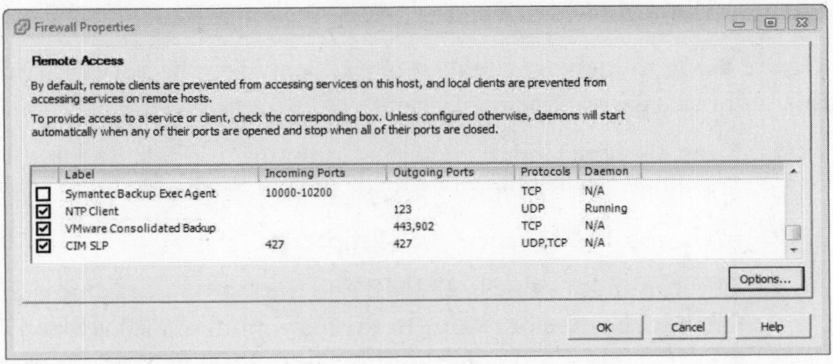

b. For ESXi, click Properties in the top-right corner.

This window is clearly different from the one for ESX, but it functions in much the same way. You can see that ESXi has a much smaller security footprint than its big brother ESX (see Figure 2.33).

Figure 2.33: ESXi firewall properties

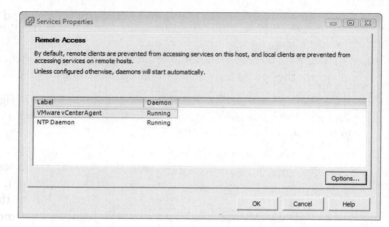

Configure the Service Console

The Service Console is the first virtual machine on an ESX host. Unlike in ESX, on an ESXi host the Service Console isn't nearly as prominent. Nonetheless, there are some configuration tasks that will help make regular maintenance or your ESXi host a lot easier.

Service Console Memory

We are going to increase the memory allocated to the Service Console; this will increase our performance.

1. From vSphere Client, click the Configuration tab, and under Hardware click Memory.

2. In the top-right corner, click Properties.

3. The minimum value is 272MB and the maximum value is 800MB. Change the memory value to the maximum of 800MB and click OK. (Changes will not take effect until after you reboot the host.)

Remember, a host has to be able to juggle a multitude of tasks at any one point in time. It is advisable to max out the memory by changing it to 800MB. This will help keep the host from disconnecting under times of stress, keep the performance high, and minimize any kind of service interruptions. All things considered, 800MB is a small price to pay to keep the infrastructure running at peak performance.

Service Console Networking

Many large organizations have a strategy of teaming their NICs and sometimes their power on key servers. In this way, an organization can bring down half of their network for routine maintenance without impacting networking or power on a server. Obviously this is a highly desirable way to run a successful operation because there is limited downtime. With VMware virtualization, and specifically High Availability (HA), you must keep a special consideration in mind as well. If the Service Console has only one physical NIC, if something happens to that one piece of hardware and HA is enabled, vCenter will see the host as down and potentially restart the virtual machines that were on that host on another host. If the host were to go down, this would be desirable; if only the physical NIC were to go down, this would clearly be bad, as virtual machines may be trying to run in more than one location.

To solve this issue, take the following steps to attach two or more physical NICs to the Service Console so that networking can be achieved through two different channels if necessary:

1. Click the Configuration tab, and under Hardware click Networking; then find the vSwitch that has the Service Console and click its Properties link (as shown in Figure 2.34).

Figure 2.34: Service Console networking

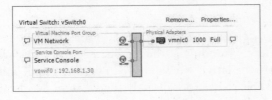

> **NOTE**   Adding or removing NICs does not affect the underlying virtual machines in the vSwitch you're working on, as long as they have at least one NIC to communicate with.
>
> If all NICs are removed from a vSwitch, the underlying virtual machines can still communicate among themselves, but not to the outside world.

2. Click the Network Adapters tab, click Add, and put a checkmark in the box next to the VMnic that will be the second in the team. Obviously, unclaimed adapters (as shown in Figure 2.35) are not being used by any other networking; an adapter can be used by only one vSwitch at a time.

3. Click Next. If the order of the NIC is important, adjust it here.

4. Review the changes and click Finish.

Figure 2.35: Adding unclaimed adapters

Now our Service Console has two physical channels to which it can communicate with vCenter and HA (as you can see in Figure 2.36).

Figure 2.36: Two NICs for our Service Console

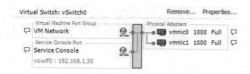

Before moving on to configuring the Service Console, we have to be able to get into it, either by standing at the Service Console or by remoting into it. If we choose the latter, we will have to perform some initial steps if we want to be able to use root directly. Those steps are detailed in the following sections.

Elevate Privileges to Root Access

Root access to the Service Console is disabled by default. When security is important and root access is to be protected, most VMware administrators will have a secondary login to a host and then they will elevate (su -) their privileges up to root. su - is the command used to elevate from a non-root account to the root account. While adding a user account to a host is not necessarily part of configuring the Service Console, it is still a better strategy than allowing root access.

Create an Account with SSH Access

To create an account on a host, log into the host via vSphere Client; the Users And Groups tab is not available in vCenter. Then take the following steps:

1. Click the Users & Groups tab, and then click Users (see Figure 2.37).

Figure 2.37: Adding users to secure root from SSH sessions

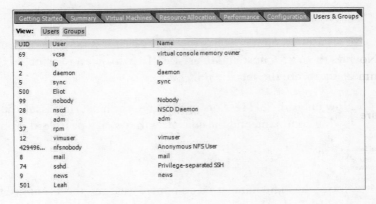

2. Right-click in the whitespace and select Add.

3. Fill in the login, username, and password, and select the option Grant Shell Access To This User (as shown in Figure 2.38). Under Group Membership, use the drop-down box to assign this user to the Users group. (Be very aware of the syntax of the username. In VMware usernames are case sensitive.)

Figure 2.38: Adding a new user

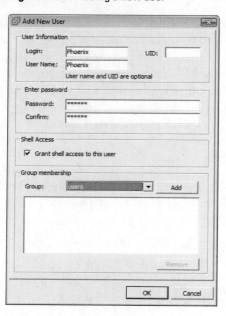

This user account now has the ability to use WinSCP to transfer files to an ESX host and to use PuTTy (which is a form of SSH) to connect into the specific ESX host.

4. Now open an SSH session and log into the host; then issue the following command and the console will return a password prompt:

```
su -
```

Notice the login name used an uppercase P and the $ changed to a #, which is the sign of root (as shown in Figure 2.39).

Figure 2.39: Elevating to root

5. Instead of clicking the X to log out, type **exit** to drop the session back down to regular user status. This is helpful if additional non-administrator-level tasks need to be completed rather than just logging back in. Typing **exit** again will drop the session altogether.

Permit Root Access via SSH (puTTy)

This next task is somewhat controversial. In ESX 3.5 newly built hosts had this feature enabled (meaning remote access by root was disabled) by default for security reasons. This edition is no different; however, the feature can be disabled. A better strategy is to create another login account on the ESX host and then elevate to root access.

Now we will disable the security feature and allow remote access by root.

1. Now that there is an account that has SSH permission, log into the Service Console with it.

2. Elevate your privileges to root using the su - command and navigate to

```
cd /etc/SSH
nano SSHd_config
```

This will open the file that needs to be configured. You can use any text editor.

3. Scroll down to PermitRootLogin and change no to yes (see Figure 2.40).

Figure 2.40: Permit root login

```
#LoginGraceTime 2m
PermitRootLogin no
#StrictModes yes
#MaxAuthTries 6
```

4. To save your changes, press Ctrl+X, and then press Y to save changes. Press Enter to keep the same name on the file. A great rule of thumb is to go back into the file and verify the change was saved. You can see in Figure 2.41 that yes now appears next to PermitRootLogin.

Building a VMware vSphere Environment

PART I

Figure 2.41: yes now appears next to `PermitRootLogin`.

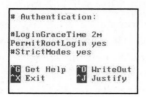

5. To make the change active, issue the following command to restart the service, as shown in Figure 2.42:

```
service sshd restart
```

Test the change and verify that root has SSH login.

Figure 2.42: Restart the sshd service.

```
[root@vsphere01 ssh]# service sshd restart
Stopping sshd:                                          [  OK  ]
Starting sshd:                                          [  OK  ]
[root@vsphere01 ssh]# _
```

Configure Active Directory Authentication

Even in many large organizations, VMware administrators and departments often choose not to integrate VMware ESX hosts into Active Directory (AD). Instead, they choose to keep the host as streamlined as possible; remember that many hosts run 20 to 40 virtual machines, so that the workloads they are responsible for get as much processing power with as little drag as possible. Loading too many additional features or software into the host and Service Console can slow down communication to and from vCenter and, in rare cases, bring down a host. When AD integration is not used, usually only a handful of administrators have access to the internal workings of any ESX host. For the most part, all work can be done from vCenter and so there is no need for admins to have access to ESX hosts. The more admins who have access to hosts, the less security there is on the virtual infrastructure. Ask yourself how many administrators in your environment have Enterprise Administrator Access to the domain. Also keep in mind that AD authentication on ESX is not as clean as it could be if it were a Windows server. If the organization or VMware administrators are not diligent in keeping up with the extra amount of overhead, pursuing integration should be a key decision—don't proceed lightly.

The reason you would want to add AD authentication is to make it easier to add administrators to an AD group that has privileges to work with the infrastructure, rather than adding user accounts to each host or, worse, allowing generic accounts for multiple people.

To begin, let's add a user for AD authentication. First navigate to the following:

```
cd /usr/sbin
```

and issue the following command to create the username (see Figure 2.43):

```
useradd %username%
```

Figure 2.43: Remember that usernames are case sensitive.

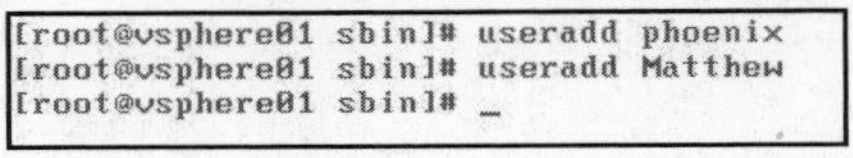

```
[root@vsphere01 sbin]# useradd phoenix
[root@vsphere01 sbin]# useradd Matthew
[root@vsphere01 sbin]# _
```

Active Directory authentication is tricky. Notice in Figure 2.43 that two users were added, one was phoenix and the other was Matthew. Prior to this another account called Phoenix (uppercase P) was added for another task: SSH access. Since Active Directory does not distinguish case in usernames, this configuration could open up a security breach. ESX may query AD for Phoenix or phoenix, and if only one exists, AD will return the same information for both accounts. Another concern to be aware of is if an account called root exists in the AD tree, whoever owns that would then have access to the VMware infrastructure.

To enable AD authentication, take the following steps:

1. If the domain is phoenix.com and the dc is ad01; then from /usr/sbin issue this command (see Figure 2.44). (Please note that the second and third lines of this code will actually be on one line.)

```
esxcfg-auth --enablead --addomain=phoenix.com --addc ad01
.phoenix.com --krb5realm=phoenix.com --krb5kdc
ad01.phoenix.com --krb5adminserve
r=ad01.phoenix.com --enablekrb5
```

Figure 2.44: Enabling AD

```
[root@vsphere01 sbin]# esxcfg-auth --enablead --addomain=phoenix.com --addc ad01
.phoenix.com --krb5realm=phoenix.com --krb5kdc ad01.phoenix.com --krb5adminserve
r=ad01.phoenix.com --enablekrb5_
```

2. If there are no errors, restart the firewall by issuing this command:

   ```
   service firewall restart
   ```

3. Now add the user account Matthew (or whichever account you are working with) to the admin group on vCenter; this account will be able to log into the Service Console and vCenter using vSphere Client.

   Once the firewall restarts, additional services, such as Active Director Kerberos, will be listed (see Figure 2.45).

Figure 2.45: Firewall additions

Security Profile

Firewall

Incoming Connections	
CIM SLP	427 (UDP,TCP)
CIM Secure Server	5989 (TCP)
CIM Server	5988 (TCP)
SSH Server	22 (TCP)
Outgoing Connections	
VMware License Client	27000,27010 (TCP)
CIM SLP	427 (UDP,TCP)
Active Director Kerberos	464,88 (TCP,UDP)
NTP Client	123 (UDP)
VMware vCenter Agent	902 (UDP)
SSH Server	22 (TCP)
VMware Consolidated Backup	443,902 (TCP)
Kerberos	749,88 (TCP,UDP)

4. If the account added still cannot log into the Service Console, verify that the date and time is accurate within 5 minutes. Kerberos has a very slim margin of error; if the time is 5 minutes out of synchronization with Active Directory, there will be no login.

vSphere Client Installation for ESX or ESXi

Follow these steps to install vSphere Client on your computer. Doing so will allow you to use a GUI to remote into either vCenter or an ESX or ESXi host.

1. Open your browser.

2. Note the IP address on the ESXi console window and enter your IP address into your web browser, like this:

   ```
   http://192.168.1.2/
   ```

3. If the Choose A Digital Certificate window appears, click OK.

4. If the browser is IE 7, the next window to appear is a security certificate window; click Continue To This Website (Not Recommended).

5. The Choose A Digital Certificate window may reappear; if so, click OK a second time. The following are the contents of what you will see if you connect to an ESX host, or if you connect to an ESXi host, and what you can expect to see on each:

   ESX: vSphere Client/vSphere Web Services SDK   This browser page contains links to the host to download and install each of these management tools. Datastores and managed objects on the host can also be browsed here.

   ESXi: vSphere Client/vSphere Web Services SDK/vSphere Remote Command Line (virtual appliance, tar.gz, or .exe**)** This browser page contains links to the host to download and install each of these management tools. This list even includes a virtual appliance to use as a remote command-line tool. This page also allows an administrator to browse datastores and managed objects in this host's inventory (as shown in Figure 2.46). Figure 2.47 shows what the output looks like.

Figure 2.46: Web-based datastore browser

Web-Based Datastore Browser

Use your web browser to find and download files (for example, virtual machine and virtual disk files).

• Browse datastores in this host's inventory

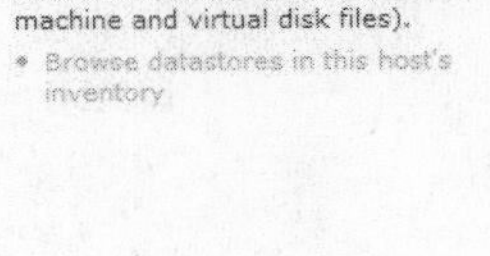

Figure 2.47: Index of datastores from web browser

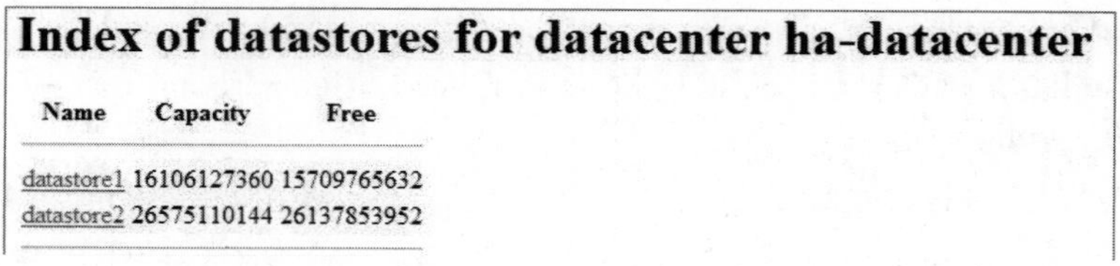

Index of datastores for datacenter ha-datacenter

Name	Capacity	Free
datastore1	16106127360	15709765632
datastore2	26575110144	26137853952

6. Click Download vSphere Client (as shown in Figure 2.48).

Figure 2.48: Download vSphere client

Getting Started

If you need to access this host remotely, use the following program to install vSphere Client software. After running the installer, start the client and log in to this host.

• Download vSphere Client

7. When the Do You Want To Run Or Save This File window opens, choose Run. This file will download approximately 68MB. Follow the prompts to finish the install.

3

Installing and Configuring vCenter Server

IN THIS CHAPTER, YOU WILL LEARN TO:

▶ **PREPARE FOR INSTALLATION** (Pages 70–77)

- Identify Hardware Requirements (Page 71)
- Identify Operating System Requirements for vCenter Server and vSphere Client (Page 71)
- Identify Database Requirements (Page 74)
- Identify Networking Requirements (Page 75)
- Identify Authentication Requirements (Page 77)

▶ **INSTALL A DATABASE** (Pages 77–83)

- Create a vCenter Database in Microsoft SQL Server 2005 (Page 77)
- Create a vCenter Database in Oracle (Page 81)

▶ **INSTALL VCENTER SERVER** (Pages 83–99)

- Prepare for Installation (Page 84)
- Install vCenter Server (Page 84)
- Install Additional Components (Page 89)

▶ **INSTALL VSPHERE CLIENT** (Pages 99–100)

▶ **CONFIGURE VCENTER** (Pages 100–120)

- Connect to vCenter Server (Page 101)
- Install Plug-ins in vSphere Client (Page 102)
- Configure Advanced vCenter Server Settings (Page 104)
- Create a Datacenter (Page 106)
- Add a Cluster (Page 107)
- Add a Host (Page 116)

V Center Server is the central management component in a vSphere environment. Without vCenter Server, ESX and ESXi hosts are simply hypervisors with the ability to run virtual machines, commonly referred to as guests. When coupled with appropriate host licensing, vCenter Server can significantly extend the capabilities of the ESX and ESXi hosts it manages. Some of the extended capabilities that vCenter Server includes are VMotion, Storage VMotion, High Availability, and Distributed Resource Scheduling. Keep in mind that vCenter Server does not enable these features but rather leverages these capabilities when hosts are assigned licenses that include those features.

You should become familiar with vCenter Server's requirements as well as the proper installation method. A well-configured vCenter Server installation provides a solid administrative platform to manage vSphere to its fullest potential.

Prepare for Installation

One of most important components of the vSphere environment is vCenter Server. vCenter Server acts as a central management point for managing ESX and ESXi hosts, and additional components like the Guided Consolidation Service, vCenter Update Manager, and user permissions.

Installing vCenter Server can be broken into three steps.

1. Ensure that your system is capable of running vCenter Server.

2. Install vCenter Server and any additional components.

3. Perform basic configuration of vCenter Server and some additional components.

As of this writing, vCenter Server is available only for Microsoft Windows systems. This has been a sore subject for administrators in IT shops that primarily run operating systems other than Windows. VMware has listened, and currently there is a technical preview of vCenter Server for Linux, available for download at http://www.vmtn.net/ as a virtual appliance.

vCenter Server must operate on the Microsoft Windows platform. What else does it require? To ensure that vCenter Server can accommodate the performance necessary to efficiently manage ESX and ESXi hosts, VMware has provided some preliminary requirements for the hardware, operating system, and database required to support vCenter Server.

Identify Hardware Requirements

VMware vCenter Server can be installed on a physical or virtual machine that meets the requirements listed in Table 3.1

Table 3.1: Hardware Requirements

Component	Requirement
Processor	2.0GHz or greater Intel or AMD x86 based processor. It is a best practice to use a faster processor if the vCenter Database runs on the same server.
Memory	2GB of RAM. Again, it is a best practice to use more RAM if the database is running on the same server. The VMware vCenter Management Webservices require from 128MB to 1.5GB of additional memory. The memory is allocated at system startup.
Database	A minimum of 1GB of additional storage is required in addition to the storage required for the operating system installation. If the VMware vCenter Update Manager service is installed on the same system, an additional 22GB of space is required to accommodate storage of patches. If Microsoft SQL Server 2005 Express is installed as the database, 2GB of disk space is required during the installation, with 1.5GB reclaimed after the installation is complete.
Networking	A 100MB network connection can be used, but a 1GB network connection is recommended.

Meeting these requirements will ensure proper operation of vCenter Server and any additional components. When designing the environment, give additional thought to future growth or scalability of vCenter Server.

Identify Operating System Requirements for vCenter Server and vSphere Client

Due to the fact that vCenter Server was developed to operate on a Windows platform, VMware supports this product on only a limited number of operating system configurations. Some operating systems, such as Windows 2000, are no longer supported, or are referred to as end of life, while others, such as 64-bit versions, are not yet supported 100 percent natively. Additionally, some operating systems were not originally designed for this type of workload, such as Windows 2003 Web Edition. Table 3.2 lists the operating systems for which VMware vCenter Server is supported, their versions, and supported Internet Protocol modes.

Table 3.2: Operating System Requirements for vCenter Server

Operating System	IPv4?	IPv6?	Mixed IPv4 and IPv6?
Windows XP Pro (SP2 or greater, x86)	Yes		Yes
Windows 2003 Server (SP1 or greater x86)	Yes		Yes
Windows 2003 Server R2	Yes		Yes
Windows 2003 Server x64	Yes		Yes
Windows Server 2008 x86	Yes	Yes	Yes
Windows Server 2008 x64	Yes	Yes	Yes

VMware has tested the operating systems in Table 3.2 and certified their use for vCenter Server. Older operating systems, such as Windows NT 4.0, Windows 2000, and Windows 2003 without any service pack, have failed to meet the minimum requirements of vCenter Server.

To manage VMware vCenter Server, you use vSphere Client to configure, manage, and monitor the environment. vSphere Client was developed using Microsoft .NET technologies and is also limited to Microsoft operating systems. Table 3.3 lists the operating systems on which vSphere Client may be installed to manage a vCenter Server.

Table 3.3: vSphere Client System Requirements

Operating System	IPv4?	IPv6?	Mixed IPv4 and IPv6?
Windows XP Pro (SP2 or greater, x86)	Yes	No	Yes
Windows XP Pro (SP2 or greater, x64)	Yes	No	Yes
Windows 2003 Server (SP1 or greater x86)	Yes	No	Yes
Windows 2003 Server R2	Yes	No	Yes
Windows 2003 Server x64	Yes	No	Yes
Windows 2003 Server Standard and Web Edition x86 or x64	Yes	No	Yes

Table 3.3: vSphere Client System Requirements *(continued)*

Operating System	IPv4?	IPv6?	Mixed IPv4 and IPv6?
Windows Vista Business with SP1	Yes	Yes	Yes
Windows Vista Enterprise with SP1	Yes	Yes	Yes
Windows Vista Business with SP1 x64	Yes	Yes	Yes
Windows Vista Enterprise with SP1 x64	Yes	Yes	Yes
Windows Server 2008 x86	Yes	Yes	Yes
Windows Server 2008 x64	Yes	Yes	Yes

There are also some best practices with regard to the domain membership of a server running vCenter Server. Following these guidelines will ensure installation and operation run more smoothly:

- Microsoft strongly recommends that vCenter Server be joined to a Microsoft Windows domain. This will provide better security and domain capabilities to services that require it.

- vCenter Server 4.0 adds the ability to use distributed vCenter Servers, referred to as Linked Mode vCenter Servers. If you are using Linked Mode vCenter Servers, the individual vCenter Servers may be in different domains, provided there is a two-way trust between the two domains.

In addition to vSphere Client, vSphere Web Access may be used to manage the vCenter Server installation, and it has some minimum requirements as well. The following browsers have been tested by VMware to verify proper operation of vSphere Web Access:

Microsoft Windows Internet Explorer 6.x

Microsoft Windows Internet Explorer 7.0

Mozilla 1.x for Windows/Linux

Mozilla Firefox 2.0.x

Mozilla Firefox 3.0.x

Ensuring that the hardware and software requirements are met will ensure that the configuration used for vCenter Server, vSphere Client,

Building a VMware vSphere Environment

PART I

and vSphere Web Access will provide a trouble-free installation and management platform for the vSphere environment.

Identify Database Requirements

At the heart of VMware vCenter Server and its ancillary components lie a number of databases. Separate databases are recommended for vCenter Server and ancillary components, such as vCenter Update Manager, although it is not required for each additional component to be installed using a separate database. Separate databases add levels of separation of the data and can result in better performance levels. These databases do not have to be on the same machine as vCenter Server, nor do they have to reside on the same remote server. It is possible to have a vCenter instance installed on one server, with its SQL database residing on another server, while having the vCenter Update Manager database on a third server. The choices are wide and depend on your operational needs. The default installation will load vCenter and required databases on the same system. The vCenter Server installation routine includes Microsoft SQL Server 2005 Express Edition.

If you accept the defaults, the instance of Microsoft SQL Server 2005 Express that is bundled with vCenter Server is used, and user authentication defaults to the rights of the user account performing the installation. If another supported database is used, administrative credentials are required.

NOTE Although not required, as a best practice, ensure that the database service on either the local or remote machine is also running as a domain account to aid in authentication if you are using any edition of Microsoft SQL Server 2005.

The following databases are supported for vCenter Server and vCenter Update Manager installations.

- Microsoft SQL Server 2005 Express
- Microsoft SQL Server 2005 Standard Edition SP2
- Microsoft SQL Server 2005 Enterprise Edition SP2
- Microsoft SQL Server 2005 Enterprise Edition SP2 x64
- Microsoft SQL Server 2008 Standard Edition

- Microsoft SQL Server 2008 Enterprise Edition
- Microsoft SQL Server 2008 Enterprise Edition x64
- Oracle 10g Standard Edition, Release 1 (10.1.0.3.0)
- Oracle 10g Enterprise Edition, Release 1 (10.1.0.3.0)
- Oracle 10g Standard Edition, Release 2 (10.2.0.1.0)
- Oracle 10g Enterprise Edition, Release 2 (10.2.0.1.0)
- Oracle 10g Enterprise Edition, Release 2 (10.2.0.1.0) x64
- Oracle 11g Standard Edition
- Oracle 11g Enterprise Edition

Identify Networking Requirements

Because vSphere is not a single stand-alone server, application, or isolated computing system, the pieces of the puzzle will require some form of communication between them. There are many possible configuration scenarios depending on the environment in which vSphere is being deployed.

A vCenter Server must be able to communicate with each host and each vSphere client. Furthermore, if a remote database server is utilized rather than a local instance of the database, the required TCP/IP ports for that database installation are also required.

If an instance of vCenter Server is installed on Windows Server 2008, you must either disable the Windows Firewall or make an exception to allow communication between all of the required pieces of the environment.

vCenter Server requires several ports to be open when you select a default installation. Each of these ports will be used for a different portion of the overall communications path. To enable proper communication between each of the components, consult a network engineer to ensure the appropriate ports are open for communication.

Web ports that are required to be open include the following:

- Port 80 is required for the purpose of redirecting nonsecure requests to vCenter Server on a secure port.
- Port 443 is the default port used to communicate with vSphere Client and to look for data from vSphere Web Access Client and

other VMware Software Development Kit (SDK) applications such as the VI Toolkit. You can change this port, but vSphere Client and any SDK applications must use the vCenter Server name, followed by the nondefault port number.

- Port 8080 is the port used by Web Services HTTP.

- Port 8443 is the port used by Web Services HTTPS.

Directory Services ports that are required to be open include the following:

- Port 389 is the standard port number used for Lightweight Directory Access Protocol (LDAP) services. This port is used for the Directory Services component of vCenter Server. It must be available to vCenter Server, even if vCenter Server is not part of a Linked Mode Group. You can change from port 389 to any available port ranging from 1025 to 65535. This is the normal LDAP port that the vCenter Server Active Directory Application Mode (ADAM) instance listens on.

- Port 636 is also used when using vCenter in Linked Mode. This is the Secure Sockets Layer (SSL) port of the local vCenter Server ADAM Instance. It is the preferred port number, but it can also be changed to any available port ranging from 1025 to 65535.

Host and client ports that are required to be open include the following:

- Port 902 is used for multiple tasks. It is used to manage ESX and ESXi hosts and send data to them. vCenter Server also receives a heartbeat at regular intervals from hosts on port 902 over User Datagram Protocol (UDP). This port must not be blocked between vCenter Server and hosts, or between hosts. Port 902 is also used for providing remote console access to virtual machines from vSphere Client.

- Port 903 is used in the same fashion as 902: it provides remote console access of virtual machines to vSphere Client. These ports must be open for proper communication to occur between vCenter Server and vSphere Client, as well as from vSphere Client and the ESX and ESXi hosts.

Identify Authentication Requirements

Initial authentication in vCenter Server is handled through local user accounts on the system that vCenter Server is installed on. Authentication to managed ESX and ESXi servers is handled through vCenter Server as hosts are added to the vSphere configuration. Additionally, local accounts on each host may be created. Accounts local to ESX and ESXi hosts do not have permissions in the vCenter Server interface, even though they may have elevated privileges at the host level.

Install a Database

As previously mentioned, VMware utilizes industry-standard databases for vCenter Server. Administrators cannot easily use or access the raw data contained in the vCenter Server database; instead, they must use vSphere Client. Components like the datacenters, clusters, resource pools, hosts, and virtual machines, along with their associated configuration and performance data, are stored in the backend database that vCenter Server is connected to. As mentioned, the default installation includes Microsoft SQL Server 2005 Express Edition. The vCenter Server installer automatically creates a data source name (DSN), the database, and the database schema when using the embedded SQL Server 2005 Express. We'll cover installation of the default database when we discuss vCenter Server installation.

We will examine a few alternate database installations—Microsoft SQL Server 2005 (other than Express Edition) or Oracle 10*g* or 11*g*—in the following sections.

Create a vCenter Database in Microsoft SQL Server 2005

The default Microsoft SQL Server 2005 Express Edition installation with vCenter Server supports up to 5 hosts and 50 virtual machines. It is not considered as robust as its cousins, Microsoft SQL Server 2005 Standard and Enterprise Editions. In many cases the Standard and Enterprise Editions are chosen due to their enhanced feature set, which they do not share with the Express Edition.

Tables listing the differences among the various editions of Microsoft SQL Server 2005 can be found on Microsoft's website:

```
http://www.microsoft.com/Sqlserver/2005/en/us/
compare-features.aspx
```

Whether you have chosen to utilize Standard or Enterprise Edition, Microsoft recommends certain configuration settings when you're creating the vCenter Server database. The database can reside on the local system or can be accessed remotely. This database can be created automatically using the SQL 2005 management tools. Using the automatic method will require some additional configuration. To accomplish this easily, use the following steps:

1. If vCenter Server is part of a Windows domain, create a domain account that will be used to access the SQL Server instance.

NOTE   It is not a best practice to use a Domain Admin account for this purpose but rather a dedicated domain account. Make sure this user has db_datawriter and db_datareader permissions on the SQL instance.

---

2. During initial installation and upgrades, the vpxuser account must have db_owner rights on the MSDB database. This access can be revoked after an installation or upgrade.

3. Load SQL Query Analyzer with a user that has DBO privileges, and run the following instructions:

```
use [master]
go
CREATE DATABASE [VCDB] ON PRIMARY
(NAME = N'vcdb', FILENAME = N'C:\VCDB.mdf' , ➡
SIZE = 2000KB , FILEGROWTH = 10% )
LOG ON
(NAME = N'vcdb_log', FILENAME = N'C:\VCDB.ldf' , ➡
SIZE = 1000KB , FILEGROWTH = 10%)
COLLATE SQL_Latin1_General_CP1_CI_AS
go
use VCDB
go
```

```
sp_addlogin @loginame=[vpxuser], @passwd=N'vpxuser', ➡
@defdb='VCDB', @deflanguage='
go
ALTER LOGIN [vpxuser] WITH CHECK_POLICY = OFF
go
CREATE USER [vpxuser] for LOGIN [vpxuser]
go
sp_addrolemember @rolename = 'db_owner', ➡
@membername = 'vpxuser'
go
use MSDB
go
CREATE USER [vpxuser] for LOGIN [vpxuser]
go
sp_addrolemember @rolename = 'db_owner', ➡
@membername = 'vpxuser'
go
```

Remember that you can change the database user, location, and database name within this script. Keep in mind that these values will need to match the DSN created to access the database.

4. Use the same SQL Query Analyzer window to run the following scripts in the order they are listed. These scripts, which create the database schema, can be located and run from the vpx/dbshema directory of the installation media.

```
VCDB_mssql.SQL
purge_stat1_proc_mssql.sql
purge_stat2_proc_mssql.sql
purge_stat3_proc_mssql.sql
purge_usage_stats_proc_mssql.sql
stats_rollup1_proc_mssql.sql
stats_rollup2_proc_mssql.sql
stats_rollup3_proc_mssql.sql
 cleanup_events_mssql.sql
 delete_stats_proc_mssql.sql
```

5. There are some additional scripts that work with the SQL Server Agent to handle job scheduling and similar tasks. They are not

supported when you're using Microsoft SQL Server 2005 Express Edition, as that edition does not natively provide any scheduling functions. Again, using the same SQL Query Analyzer, load and run each of these scripts in the order listed. Before running the scripts, confirm that the SQL Server Agent is running.

```
job_schedule1_mssql.sql
job_schedule2_mssql.sql
job_schedule3_mssql.sql
job_cleanup_events
```

6. The database and database schema have now been created and are ready for a DSN to connect to the VCDB instance.

7. On the vCenter Server system, open the Windows ODBC Data Source Administrator by choosing Settings ➤ Control Panel ➤ Administrative Tools ➤ Data Sources (ODBC).

NOTE   If you're using a 64-bit operating system, you are required to run the 32-bit ODBC Administrator application, which is located at C:\Windows\SysWOW64\odbcad32.exe.

---

8. Select the System DSN tab.

9. Click Add, select SQL Native Client, and click Finish.

10. Type an ODBC DSN name in the Name field, something like **vCenter Server**.

11. Select the server name from the Server drop-down menu and click Next. This can be the local system or a remote system.

NOTE   With a default installation of SQL Server, only a single instance or installation of SQL is present. If multiple SQL Server installations are present on a server, each additional installation is referred to as a named instance. The primary instance does not have a specific name, other than the server name, while named instances are typically signified as *SERVERNAME\InstanceName*.

---

12. Type the SQL Server machine name in the Server text field (or select it from the Server drop-down list).

Building a VMware
vSphere Environment

PART I

13. Select Windows Authentication.

14. Select the database created for the vCenter Server system from the Change The Default Database To menu and click Next.

15. Click Finish.

A DSN that is compatible with vCenter Server is now available. When the vCenter Server installer prompts for the DSN of the database, select vCenter Server, or whatever value you entered in step 10.

Microsoft SQL Server 2005 is a popular database, and as you can see in steps 1 through 15, it is relatively simple to configure.

Create a vCenter Database in Oracle

Not every environment uses Microsoft SQL Server 2005. For various reasons, administrators are often forced to choose databases already being used in their environment. Oracle is a popular database choice, and VMware supports several versions of Oracle, including 10*g* and 11*g*. Oracle has another appeal to environments that have a limited Microsoft footprint: it is available for many other platforms, including Linux, Solaris, and HP-UX. You don't have to have Oracle installed locally on the vCenter Server. Just as with Microsoft's database offering, when you're using Oracle, certain configurations are considered best practices when creating the database. Perform these steps to create the database:

1. Log on to a SQL*Plus session with the system account.

2. Run the following commands, or script, to create the database:

```
CREATE SMALLFILE TABLESPACE "VPX" DATAFILE
 '/u01/app/oracle/oradata/vcdb/vpx01.dbf' ➥
SIZE 1G AUTOEXTEND ON NEXT 10M MAXSIZE
 UNLIMITED LOGGING EXTENT MANAGEMENT ➥
LOCAL SEGMENT SPACE MANAGEMENT AUTO;
```

NOTE The datafile path ('/u01/app/oracle/oradata/vcdb/vpx01.dbf' in this case) must be a valid path on your Oracle system; change this to match your particular environment.

---

3. Open a SQL*Plus window with a user that has schema owner rights on the vCenter Server database to create the database schema.

4. Locate the dbschema scripts in the vCenter Server installation package bin/dbschema directory.

5. In SQL*Plus, run the scripts in sequence on the database. *<path>* is the directory path to the bin/dbschema folder.

   ```
   @<path>/VCDB_oracle.SQL
   @<path>/purge_stat1_proc_oracle.sql
   @<path>/purge_stat2_proc_oracle.sql
   @<path>/purge_stat3_proc_oracle.sql
   @<path>/purge_usage_stats_proc_oracle.sql
   @<path>/stats_rollup1_proc_oracle.sql
   @<path>/stats_rollup2_proc_oracle.sql
   @<path>/stats_rollup3_proc_oracle.sql
   @<path>/cleanup_events_oracle.sql
   @<path>/delete_stats_proc_oracle.sql
   ```

6. All supported editions of Oracle Server require that these additional scripts be run to set up scheduled jobs on the database:

   ```
   @<path>/job_schedule1_oracle.sql
   @<path>/job_schedule2_oracle.sql
   @<path>/job_schedule3_oracle.sql
   @<path>/job_cleanup_events_oracle.sql
   ```

7. Oracle can use a local or remote Oracle instance. From the same SQL*Plus window, run the following script (where *VPXADMIN* is the user):

   ```
   CREATE USER "VPXADMIN" PROFILE "DEFAULT"
   IDENTIFIED BY "oracle" DEFAULT TABLESPACE
   "VPX" ACCOUNT UNLOCK;
   grant connect to VPXADMIN;
   grant resource to VPXADMIN;
   grant create view to VPXADMIN;
   grant create sequence to VPXADMIN;
   grant create table to VPXADMIN;
   grant execute on dbms_lock to VPXADMIN;
   grant execute on dbms_job to VPXADMIN;
   grant unlimited tablespace to VPXADMIN;
   ```

8. If the Oracle database is not installed on the same system as vCenter Server, download and install the Oracle client.

9. On the vCenter Server system, open the Windows ODBC Data Source Administrator by choosing Settings ➤ Control Panel ➤ Administrative Tools ➤ Data Sources (ODBC).

NOTE   If you are using a 64-bit operating system, run the 32-bit ODBC Administrator application, which is located at `C:\Windows\SysWOW64\odbcad32.exe`.

---

10. Select the System DSN tab and click Add.

11. Select the appropriate Oracle driver for your installation and click Finish.

12. Enter the name of the DSN, such as **vCenter Server**.

13. Ensure that appropriate values appear in the TNS Names field referencing the local or remote Oracle instances. Select the appropriate TNS Service name.

14. Enter the username created in the Create User section.

15. Click OK. An Oracle database is now available for the vCenter Server installer.

Like SQL Server, Oracle is a popular database and is also relatively simple to configure for use with vCenter Server.

Install vCenter Server

Now that you have configured a database, you can begin installing vCenter Server. Remember that vCenter Server includes an installation of Microsoft SQL Server 2005 Express Edition, and if a database has not previously been installed, the vCenter installation will provide the ability to set up an initial database.

Installing vCenter Server consists of these steps:

1. Prepare for installation.

2. Install vCenter Server.

3. Install additional components.

4. Install vSphere Client.

5. Configure vCenter.

The steps have been segmented in this way to provide a better logical flow of how the process works. Each step is dependent on the previous task, and all the steps are detailed in the following sections.

Prepare for Installation

Before attempting to install the vCenter Server, make sure that your server meets the following criteria:

- The server must meet the hardware requirements (see Table 3.1).

- The server must be configured with a static IP address.

- The computer name must consist of fewer than 15 characters. To conform with best practice, ensure that the computer name matches the hostname in the fully qualified domain name of the system.

- The system must be joined to a domain, and not a workgroup. This will ensure that when you're using advanced features like the vCenter Guided Consolidation Service, it will be able to find all domains and systems on the network for the purpose of converting physical systems to virtual machines.

- A supported database must already be created, unless you're using the bundled SQL Server 2005 Express Edition.

- A valid DSN must exist to allow vCenter Server to connect to the created database.

- The vCenter Server must be able to directly access the hosts it will manage without any type of network address translation between the server and the hosts.

- The vCenter Server must be able to communicate with the ADAM (LDAP) server.

Install vCenter Server

To start leveraging the capabilities and enterprise-class features of vSphere, you must install vCenter Server. The installer will guide you through each step of the process:

1. Because VMware does not typically ship software to its customers, to get started you must download the vCenter Server

installation media from the VMware site (Figure 3.1). The download area is located at `http://www.vmware.com/download/`.

NOTE To download the software, you must set up an account at the VMware store, which you typically do upon purchase of VMware products. vCenter Server is available in two formats: ISO format (DVD-ROM image file) or a `.zip` (compressed) file.

Figure 3.1: vCenter 4 Download Links

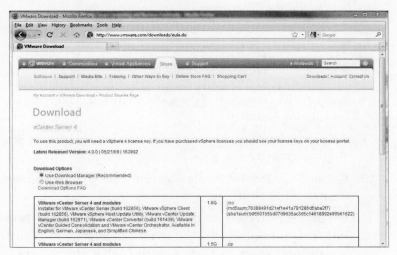

Either format will install all of the components necessary, but there are differences. The `.iso` file may need to be burned to a DVD-ROM for the purpose of installing the software, while the `.zip` file must be extracted to a location large enough to accommodate the decompressed files.

2. vCenter Server can be installed from a DVD-ROM, local path, mapped drive, or network share, but the software can only be installed to the local machine on a local drive. Select `autorun.exe` to start.

3. On the splash screen shown in Figure 3.2, click vCenter Server to begin.

Building a VMware vSphere Environment

PART I

Figure 3.2: vCenter Server installer splash screen

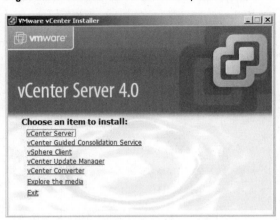

4. On the next screen, select the appropriate language for your installation and click OK.

5. Accept the license agreement by choosing "I agree to the terms of the license agreement," and then click Next.

6. On the Customer Information screen, enter your name and organization; then click Next.

7. On the next screen, enter your license key; vCenter Server will be installed in evaluation mode if you fail to enter a key. (You can update the licensing at a later time through vSphere Client.) Click Next.

8. On the Database Options screen shown in Figure 3.3, select the Use An Existing Supported Database radio button, and from the Data Source Name (DSN) drop-down list, select the ODBC connection you set up in the previous section "Create a vCenter Database in Microsoft SQL Server 2005" or "Create a vCenter Database in Oracle," depending on the database platform chosen. Select the Install A Microsoft SQL Server 2005 Express Instance option if no other supported database is available. Click Next.

Figure 3.3: Database Options screen

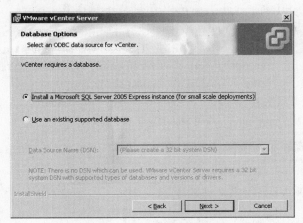

9. You'll install the vCenter Service next, as shown in Figure 3.4. This service is the core of vCenter Server. For our example, leave the Use SYSTEM Account radio button deselected, and fill in the Account Name, Account Password, and Confirm The Password text boxes. It is considered a best practice to use a Windows domain account, especially if the database is utilizing SQL Server 2005, as you can then use Windows authentication when connecting to the database. Click Next to continue.

Figure 3.4: The vCenter Service screen

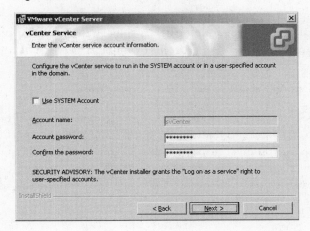

10. On the next screen, accept the default installation path as recommended, unless you wish to modify it, and then click Next.

11. A new component of vCenter Server is the ability to run Linked Mode vCenter Servers for additional scalability. During an initial installation, you must install the first instance for vCenter Server, as shown in Figure 3.5. After you select the first option, click Next.

Figure 3.5: The vCenter Linked Mode Options screen

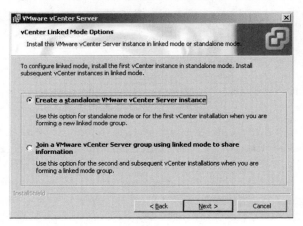

vCenter Server now uses Microsoft ADAM to handle Directory Services.

12. The Configure Ports screen appears next, as shown in Figure 3.6. The default ports appear in the fields; you can modify these ports to fit your environment, but for this example, accept the default values by clicking Next.

13. Click Next on the last screen to kick off the installation.

When the vCenter Server installation is complete, vCenter will be ready for you to configure to manage ESX and ESXi hosts. To perform management tasks, you must install vSphere Client. Additional components can be installed before or after the installation of vSphere Client. To make the process flow more evenly, let's start by installing the additional components first.

Figure 3.6: The Configure Ports screen

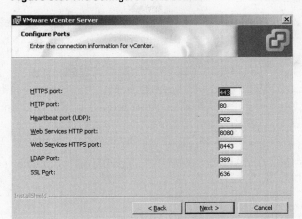

Install Additional Components

To extend the functionality of vCenter Server, several additional components are included. These add-ons give vCenter greater functionality in the area of ESX and ESXi patching, as well as the ability to convert physical, or other virtual, systems into a vSphere environment. These add-ons include

vCenter Guided Consolidation   This add-on is used to determine whether systems are good candidates for virtualization. It works hand in hand with vCenter Converter Enterprise to import systems into vSphere.

vCenter Converter Enterprise   This add-on is used to perform a physical-to-virtual (P2V) conversion or a virtual-to-virtual (V2V) conversion of systems into vSphere.

vCenter Update Manager   This add-on is used to manage security updates, or patches, for ESX and ESXi hosts, Windows guests, and various Linux guests.

Now that you are familiar with some of the additional components, let's see how they are installed.

Install vCenter Guided Consolidation

vCenter Guided Consolidation is a lightweight version of VMware's Capacity Planner service. It analyzes systems that you want to virtualize in a vSphere environment.

vCenter Guided Consolidation cannot function without the foundation of vCenter Server. Once vCenter Server is installed, you can install vCenter Guided Consolidation, thus extending the functionality of vCenter Server.

To install vCenter Guided Consolidation Manager:

1. Select vCenter Guided Consolidation Service on the splash screen, shown in Figure 3.7.

Figure 3.7: VMware vCenter installer splash screen

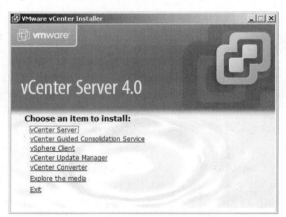

2. On the next screen, select the appropriate language setting and click Next.

3. On the next screen, accept the license agreement by choosing "I agree to the terms of the license agreement," and then click Next.

4. On the next screen, accept the default installation path, unless you wish to modify it, and then click Next.

5. The VMware vCenter Collector Service screen shown in Figure 3.8 opens. This service requires an account that will have local administrator rights on the systems it is evaluating for possible P2V conversion. The account may be a domain account, but Microsoft doesn't

recommend that you use a domain admin account. Enter an account and password with local administrator rights, and then click Next.

Figure 3.8: The VMware vCenter Collector Service screen

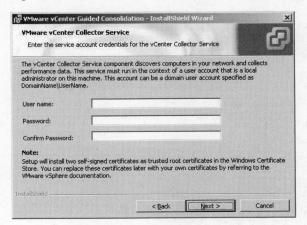

6. On the next screen (Figure 3.9), review the port information. The Guided Consolidation Service requires two additional TCP/IP ports for the Collector Service and the Provider Service. These ports are set to 8181 and 8182 by default. Click Next.

Figure 3.9: Reviewing the port information

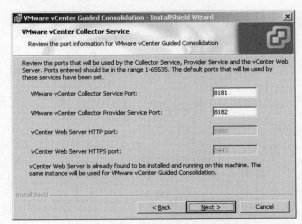

7. On the VMware vCenter Server Registration screen shown in Figure 3.10, enter the name or IP address of the vCenter Server,

along with the SSL port number (443 by default). Then enter the credentials required to register the extension with vCenter Server. The credentials you use must have the extension registration privilege. Click Next once you've entered this information.

Figure 3.10: The VMware vCenter Server Registration screen

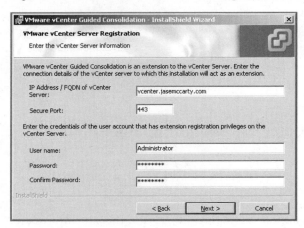

8. On the Server Identity screen shown in Figure 3.11, specify either the FQDN or the IP address of your vCenter Server and click Next.

Figure 3.11: The Server Identity screen

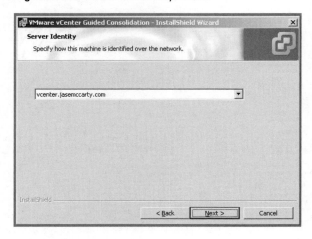

9. Click Install on the next screen to begin the Guided Consolidation Service.

The vCenter Guided Consolidation Service will now be available to you through vSphere Client; just select the Consolidation tab.

Install vCenter Converter Enterprise

vCenter Converter Enterprise is the natural progression from vCenter Guided Consolidation. The information vCenter Consolidation gathers is only useful if it can be acted upon—in other words, if you want to convert a physical system into a virtual system. vCenter Converter Enterprise handles the task of converting a physical system that has been determined to be a good virtualization candidate into the vSphere world.

To add the ability to perform P2V conversions from within vCenter Server:

1. Select vCenter Converter from the splash screen shown earlier in Figure 3.7.

2. Select the appropriate language setting on the next screen and click Next.

3. Choose "I agree to the terms of the license agreement" on the next screen and click Next.

4. Accept the default installation path, unless you wish to modify it, and click Next.

5. On the Setup Type screen, shown in Figure 3.12, click the Custom radio button. This way, you can control which components are installed.

Figure 3.12: The Setup Type screen

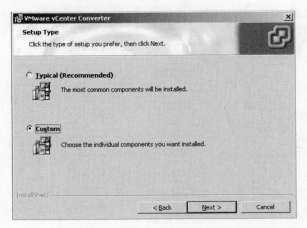

Building a VMware
vSphere Environment

PART I

6. The screen shown in Figure 3.13 appears. Note that Converter Agent is only required if the server that vCenter Converter is installed on is going to be converted. Click Next.

Figure 3.13: Custom Setup screen

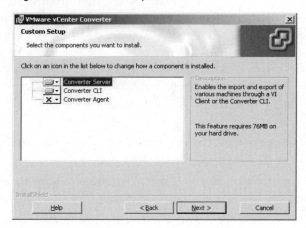

7. On the next screen, shown in Figure 3.14, enter the IP address and port of the vCenter Server, along with a user account that has appropriate permissions in vCenter Server and the password associated with it. This will ensure that Converter Enterprise can effectively integrate with vCenter Server.

Figure 3.14: The Specify The vCenter Server To Connect To screen

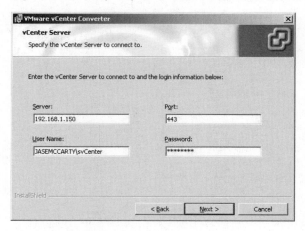

8. Select the default ports on the next screen (Figure 3.15) by clicking Next.

Figure 3.15: The vCenter Server Port Configuration screen

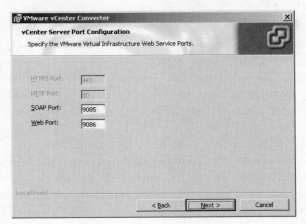

9. On the screen shown in Figure 3.16, specify the vCenter Server identity to verify which vCenter Server instance will be used. Click Next.

Figure 3.16: vCenter Server Identification

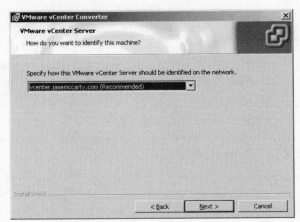

10. Click Install to begin the installation.
11. On the final screen, click Finish to complete the installation.

With vCenter Converter Enterprise installed, growing the vSphere environment can be accomplished quickly and easily.

Install vCenter Update Manager

As the vSphere environment grows, additional ESX and ESXi servers may be added. As the numbers of hosts grow, maintenance, and specifically patching, can become a burden. In the days of ESX 2.x, patches had to be copied to hosts, hosts had to be rebooted into a Linux single-user mode, and then patches were installed. The majority of times, it was easier to simply rebuild hosts using some type of automated scripting.

This manual patching process required VMware administrators to have some Linux command-line knowledge or at least familiarity. VMware released VMware Update Manager with the launch of Virtual Infrastructure 3 with the aim of making the patching process significantly easier. vCenter Update Manger also has the ability to patch Windows and Linux guests in a similar fashion to ESX and ESXi hosts. It is a complete solution for the patching of VMware hosts, Windows guests, and Linux guests. In vSphere, this product has been rebranded as vCenter Update Manager.

To take advantage of the abilities of vCenter Update Manager:

1. Select vCenter Update Manager from the splash screen shown earlier in Figure 3.7.

2. On the next screen, select the appropriate language setting and click Next.

3. On the next screen, click "I agree to the terms of the license agreement" and click Next.

4. On the next screen, shown in Figure 3.17, enter the IP address and port of the vCenter Server installation, followed by a username and password so that vCenter Update Manager can properly communicate with vCenter Server. Click Next.

5. On the next screen (see Figure 3.18), select the database to be used for the vCenter Update Manager. If the default SQL Server 2005 Express database was installed during the vCenter Server installation, select Install A Microsoft SQL Server 2005 Instance; otherwise select Use An Existing Supported Database radio button, and

select the preconfigured DSN from the Data Source Name (DSN) drop-down menu.

Figure 3.17: Entering the vCenter Server information

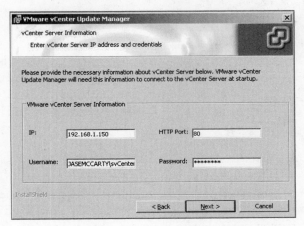

Figure 3.18: Specifying a database

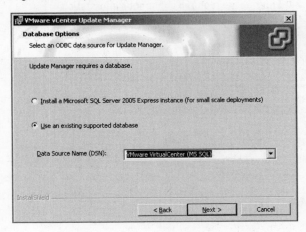

6. As you can see on the next screen (Figure 3.19), vCenter Update Manager requires authentication. If the DSN created uses NT Authentication, then a username and password is not required. If the database uses database authentication, then enter a username and password and then click Next.

Figure 3.19: You can leave these fields blank if the DSN uses NT Authentication.

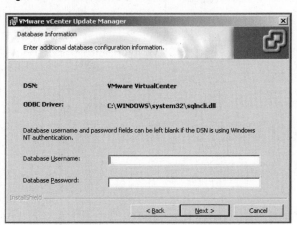

7. On the next screen (see Figure 3.20), enter the required connection information, which tells vCenter Server, ESX, and ESXi hosts how to talk to vCenter Update Manager. Then click Next.

Figure 3.20: Entering the required connection information

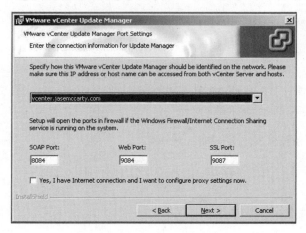

8. On the screen shown in Figure 3.21, if the vCenter Update Manager service is behind a proxy server, select Configure Proxy Settings and enter the required information. Otherwise, click Authenticate Proxy Using The Credentials Below and complete those fields. Once you've entered the information, click Next.

Figure 3.21: Configure Proxy Settings

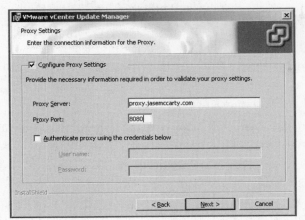

This information will give vCenter Update Manager the ability to access and download patches when connected to the Internet behind a proxy server.

9. Use the default installation paths and click Next.

10. Click Install to start the installation.

11. Click Finish to complete the installation.

Now that the additional components for vCenter Server have been installed, the installation of vSphere Client will provide you with the ability to manage vCenter Server and the additional components.

Install vSphere Client

vSphere Client is the next iteration of the VI Client. When the VI Client was introduced with the 1.0 version of VMware Virtual Center, it lacked the ability to directly manage the vast majority of settings in ESX 2.x hosts. When version 2.0 was introduced to manage ESX 3.0, and later ESXi, the VI Client was given the ability to manage either vCenter Server or ESX and ESXi hosts directly. The release of the 2.5 version of the Client, which was coupled with the release of vCenter

Server 2.5, added the ability to use custom plug-ins for the purpose of better integrating all the features and offerings into a single interface.

vSphere Client is similar to the VI Client, version 2.5, in operation. Here's how to get started using it:

1. Select vSphere Client from the splash screen shown earlier in Figure 3.7.

2. Select the appropriate language setting and click Next.

3. On the next screen, click "I agree to the terms of the license agreement" and click Next.

4. Enter the appropriate customer information on the next screen and click Next.

5. vSphere Client will present an option to install the vSphere Host Update Utility 4.0. This utility allows administrators to patch, or update, ESX and ESXi hosts without using the vCenter Update Manager. This is an optional component that extends the ability to upgrade ESX and ESXi hosts without using Update Manager.

6. On the next screen, choose the default installation path, unless you wish to modify it, and click Next.

7. Click Install to start the installation.

   Microsoft Visual J# 2.0 Second Edition is installed as a required component of vSphere Client.

8. On the final screen, click Finish to complete the installation.

vSphere Client is installed. Plug-ins for additional components that were installed will have to be added upon connecting to vCenter Server.

Now that vSphere Client is installed, the initial setup of the vSphere environment can begin. vSphere Client is the administrator's window into the vSphere world.

Configure vCenter

Configuring vCenter includes these steps:

- Connecting to vCenter
- Installing plug-ins in vSphere Client

- Configuring Advanced Settings
- Creating a datacenter
- Creating clusters
- Adding hosts

Each of these steps must be accomplished to leverage the complete feature set of vSphere. For example, enterprise features such as VMware High Availability and Distributed Resource Scheduling cannot be used unless you've configured a cluster.

Connect to vCenter Server

As you know, vCenter Server operates as a Windows service on the vCenter Server system. There is no native interface in Windows to access the vCenter installation. This function is achieved via vSphere Client.

To connect to vCenter Server:

1. Launch the VMware vSphere Client by choosing Start ➢ Programs ➢ VMware ➢ VMware vSphere Client, or double-click the VMware vSphere Client on the Desktop.

2. When vSphere Client login dialog box (see Figure 3.22) opens, enter the IP address or hostname of the vCenter Server, along with a valid username and password. Alternatively, select the Use Windows Session Credentials check box to use the context of the current user account logged into the system.

Figure 3.22: vSphere Client login dialog box

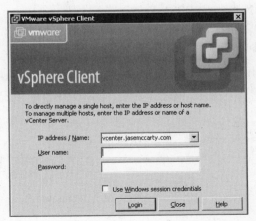

Building a VMware vSphere Environment

PART I

3. A Security Warning dialog box (see Figure 3.23) appears. This box simply states that you have not chosen to trust the certificate that the vCenter Server is configured to use. Select the option Install This Certificate And Do Not Display Any Security Warnings for "*IP/hostname*". Then click Ignore to continue.

Figure 3.23: Security warning

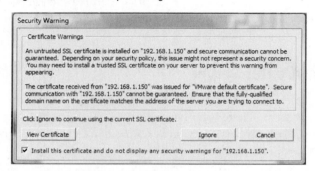

4. When vSphere Client loads, if you have not configured licensing for your environment, you will be presented with an Evaluation Notice, warning you about the evaluation period, and what will occur if you do not install your licenses. Click OK.

Once you're connected to vCenter Server, configuration can begin.

Even though vSphere Client is installed, if any additional components have been installed, their associated plug-ins will have to be loaded in order for you to leverage the additional capabilities.

Install Plug-ins in vSphere Client

Plug-ins extend the abilities of vSphere Client. VMware-provided plug-ins are installed through the Plug-ins drop-down menu in vSphere Client interface.

Not all of the previously installed additional components require a plug-in, but the vCenter Converter Enterprise and vCenter Update Manager components do to have a plug-in associated with them. Here's how to install them:

1. In vSphere Client, select Plug-ins ➤ Plug-in Management, as shown in Figure 3.24.

Figure 3.24: Select Manage Plug-ins from the Plug-ins menu.

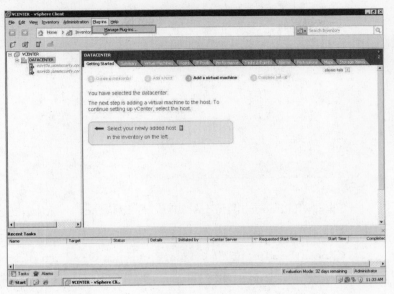

The Plug-in Manager shown in Figure 3.25 appears. The installed plug-ins are listed, and there are two additional plug-ins available for download and installation. These additional plug-ins are for vCenter Converter Enterprise and vCenter Update Manager.

Figure 3.25: Plug-in Manager

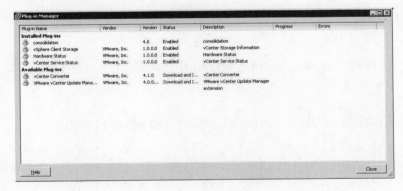

2. Click Download And Install next to vCenter Converter in the Status column, as shown in Figure 3.26.

Figure 3.26: Installing the vCenter Converter plug-in

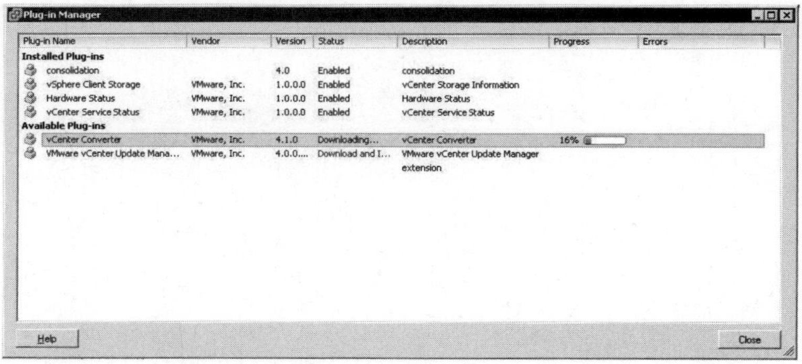

This will download the installation and launch the installation process.

3. Choose the appropriate language and click OK. Then click Next.

4. On the next screen, click Install.

5. Click Finish to complete the plug-in installation.

6. Click Download And Install in the Status column next to vCenter Update Manager. Again, this will download the installation and launch the installation process.

7. Choose the appropriate language, then click OK and Next; select the license agreement and click Next; and then click Install.

8. Click Finish to complete the installation.

9. When you see the security dialog box, click Ignore.

10. Click Close to close the Plug-in Manager.

Now that all of the plug-ins have been installed, you will be able to use the additional components.

Configure Advanced vCenter Server Settings

The basic installation of vCenter Server is complete. You can configure some additional settings to add to the overall usefulness of the installation.

These advanced settings affect the way vCenter Server behaves under normal operation. Some of these settings can be configured once, and others may need to be modified depending on how the environment is managed.

To configure vCenter Server settings, first select Administration ➤ vCenter Server Settings. The settings include the following:

License Settings   These settings are used to manage licenses for vCenter Server, ESX, and ESXi hosts, as well as legacy ESX and ESXi hosts. This topic will be discussed in more detail in Chapter 4.

Statistics   These settings are used to modify the view or the statistics parameters for data collection, and provide database sizing estimations.

Runtime Settings   The Runtime settings—Unique ID, Managed IP, Name Used—distinguish this vCenter Server installation from another installation when you're using vCenter Server in Linked Mode.

Active Directory   These settings are used to set up AD timeout, query limit, validation, and validation timeout. The settings are especially important when vCenter Server is part of a large domain environment.

Mail   These settings are used to configure a Simple Mail Transfer Protocol (SMTP) server for the purpose of sending out email alerts when alarms are triggered by issues occurring in clusters, hosts, guests, and the like.

SNMP   Use these settings to configure Simple Network Management Protocol (SNMP) to send data to external monitoring services, or to allow for the querying of information from vCenter Server by external monitoring services.

Web Service   Use these settings to configure the web service ports for vCenter Server. The defaults are 80 and 443, and you should change them only if there are conflicts with other services operating on the same ports on vCenter Server.

Timeout Settings   These settings are used to manage the amount of time vSphere clients should wait for a response for long and short operations. The settings can be used to tweak the timeouts when you're using vSphere Client over low-bandwidth networks.

Logging Options   These settings are used to modify the logging level for vCenter Server log files. You can change the level of logging to enhance troubleshooting when there are issues in the vSphere environment.

Database   The total number of connections to the database is configured here. This setting can be changed to increase or decrease the number of connections, which can increase or decrease the performance of vCenter Server.

Database Retention Policy   As events occur in the vSphere environment, they are logged in the vCenter Server database. Collection of these events over time can increase the size of the database. The retention policy will allow you to purge events that are older than the number of days you configure here.

SSL Settings   These settings are used to view and require SSL certificate checking between ESX and ESXi hosts when you're adding them to vCenter Server, as well as when you're using vSphere Client to connect to the console of guests.

Not all of the advanced features will have to be modified, but some will need to be changed to enable communication with the environment in which vSphere will be operating.

Create a Datacenter

To begin configuring the virtual environment, you need a datacenter. A datacenter is the logical container of clusters, ESX and ESXi hosts, resource pools, and virtual machines. Multiple datacenters are typically created when a vCenter Server instance is managing hosts and guests in multiple locations, but this is not a required configuration.

Create a datacenter using one of the following methods:

- Selecting File ➢ New ➢ Datacenter
- Pressing Ctrl+D
- Right-clicking on the vCenter Server name in the left panel and choosing New Datacenter from the initial logon screen.
- Clicking Create A Datacenter on the Getting Started tab in the right panel, as shown in Figure 3.27

The datacenter will be named New Datacenter, and the name will be highlighted, allowing you to rename the datacenter to a name appropriate for your environment or to coordinate with your environment's naming standards.

Figure 3.27: Click Create A Datacenter.

To get started, click Create a datacenter.
 Create a datacenter

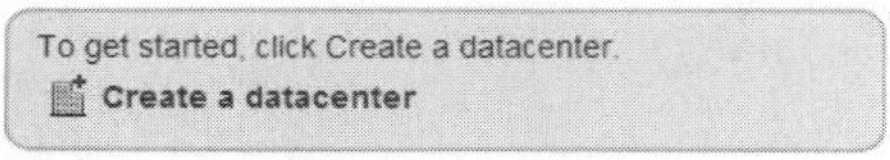

To change the datacenter name, while it is highlighted, simply type the new name, and then press Enter.

Add a Cluster

Clusters are not actually a requirement in the vSphere environment, but they do provide for additional capabilities in vSphere. Without a cluster, additional features such as High Availability (HA) and Dynamic Resource Scheduling (DRS) across ESX and ESXi hosts would be unavailable.

To leverage these features, let's configure a datacenter:

1. After selecting the datacenter object, add a cluster by using one of the following methods:

   - Select File ➢ New ➢ Add Cluster.

   - Press Ctrl+L.

   - Right-click on the datacenter you created, and select New Cluster.

2. When the New Cluster Wizard open, as shown in Figure 3.28, enter a name for the cluster in the Name text box.

Figure 3.28: Enter a name on the first screen of the New Cluster Wizard.

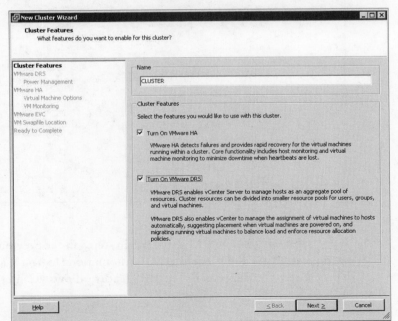

3. As cluster features are selected, the list of steps in the left panel will add additional components for configuration.

4. To enable VMware High Availability features, select the Turn On VMware HA check box.

5. To enable VMware Distributed Resource Scheduling, select the Turn On VMware DRS check box.

6. Click Next to continue.

We'll continue these steps in the next section.

Configure VMware DRS

VMware DRS options are shown in Figure 3.29. Follow these steps:

Figure 3.29: VMware DRS

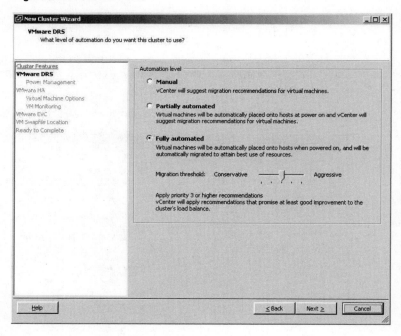

1. If you selected Turn On VMware DRS in step 5 in the previous section, you'll see the What Level Of Automation Do You Want This Cluster To Use? screen. The DRS feature allows vCenter to

load-balance guests across hosts to make sure that there is an even load across all hosts. Select one of the available radio buttons on this screen, depending on the configuration desired:

Manual: Choose this option to have vCenter suggest when guests need to be migrated between hosts, as well as automatically placing guests on hosts when they are powered on.

Automatic: Choose this option to allow vCenter to automatically migrate guests between hosts in the cluster for the best use of available resources.

Migration Threshold: Use the mouse to slide the pointer either left or right, depending on whether vCenter should use aggressive or conservative decisioning for the movement of guests between hosts in the cluster.

2. Click Next after you make your choice.

3. The Power Management screen (Figure 3.30) is next. Power Management allows vCenter to power hosts on or off as required for a cluster's workload. Select one of the available radio buttons, depending on the configuration desired:

   Manual: Choose this option for vCenter to recommend which hosts should have guests evacuated and powered off, as well as powering the hosts back when the workload suggests powering the hosts on.

   Automatic: Choose this option to have vCenter automatically evacuate guests from one or more hosts, and power the host off when the workload does not require the hosts. This will also automatically power hosts on when the workload requires additional host resources.

   DPM Threshold: Use the mouse to slide the pointer either left or right, depending on whether vCenter should use aggressive or conservative decisioning for the powering on or off of hosts depending on workload.

4. Click Next to continue.

Figure 3.30: Power Management

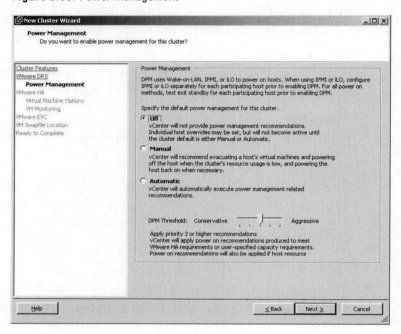

We'll continue these steps in the next section.

Configure VMware HA

VMware HA options are shown in Figure 3.31.

The High Availability feature lets ESX and ESXi hosts restart virtual machines when the failure of an ESX or ESXi host occurs. The guests will be restarted on other hosts in the cluster.

To continue with the wizard:

1. If you selected Turn On VMware DRS in step 5 in the section "Add a Cluster" earlier in this chapter, you'll see the admission control options. Select one of the available radio buttons, depending on the configuration desired:

    Host Monitoring Status: Select this check box to have vCenter monitor hosts through heartbeats. This option can be deselected during maintenance schedules to prevent host isolation issues, resulting in unnecessary HA failovers.

Figure 3.31: VMware HA

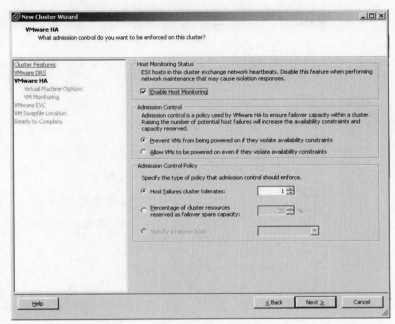

Admission Control: Select one of the two radio buttons to allow (or prevent) guests to be powered on even if they violate the available resources. If you click the Prevent option, guests will not be powered on if they require more resources than are available.

Admission Control Policy: Select one of the available radio buttons to choose the number of allowed host failures that can occur, the percentage of cluster resources that should be reserved for HA, or to specify a specific host to fail over to.

2. Click Next to continue.

3. Next you'll see the Virtual Machine Options screen (Figure 3.32):

   VM Restart Priority: This option determines the default order in which guests are restarted. A higher value will attempt to start more guests simultaneously.

   Host Isolation Response: This option determines what a host should do with guests if it loses connectivity with vCenter and/or the default

gateway. The default is Shut Down. This selection ensures that
if the host can access the shared storage, guests are cleanly shut
down and the virtual disk file locks are released before another
host attempts to power them on as a result of an HA error condi-
tion. This is especially important when using iSCSI or NFS-based
shared storage.

Figure 3.32: Virtual Machine Options

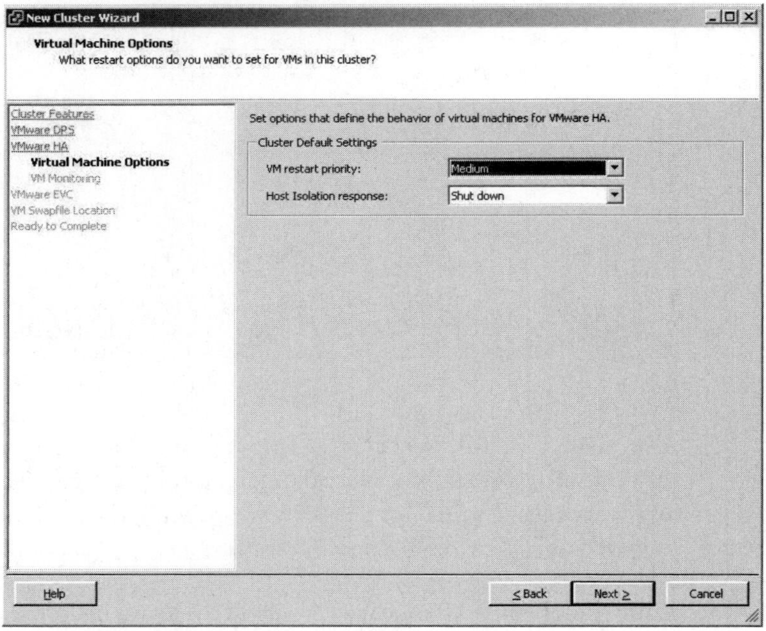

4. Click Next to continue.

5. The VM Monitoring options (Figure 3.33) appear next. Select the
Enable VM Monitoring check box if you want to restart guests
when VMware tools heartbeats are not received in a given amount
of time. Use the mouse to slide the Monitoring Sensitivity pointer
to the left or right to change the time threshold for monitoring the
VMware tools in each guest.

Figure 3.33: VM Monitoring options

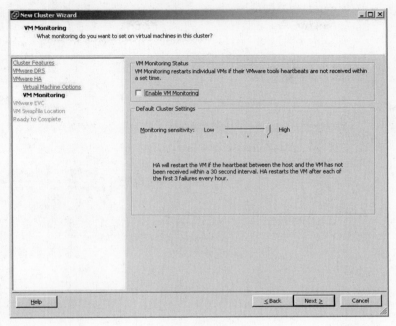

6. Click Next to continue.

7. The next screen (Figure 3.34) asks if you want to enable Enhanced VMotion Compatibility (EVC) for this cluster. This feature allows you to maximize VMotion compatibility and ensures that only hosts that are compatible with those in your cluster can be added to the cluster. EVC will only present the CPU instruction set of the least capable processors to each guest. Select the appropriate radio button:

   Disable EVC: Select this option to disable EVC.

NOTE   When you select either of the Enable options, a drop-down box is provided so you can select the type of hosts being used. Your selection will determine which processor instruction sets are required for a host to become part of the cluster.

Enable EVC For AMD Hosts: Select this option to enable EVC for supported AMD hosts.

Enable EVC For Intel Hosts: Select this option to enable EVC for supported Intel hosts.

Figure 3.34: VMware EVC options

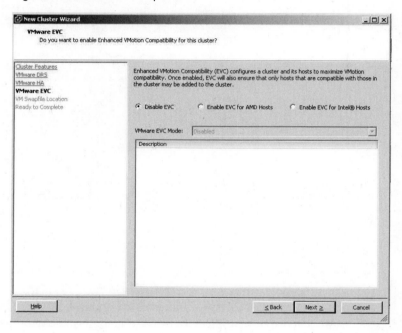

8. Click Next to continue.

9. The Swapfile Location configuration options (Figure 3.35) are next. Here you specify whether a guest's swap file is stored with the guest on shared storage or on a dedicated datastore. Microsoft recommends that you keep the swap file in the same location as the guest. Choose the desired option and click Next.

10. When you see the Ready To Complete screen (Figure 3.36), make sure the configuration settings are correct and click Finish.

Figure 3.35: The Virtual Machine Swapfile Location screen

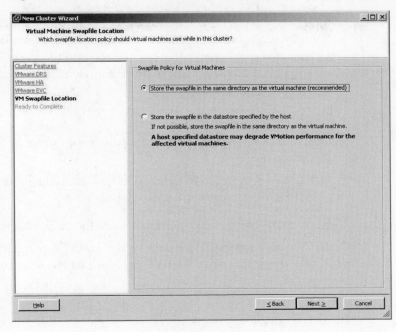

Figure 3.36: The Ready To Complete screen

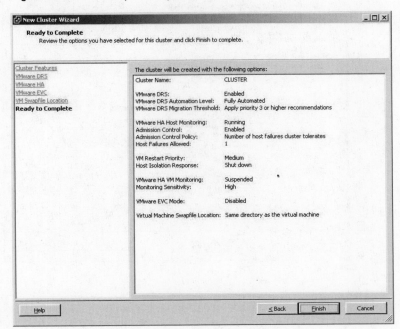

Add a Host

While vCenter Server is the central management point of vSphere, ESX and ESXi hosts are the workers of the environment. To use hosts in a managed vSphere environment, you must add them to the vCenter Server installation. Add a host using one of the following methods:

- Select File ➤ New ➤ Add Host.

- Press Ctrl+H.

- Right-click on the datacenter you created, and select Add Host.

- Click Add A Host on the Getting Started tab in the right panel when a given datacenter is selected.

Once you complete one of these steps, the Add Host Wizard opens:

1. On the Specify Connection Settings screen, enter either the IP address or the hostname of the ESX or ESXi host you want to add, as shown in Figure 3.37.

Figure 3.37: The Specify Connection Settings screen

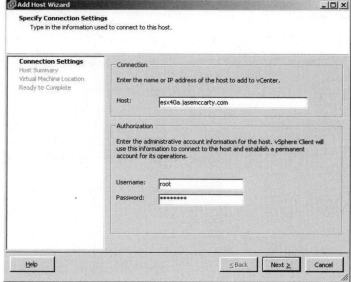

You will have to also add **root** as the username, as well as the appropriate password for the root user on the host you want to add.

2. Click Next to add the host.

3. Click Yes when presented with a security alert. This alert is shown because a self-generated, self-signed certificate (provided by VMware), which has not been trusted by the Windows system yet, has been installed on the host installation.

4. The Add Host Wizard will show a summary of the ESX or ESXi host you are adding and any virtual machines that may already reside on it (see Figure 3.38). Click Next.

Figure 3.38: Host information

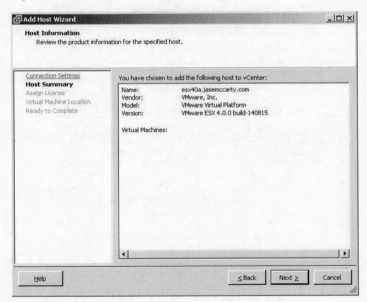

5. You will now be prompted to add a license key. If you have not installed your licenses, you can choose Evaluation Mode, as shown in Figure 3.39. Click Next when finished.

6. On the next screen (shown in Figure 3.40), you specify a location for the host's VMs.

Figure 3.39: The Assign License screen

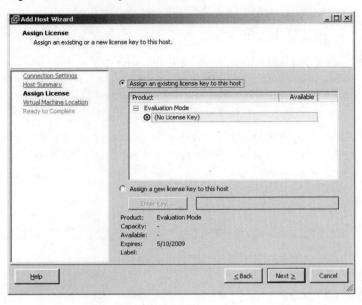

Figure 3.40: Specifying a location for the host's VMs

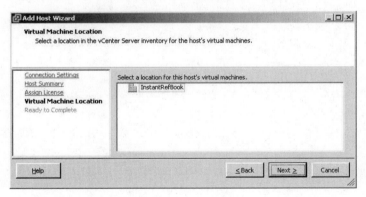

7. If you chose to put the host in an existing cluster in the previous step, the next screen (Figure 3.41) asks you to specify a location for your host's VMs in the resource pool hierarchy. Once you do, click Next.

8. On the Ready To Complete screen (Figure 3.42), click Finish to add the host to the datacenter, and if you specify one, the selected cluster.

Figure 3.41: The Choose The Destination Resource Pool screen

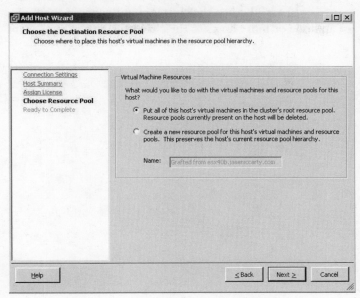

Figure 3.42: Click Finish on the Ready To Complete screen.

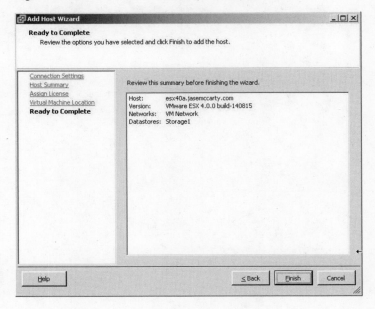

Now that you've added a host to the cluster, your work is not done. Clusters are only useful when the cluster contains more than one host. You can add one or more hosts to the cluster using the same steps.

4

Understanding Licensing

IN THIS CHAPTER, YOU WILL LEARN TO:

S oftware has become a critical component in today's business environment. Most software vendors include a licensing mechanism to
prevent users from installing as many instances, or copies, of their product as they want to. From the vendor's perspective, the ability to limit
the number of installations is vital to their revenue. If an enterprise only
had to purchase a single copy of a software package simply to obtain
the technology, additional purchases from a technical standpoint would
not be required. The licensing model that VMware uses allows for one
installation of the software for every license purchased. This chapter
will discuss all the vital components of VMware licensing.

Become Familiar with VMware Licensing

How does VMware limit the number of installations a customer has in
place? A manageable licensing process is necessary to enforce licensing
compliance. Two methods can be used to enforce licensing:

Serial Numbers   Serial numbers are typically a complex alpha-
numeric code that enables software functionality and features. In
some cases, serial numbers are associated with a particular email
address or user's name to ensure that the serial number cannot be
validated without both pieces of information.

VMware has many different products in their virtualization arse-
nal. Some products are targeted toward desktop use, while others
are targeted at server, or enterprise, use. VMware Workstation, for
instance, is a desktop-targeted application. As many other desktop
applications are often licensed, VMware Workstation uses a simple
serial number to unlock the product. This licensing method does
not limit the number of systems the application may be installed on.
The intended audience for VMware Workstation consists of systems
administrators, software developers, and users who wish to use virtual appliances locally.

VMware originally licensed ESX servers using serial numbers, just
as VMware Workstation does. Additional features like virtual symmetric multiprocessing (VSMP) or VMotion required additional
license keys. Unfortunately, this licensing model does not prevent
unauthorized product installations.

Since the introduction of Virtual Infrastructure 3 (VI3), basic
serial numbers installed on a host are designated as *host licenses*.

Host licenses behave in the same fashion as Workstation licenses; they can be installed many times, on separate servers. Licensing ESX in this fashion is not much different than licensing VMware Workstation.

One of the drawbacks of host licensing is that advanced features are not available. This is because host licenses provide ESX servers with the ability to function with only the basic set of features. VMware ESX or ESXi can be installed with a host license, but advanced features are unavailable. When coupled with a vCenter Server installation, only the number of licensed hosts can be managed. In a limited fashion, this somewhat restricts the number of host installations that can be used in an enterprise.

Licensing Server   Without a central licensing model, it is difficult to manage advanced features such as High Availability, Distributed Resource Scheduling, and VMotion. Advanced features provide capabilities that are often the reason vSphere is chosen over many of the other virtualization platforms on the market today. If VMware had no way to limit their use, it would be very difficult for VMware to have an effective business model. A central location was needed to manage licensing of all of the ESX servers in the environment and to provide the ability to limit advanced features.

To make license management more flexible, and to enable management of these advanced features, VMware introduced server-based licenses in conjunction with a licensing server. Serial numbers, or a license file, are loaded into a license server. The sole purpose of this license server is to answer network requests from hosts, grant a license, and enable any advanced features licensed. A VMware host will query the license server upon bootup for authorization to enable use as well as unlock licensed features. The license server option ensures that only the number of licenses purchased can be used. When all available licenses have been issued, no additional licenses may be granted.

VI3 used a Macromedia FlexNet service to listen for requests from hosts and to provide available licenses to them. This worked well when communication was not interrupted but lacked flexibility when using different licensed editions together. When VI3 had Standard and Enterprise licenses installed, it was difficult to specify which hosts received which licenses, and in turn, advanced features.

VSphere addresses the central management of licenses somewhat differently than VI3 did. When vCenter Server 4.0 is used with version

4.0 ESX and ESXi hosts, the vCenter Server handles the task of issuing licenses to hosts. Licenses can be distinctly assigned to 4.0 hosts, providing additional flexibility when many licenses for multiple editions are used. When vCenter Server 4.0 has the task of managing version 3.x ESX and ESXi hosts, a VI3 license service is required. VCenter Server 4.0 is aware of the license service and allows the legacy hosts to operate in a similar fashion as they did in VI3.

Review the Versions of vSphere

To determine which version of vSphere to license, you must know which features are included with which edition of vSphere. Similarly, to understand how the licensing has changed from VI3 to vSphere, you must know which editions and features were available in VI3 (Table 4.1), what is available in vSphere (Table 4.2), and how the VI3 offerings relate to the new vSphere editions (Table 4.3).

Table 4.1: Virtual Infrastructure 3 Editions

Feature	Foundation	Standard	Enterprise
Cores per Processor	4	4	4
Virtual SMP	X	X	X
ESX or ESXi	X	X	X
Consolidated Backup	X	X	X
Update Manager	X	X	X
vCenter Agent	X	X	X
VMFS	X	X	X
High Availability		X	X
VMotion			X
Storage VMotion			X
vCenter Server	3 hosts and 6 total processors	Unlimited hosts and processors	Unlimited hosts and processors

VSphere has expanded the number of editions from three to six in an effort to provide more licensing options for enterprises. The additional editions allow for more flexible choices when licensing vSphere. Table 4.2 outlines the vSphere editions and their features.

Table 4.2: vSphere Editions

Features	Essentials	Essentials Plus	Standard	Advanced	Enterprise	Enterprise Plus
Cores	6	6	6	12	6	12
Virtual SMP	4-way	4-way	4-way	4-way	4-way	8-way
Host RAM	256 GB	256 GB	256 GB	256 GB	256 GB	Unlimited
Thin Virtual Disks	X	X	X	X	X	X
vCenter Agent	X	X	X	X	X	X
Update Manager	X	X	X	X	X	X
VMSafe	X	X	X	X	X	X
vStorage APIs	X	X	X	X	X	X
High Availability		X	X	X	X	X
Data Recovery		X		X	X	X
Hot Add Hardware to Guests				X	X	X
Fault Tolerance				X	X	X
vShield Zones				X	X	X
VMotion				X	X	X
Storage VMotion					X	X

Building a VMware vSphere Environment

PART I

Table 4.2: vSphere Editions *(continued)*

Features	Essentials	Essentials Plus	Standard	Advanced	Enterprise	Enterprise Plus
DRS					X	X
vNetwork Distributed Switch						X
Host Profiles						X
Third party multipathing						X

As you can see, with the new editions, many new features have been added. All vSphere editions have many features included by default. Two of the features included in all editions are carried over from VI3, including a vCenter Agent and the ability to use Update Manager. New features that are included in all editions are thin virtual disks, VMSafe, and vStorage APIs. If the High Availability feature is preferred, all editions, with the exception of Essentials, will suffice. For users wishing to leverage the new VMware Data Recovery feature for backing up virtual machines, all editions other than Standard and Essentials provide this capability. For environments where more advanced features are desired, Advanced, Enterprise, and Enterprise Plus editions include VMotion, the ability to add hardware to running guests, Fault Tolerance, and vShield Zones. While the Enterprise edition adds Distributed Resource Scheduling and Storage VMotion [SVMotion], it lacks the 12-processor core support that Advanced Edition includes. Enterprise Edition is limited to only 6-processor core support. The top-tier edition, Enterprise Plus, includes all of the features of the other editions, with a few additions. These additions include the ability to configure vNetwork Distributed Switches, Host Profiles, and third-party multipathing. For those interested in purchasing new or additional licenses, it is important to know which edition is the best fit. This is because editions have changed somewhat from VI3 to vSphere.

For users who already have VI3, it is important to know how licensing has changed. VMware Support and Subscription (SNS) is required for upgrading from VI3 to vSphere. Table 4.3 lists the editions entitled to users who have a current SNS agreement.

Table 4.3: VMware Edition Upgrades for SNS Entitlements

VI3 Version	vSphere Edition	Added Features
Foundation	Standard	Thin Provisioning High Availability
Foundation with VMotion	Standard with VMotion and Storage VMotion	Thin Provisioning High Availability
Foundation with VMotion and DRS	Enterprise	Thin Provisioning High Availability Fault Tolerance Hot Add vShield Zones Data Recovery
Standard	Standard	Thin Provisioning
Standard with VMotion	Standard with VMotion and Storage VMotion	Thin Provisioning
Standard with VMotion and DRS	Enterprise	Thin Provisioning Fault Tolerance Hot Add vShield Zones Data Recovery
Enterprise	Enterprise	Thin Provisioning Fault Tolerance Hot Add vShield Zones Data Recovery

As you can see in Table 4.3, there are no SNS upgrades to the Essentials Plus, Advanced, and Enterprise Plus editions. These are upgrade paths that VMware has provided to give additional features to existing users, while augmenting the VI3 product offerings.

Review the Licensing Method in vSphere

This licensing method is carried over from VI3 into vSphere. There is a significant difference between the licensing mechanism in VI3 and vSphere. In VI3, VMware employed a licensing server from Macromedia using the FlexLM licensing engine. This licensing engine acted as a central location for vCenter Server, ESX hosts, and ESXi

Building a VMware vSphere Environment

hosts. From time to time, this licensing engine proved to be problematic. As a result, many systems administrators complained to VMware about the problems and voiced their desire to have VMware discontinue the use of the FlexLM engine.

VMware has always been very responsive to customer feedback. The FlexLM licensing engine has been problematic in the VI3 environment, and many customers have expressed disdain for it. There have been many posts in the VMware Community Forums pertaining to trouble-shooting issues with this application. In an effort to ease the licensing process, in vSphere the FlexLM licensing engine is no longer used to provide licenses to vCenter Server 4.0, ESX 4.0 hosts, and ESXi 4.0 hosts. The FlexLM license server is still required if you're using vCenter Server 4.0 to manage ESX 3.x or ESX 3.5 hosts.

When vCenter Server is initially installed, if no license is provided, vCenter Server will operate with all features enabled for 60 days. If a license is provided, the features available to vCenter Server will be determined by the features associated with the license key purchased.

Licenses for ESX 4.0 and ESXi 4.0 hosts can be entered, or installed, using the licensing functions in vSphere Client interface when connected to vCenter Server. If licenses are not installed for ESX 4.0 and ESXi 4.0 hosts, they will also operate for up to 60 days with all features enabled. Additional licensed features are also installed into the vCenter Server license service using the same method used for installing licenses for ESX and ESXi hosts.

Review Licensing of Legacy ESX Hosts

vCenter Server now works as the central licensing point for the environment, in most cases. If legacy hosts are going to be used in a vSphere environment, a license server is required until those hosts are either upgraded to ESX or ESXi 4.0, or are removed from the environment. To meet the need of using legacy hosts in a vSphere environment, the VI3 FlexLM license server is still used. This is because the 3.x releases of ESX and ESXi do not know how to properly obtain licenses from the newer vCenter Server licensing process.

VMware recommends that the legacy license server be loaded on the same system as vCenter Server. Also, in order for you to use features such as the vCenter Management Agent, VMotion, High Availability, and DRS on the legacy ESX and ESXi hosts, the server license must include those features. Using a license server also requires additional networking consideration, as ports 27000 and 27010 must be open for the ESX hosts to communicate with the license server.

You may ask why it is still important to be familiar with the VI3 licensing process. Many administrators may still be using legacy hosts, at least initially, when upgrading from VI3 to vSphere. If you don't understand how vCenter Server for vSphere handles licensing for legacy hosts, you may find the upgrade process to be problematic.

Manage Licenses

In VI3, the licensing process was somewhat complicated. Licenses would be purchased from VMware, or through a reseller, and then they had to be registered on VMware's licensing portal so that a single license file could be generated. This license file would then be downloaded, or received from email, and installed in the licensing server. When new licenses were purchased, the license file would have to be re-created, and the old license file would have to be deleted. This process made it somewhat cumbersome to add additional host or feature licenses. The previous method made creating new license files dependent on the licensing portal.

The process of installing licenses has changed significantly compared to the previous generation's process. Unlike using the license server to issue licenses to vCenter Server, adding licenses is performed through vSphere Client directly into vCenter Server.

Install Licenses

As we mentioned earlier, adding new licenses is significantly easier than in earlier releases of VMware products. To add the license purchased for vCenter Server and ESX or ESXi hosts:

1. Log into the vCenter Server using vSphere Client.

2. Once connected, load Licensing Administration by selecting View ➤ Administration ➤ Licensing (see Figure 4.1), or by pressing Ctrl+Shift+L.

Figure 4.1: License administration

3. The currently installed licenses will be displayed in a licensing report, as shown in Figure 4.2, which shows a vCenter Server and two ESX hosts in Evaluation mode.

Figure 4.2: Licensing report

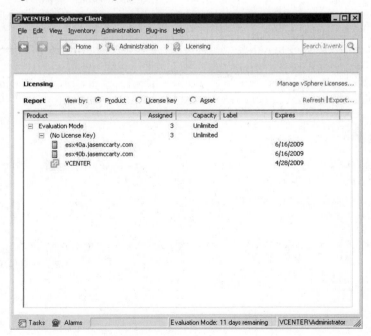

Click Manage vSphere Licenses to manage licenses in the vSphere environment.

4. The first licensing action available is Add License Keys, as you can see in Figure 4.3.

Figure 4.3: The Add License Keys menu

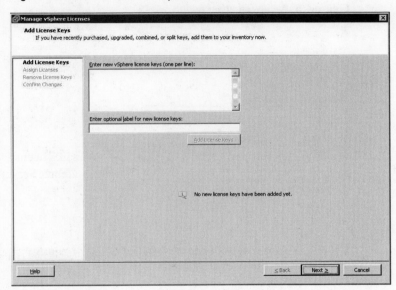

Enter a license key in the large window on the right, as shown in Figure 4.4. License keys are not case sensitive and will be automatically displayed in uppercase when entered.

Figure 4.4: Add License Keys added

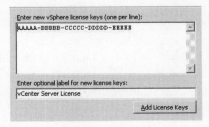

5. Enter a name for the license, such as vCenter Server License, to identify the type of license being added, and select Add License Keys.

6. Enter any additional license keys as in steps 4 and 5.

7. Review the licenses in the details window, as shown in Figure 4.5.

Figure 4.5: Review Licenses added

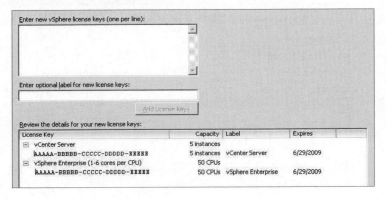

Click Next three times to get to the confirmation window. Figure 4.6 shows the licenses that have been added.

Figure 4.6: Confirmation of added licenses

8. Click Finish to complete the license installation.

During the initial installation of licenses, licenses may also be assigned to resources, including vCenter or hosts. That process will be detailed in the next section to demonstrate the process of assigning licenses; the process of assigning licenses can occur at any time after they have been installed.

Assign Licenses

For vCenter Server and hosts to be able to leverage the features purchased, licenses have to be assigned to these resources. In VI3, it was not possible from a single location to individually assign licensed features to different hosts. Let's look at an example.

A VI3 environment has one vCenter Server license, eight VI3 Standard licenses, and eight VI3 Enterprise licenses. The environment has eight dual-processor multiple-core systems. The hosts are configured in two clusters with four hosts each, with one cluster for production use and one cluster for test use. To ensure hosts designated for production use receive the Enterprise licenses, they must be assigned to those hosts, in the Licensed Features screen.

In vSphere, features are granted to hosts by assigning licenses in Licensing Administration. To assign licenses purchased for vCenter Server and ESX or ESXi hosts:

1. Log into the vCenter Server using vSphere Client.

2. Once connected, load Licensing Administration by selecting View ➤ Administration ➤ Licensing or by pressing Ctrl+Shift+L.

3. The currently installed licenses will be displayed in the Licensing screen, shown in Figure 4.7.

Figure 4.7: Licenses installed but unassigned

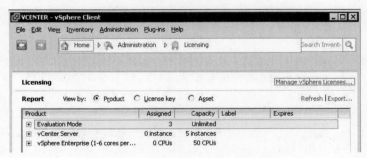

4. Click Manage vSphere Licenses to manage licenses in the vSphere environment.

5. The first licensing action available is Add License Keys. Click Next to continue to Assign Licenses. Because licenses have already been added it is not necessary to add licenses again.

6. The Assign Licenses window can display unlicensed assets, licensed assets, or all assets. Because no assets have been assigned licenses, ensure that the Show Unlicensed Assets radio button is selected.

7. To assign licenses to ESX or ESXi hosts, select the ESX tab to display hosts that are currently unlicensed. This can be seen in Figure 4.8. To assign licenses to a vCenter Server, select the vCenter tab instead, as shown in Figure 4.9.

Figure 4.8: Assigning ESX assets

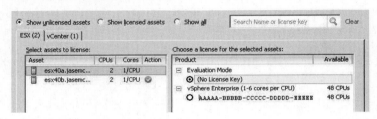

Figure 4.9: Unlicensed vCenter asset

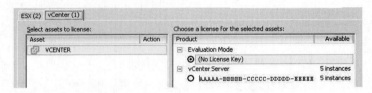

8. To assign a license to a single asset, click on a host in the Select Assets To License window, then select a radio button next to the desired product in the Choose A License For The Selected Assets window.

9. To assign a license to multiple assets, hold the Ctrl key, and click on each host in the Select Assets To License window; then select a radio button next to the desired product in the Choose A License For The Selected Assets window.

10. Once the licenses have been assigned to the hosts, a green circle with a check mark will be displayed to the right of the host in the Action field. You can see this in Figures 4.10 and 4.11.

Figure 4.10: ESX licenses added

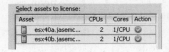

Figure 4.11: vCenter license assigned

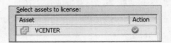

11. Select the Show Licensed Assets radio button to verify that the ESX hosts and vCenter Server or servers are properly licensed.

12. Click Next two times to proceed to the confirmation window.

13. The confirmation window will show which licenses have been assigned to which assets, as well as which previous licenses were assigned to those assets. You can see this in Figure 4.12.

Figure 4.12: Confirming the assigned licenses

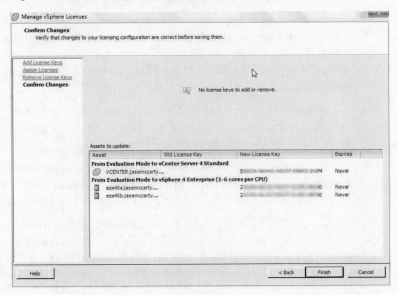

14. Click Finish to complete the license assignment process.

Remove Licenses

Removing licenses is not a common task. Typically there's only one time that licenses would be removed: to replace evaluation licenses with purchased licenses. Licenses cannot be removed while they are assigned to assets because they are currently being used. Assets such as hosts or vCenter servers must have their licenses unassigned from them before the licenses can be removed. When licenses are *unassigned*, they are disassociated from hosts or vCenter Servers. When licenses are *removed*, they are deleted from the vSphere installation.

To remove licenses for vCenter Server and ESX or ESXi hosts:

1. Log into the vCenter Server using vSphere Client.

2. Once connected, load Licensing Administration by selecting View ➤ Administration ➤ Licensing or by pressing Ctrl+Shift+L. The currently installed licenses will be displayed in Licensing Administration.

3. Click Manage vSphere Licenses to manage licenses in the vSphere environment.

4. The first licensing action available is Add License Keys; click Next to continue to Assign Licenses.

5. The Assign Licenses window will default to displaying unlicensed assets, licensed assets, or all assets. Because assets have been assigned licenses, ensure that the Show Licensed Assets radio button is selected.

6. To unassign licenses from ESX or ESXi hosts, select the ESX tab to display hosts that are currently licensed. To unassign a license from a vCenter Server, select the vCenter tab instead.

7. To unassign a license from a single asset, click on a host in the Select Assets To License window; then select a radio button next to No License Key in the Choose A License For The Selected Assets window.

NOTE   To unassign a license from multiple assets, hold the Ctrl key, and click on each host in the Select Assets To License window; then select a radio button next to No License Key in the Choose A License For The Selected Assets window.

Once the licenses have been unassigned, a green circle with a check mark will be displayed to the right of the host in the Action field.

8. Select the Show Unlicensed Assets radio button to verify that the ESX hosts and vCenter Server or servers have had their licenses unassigned.

9. Click Next to proceed to the Remove Licenses window.

   Licenses that are not currently assigned to any assets are now available to be removed from vCenter.

10. Select the check box next to each license that is to be removed. This process is shown in Figure 4.13.

Figure 4.13: Removing licenses from assigned resources

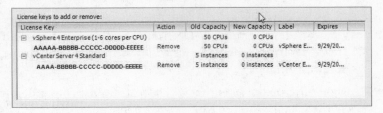

11. Click Next to proceed to the confirmation window.

12. Figure 4.14 shows licenses to be removed in the topmost pane. The licenses that have been unassigned from each of assets, as well as which previous licenses were assigned to those assets, appear in the bottom pane.

13. Click Finish to complete the license removal process.

Figure 4.14: Confirming that licenses have been removed

Assets to update:			
Asset	Old License Key	New License Key	Expires
From vCenter Server 4 Standard to Evaluation Mode			
VCENTERUPG.jasem...	AAAAA-BBBBB-CCCCC-DDDDD-EEEEE		8/27/20...
From vSphere 4 Enterprise (1-6 cores per CPU) to Evaluation Mode			
esx40a.jasemccarty....	AAAAA-BBBBB-CCCCC-DDDDD-EEEEE		9/25/20...
esx40b.jasemccarty....	AAAAA-BBBBB-CCCCC-DDDDD-EEEEE		10/3/20...

In the situation where new production licenses are to be installed, and evaluation licenses are to be removed, the process is the same, with the exception of assigning the new licenses to ESX and vCenter assets, rather than choosing No License Key during the unassign process.

Change Licenses Assigned to Assets

Changing licenses assigned to assets can be accomplished through the Manage vSphere Licenses action item, but it is not the only way to perform this task. Depending on the number of assets in the environment, going through the whole Manage vSphere Licenses process might prove to be confusing. VMware has added the ability to change licenses through the Report window in the Licensing component of vCenter Server.

To change license assigned to assets:

1. Log into the vCenter Server using vSphere Client.

2. Once connected, load Licensing Administration by selecting View ➤ Administration ➤ Licensing or by pressing Ctrl+Shift+L. The currently installed licenses will be displayed in Licensing Administration.

3. Right-click on the asset that will have its license changed, and choose Change License Key, as shown in Figure 4.15.

Figure 4.15: Selecting Change License Key

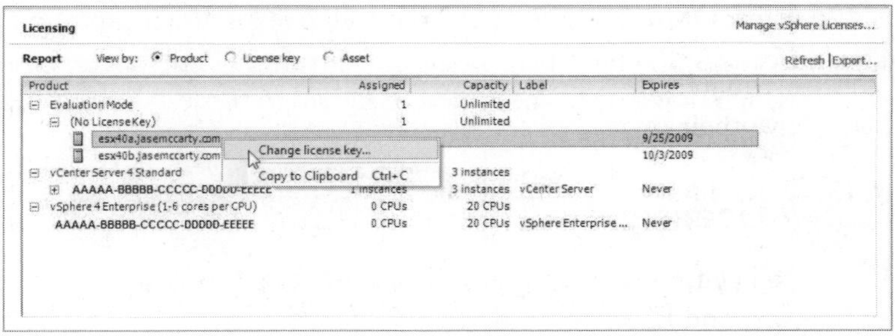

4. The Assign License dialog box will appear, as shown in Figure 4.16.

Figure 4.16: Assign License dialog box

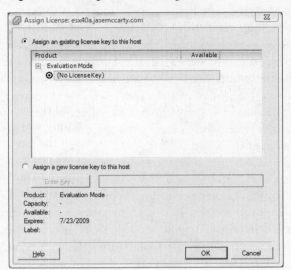

5. To assign an existing license, ensure that Assign An Existing License Key To This Asset is selected, and select the radio button next to the license that is to be used.

6. To assign a new license key, select Assign A New License Key To This Asset and press the Enter key. When prompted by the Add License Key dialog box, enter the new license key.

7. Click OK to complete the license reassignment or addition.

Unfortunately, legacy hosts cannot be managed as easily. Legacy hosts have their own license management method.

Install Licenses for Legacy Hosts

In VI3, a license server is required for the licensing of vCenter Server, ESX hosts, and ESXi hosts. This is still a requirement when using vCenter Server for vSphere with 3.0 or 3.5 ESX and ESXi hosts. This is because the previous generation of ESX does not know how to communicate with the integrated licensing of vSphere.

A typical practice when upgrading a VI3 environment is to upgrade the vCenter Server to the highest possible revision, or build, that will accommodate the newest build of ESX or ESXi in the environment. When upgrading from a VI3 environment to a vSphere environment, the vCenter server will be upgraded first. The license server from the VI3 installation is still required to facilitate the use of ESX 3.x or ESXi 3.5 hosts.

If the license server is removed from the upgraded vCenter Server, it must be downloaded from VMware's website, because it is not included with the vSphere distribution. It is a VMware best practice to install the license server on the same system as the vSphere vCenter Server. This will make the installation less complicated than using another system to host the licensing service, while keeping the requirement of only one Windows installation in the environment.

You might also ask, why not upgrade all hosts at the same time as you are upgrading the vCenter Server? Some administrators might feel more comfortable using vCenter Server for vSphere in production for a short time before upgrading hosts. In other situations, where some hosts are upgraded, some other hosts may not be able to be upgraded, due to the constraints the vSphere Hardware Compatibility List puts on some equipment. Because hosts are not inexpensive, it might be desired to continue to leverage them until it is financially feasible to replace them.

To manage legacy hosts in a vSphere environment:

1. Download the license server from the VMware website, or use the most recent distribution from vCenter Server for VI3 media.

2. Run the license server installation to begin.

3. When proceeding through the installation dialog boxes, choose all the defaults until you reach the Provide Licensing Info window. Enter the path to the license file obtained from the VMware License Portal, or an existing license file. Click Next, then Install, followed by Finish to complete the license server installation.

4. Log into the vCenter Server using vSphere Client.

5. Once connected, load vCenter Server Settings by selecting Administration ➤ vCenter Server Settings, shown in Figure 4.17.

Figure 4.17: vCenter license settings

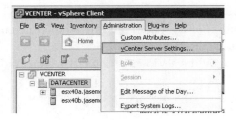

6. Select the Licensing menu from the left pane to access licensing settings.

7. In the License Server section, enter the name or IP address of the system where the license server service is running. This can be the vCenter Server or another system that is running the service, as shown in Figure 4.18.

Figure 4.18: The License Server window

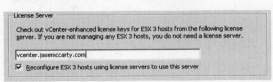

8. Also ensure that the Reconfigure ESX 3 Hosts Using License Servers To Use This Server check box is selected. Doing so ensures that vCenter Server can manage the licenses that the ESX hosts are using.

9. Click OK to accept the changes so that VI3 licenses can be used for legacy hosts.

10. To ensure the licenses are installed and recognized by vCenter Server, load the licensing window in vSphere by pressing Ctrl+Shift+L or selecting View ➤ Administration ➤ Licensing.

11. Figure 4.19 shows the License Server and any vSphere licenses. Click the plus (+) sign to the left of the License Server listed to view the licenses that are loaded by the license server.

Figure 4.19: License report

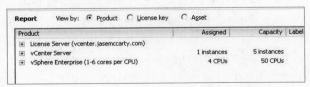

As you can see, managing licenses for legacy hosts is slightly more complicated than for ESX or ESXi version 4.0 hosts. Some additional limitations with using legacy hosts include the inability to manage which hosts use which features from a central location. Legacy hosts still have to be configured individually, through each host's configuration menu, to enable or disable features such as HA, DRS, and VMotion.

Review Installed Licenses

Now that licenses have been installed and assigned, it is important to review them for not only compliance, but to ensure they are assigned appropriately. In any environment, it is important to know which licenses are currently in use, and whether all licenses are being leveraged appropriately.

As new equipment is being implemented in an environment, often new licenses are purchased along with the new equipment. In other situations, equipment is replaced, and it is necessary to reassign licenses from older equipment to the newer equipment.

Fortunately VMware has provided a reporting function in the Licensing component of vCenter Server. Reporting can be viewed by Product, License Key, or Asset. Each of these displays information somewhat differently. This ability is a great addition to the management of licenses in vSphere. This reporting function replaces the VMware Licensing Portal, which can only be accessed with Internet connectivity to VMware's website, which provides only the ability to view purchased licenses. By using the reporting function in vSphere, you can easily determine which assets are using licenses.

View Licenses by Product

When you are reviewing licensing, it is good to know what products are installed in the environment. Reviewing this information is easy in the License Administration screen:

1. When connected to vCenter Server, load Licensing Administration by selecting View ➢ Administration ➢ Licensing or by pressing Ctrl+Shift+L.

2. The currently installed licenses will be displayed in Licensing Administration and appear according to product. By default, the different products listings only display the product names, the number assigned, and the total number of licenses or capacity. This information is only somewhat useful.

3. To get a better view of which vSphere assets are using which licenses, click the plus (+) sign to the left of the product name. For vSphere products, the license key, the number assigned, the capacity, the label assigned to the key, and an expiration of the key, if any, will be displayed.

4. For legacy clients, click the plus (+) sign to the left of the license server, and the VI3 licenses will be displayed underneath it.

5. To display which vSphere assets or VI3 legacy hosts are assigned which licenses, click the plus (+) sign to the left of either the vSphere license key or the VI3 license type.

Figure 4.20 shows a typical report, including vCenter Server, two ESX 4.0 hosts, and an ESX 3.5 host that requires a licensing server.

Figure 4.20: License report by product

Report View by: (•) Product ( ) License key ( ) Asset				
Product	Assigned	Capacity	Label	Expires
⊟ License Server (vcenter.jasemccarty.com)				
⊟ VI3 ESX Server Standard	1 CPUs	20 CPUs		
▯ esx35.jasemccarty.com	1 CPUs			
⊟ VI3 vCenter agent for ESX Server	1 CPUs	20 CPUs		
▯ esx35.jasemccarty.com	1 CPUs			
VI3 vCenter Management Server	0 instances	3 instances		
⊟ VI3 VMotion	1 CPUs	20 CPUs		
▯ esx35.jasemccarty.com	1 CPUs			
⊟ VI3 VMware Consolidated Backup	1 CPUs	20 CPUs		
▯ esx35.jasemccarty.com	1 CPUs			
⊟ VI3 VMware DRS	0 CPUs	20 CPUs		
▯ esx35.jasemccarty.com	Not used			
⊟ VI3 VMware HA	0 CPUs	20 CPUs		
▯ esx35.jasemccarty.com	Not used			
⊟ vCenter Server	1 instances	5 instances		
⊟ AAAAA-BBBBB-CCCCC-DDDDD-EEEEE	1 instances	5 instances	vCenter Server	6/29/2009
⚙ VCENTER	1 instances			
⊟ vSphere Enterprise (1-6 cores per CPU)	4 CPUs	50 CPUs		
⊟ AAAAA-BBBBB-CCCCC-DDDDD-EEEEE	4 CPUs	50 CPUs	vSphere Enterprise	6/29/2009
▯ esx40a.jasemccarty.com	2 CPUs			
▯ esx40b.jasemccarty.com	2 CPUs			

You can export this license information by clicking Export. Information organized by product will be exported to one of five different formats. These formats include comma-separated values (CSV), Microsoft Excel Workbook (XLS), Extensible Markup Language (XML), or one of two possible Hypertext Markup Language (HTML) options.

View Licenses by License Key

Another way to view licensing is by license key. This report view makes the process of seeing which products have assets assigned very easy. To view licenses and the products that have been assigned to those keys:

1. When connected to vCenter Server, load Licensing Administration by selecting View ➤ Administration ➤ Licensing or by pressing Ctrl+Shift+L.

2. The currently installed licenses will be displayed in Licensing Administration and appear according to product.

3. Click the License Key radio button to change the report to show license keys and the assets associated with them. By default, the different license keys display the license key, the product, the number assigned, the capacity, the label given, and the expiration date, if any. Again, this information is only somewhat useful.

4. To get a better view of which vSphere assets are using which licenses, click the plus (+) sign to the left of the product name. For vSphere products, the license key, the number assigned, the capacity, the label assigned to the key, and an expiration of the key, if any, will be displayed. Legacy clients will not be visible in this view, because they are not licensed by a key.

Figure 4.21 shows license information with the license key as the primary reporting item. Notice that legacy clients are not visible in this report.

Figure 4.21: License report by license key

Report	View by: ◯ Product ⦿ License key ◯ Asset					
License Key	Product	Assigned	Capacity	Label	Expires	
⊟ AAAAA-3BBBB-CCCCC-DDDDD-EEIEE Center Server		1 instances	5 instances	vCenter Server	6/29/2009	
VCENTER		1 instances				
⊟ AAAAA-3BBBB-CCCCC-DDDDD-EEIEE	ʹSphere Enterprise (1-6 cores per CPU)	4 CPUs	50 CPUs	vSphere Enterprise	6/29/2009	
esx40a.jasemccarty.com		2 CPUs				
esx40b.jasemccarty.com		2 CPUs				

View Licenses by Asset

Another way to view licensing is by asset. This report view dispenses with having to go through the process of viewing a license and expanding it to see which asset is associated with each license. This report view simplifies the process of determining which license is assigned to an asset. To view the Assets report:

1. When connected to vCenter Server, load Licensing Administration by selecting View ➢ Administration ➢ Licensing or by pressing Ctrl+Shift+L.

2. The currently installed licenses will be displayed in Licensing Administration and appear according to product.

3. Click the Asset radio button to change the report to show assets.

This is the least detailed report. This report only shows the asset, the product assigned, the license key assigned, and the expiration date.

Figure 4.22 shows each asset in the environment and the licenses associated with each asset. This report is useful when you specifically want to know how an asset is licensed without having to drill down into the product or license keys reports.

Figure 4.22: License report by asset

Asset	Product	License Key	Expires
esx35.jasemccarty.com	vCenter agent for ESX Server, VMotion,...		
esx40a.jasemccarty.com	vSphere Enterprise (1-6 cores per CPU)	AAAAA-BBBBB-CC..	6/29/2009
esx40b.jasemccarty.com	vSphere Enterprise (1-6 cores per CPU)	AAAAA-BBBBB-CC,.	6/29/2009
VCENTER	vCenter Server	AAAAA-BBBBB-CC...	6/29/2009

5

Upgrading from VI3 to vSphere

IN THIS CHAPTER, YOU WILL LEARN TO:

I t's entirely conceivable that many readers of this book are existing VMware Infrastructure 3 (VI3) customers who are preparing for the upgrade to VMware vSphere 4. This chapter provides information on how to upgrade your existing VI3 environment to VMware vSphere 4.

Prepare for the Upgrade

Before starting the upgrade from VI3 to VMware vSphere 4, a prudent administrator will take the time to properly prepare for the upgrade. This section provides some tasks that you should complete before starting the upgrade process. Completing these tasks will help ensure that your upgrade is smooth and successful with a minimum of downtime.

Verify that the vCenter Server 4.0 hardware requirements are met. vCenter Server 4.0 has more stringent hardware requirements than VirtualCenter 2.5. For example, VMware recommends a minimum of 3GB of RAM for vCenter Server 4.0. If the database server will be running on the same system, the installed RAM should be even higher. Be sure to double-check the hardware requirements for vCenter Server 4.0 and ensure that the system that is intended to run vCenter Server 4.0 meets those minimum requirements.

Verify database compatibility with vCenter Server 4.0.   vCenter Server 4.0 adds support for some databases and removes support for other databases. The databases supported for use with vCenter Server 4.0 are Oracle 10g, Oracle 11g, SQL Server 2005 Express, SQL Server 2005, and SQL Server 2008. Oracle 9i and SQL Server 2000 are no longer supported. If you are using one of these older databases, you must complete a database upgrade to a supported version before starting the upgrade to vCenter Server 4.0.

Make a complete backup of the vCenter Server database.   Because the vCenter Server 4.0 upgrade will upgrade the database scheme, you will want to have a complete backup of the VirtualCenter 2.x database before starting the upgrade.

Make a complete backup of the VirtualCenter 2.x SSL certificates. To be able to successfully "roll back" after a failed upgrade, you must have not only a copy of the database, but also a copy of the SSL certificates. Ensure that you have a complete backup of the VirtualCenter 2.x SSL certificates.

Ensure that you have sufficient database permissions to upgrade the database. The upgrade to vCenter Server 4.0 modifies the database schema, and so you need elevated permissions on the database in order for this operation to succeed. Ensure that you have the proper permissions on the external database before starting the upgrade. On an Oracle system, the user should have the DBA role; on a SQL Server database, the user should have the db_owner role on both the vCenter Server database as well as the MSDB database.

NOTE The permissions on the MSDB database are required only during the upgrade and can be removed after the upgrade is complete.

Locate and verify the username and password used by Virtual-Center to authenticate to external databases. You must have the login credentials, the database name, and the database server name used for the vCenter Server database. If this information is not available, the vCenter Server upgrade routine will not be able to upgrade the database.

Make sure the name of the vCenter Server computer is less than 15 characters long. vCenter Server 4.0 requires that the name of the computer be less than 15 characters. If the name is longer, you will need to shorten it. If the database server runs on the same computer, access to the database could be impacted by the name change. If you change the name of the computer, be sure to update the Open Database Connectivity (ODBC) Data Source Name (DSN) information appropriately.

Verify the upgrade path to vCenter Server 4.0. VirtualCenter 1.*x* cannot be upgraded to vCenter Server 4.0. You must perform a fresh installation of vCenter Server 4.0 instead. Likewise, Oracle 9*i* and SQL Server 2000 are no longer supported; these databases must be upgraded to a supported version before VirtualCenter 2.*x* can be upgraded to vCenter Server 4.0.

Ensure that all ESX/ESXi host hardware is listed on the VMware Hardware Compatibility List (HCL). Administrators should verify that all hardware in the ESX/ESXi hosts is listed on the VMware HCL for VMware vSphere 4. Hardware components that are not found on the HCL should be replaced with compatible components in order to ensure maximum compatibility and supportability.

NOTE One area that might cause a problem in upgrade scenarios is 64-bit compatibility. Earlier versions of ESX/ESXi ran on 32-bit CPUs, but ESX/ESXi 4.0 require 64-bit CPUs. Be sure to confirm that your server's CPUs are fully 64-bit compatible.

Verify the upgrade path to ESX/ESXi 4.0. Only environments running ESX 3.0 or later can upgrade to ESX/ESXi 4.0. Environments running ESX 2.5.5 might be able to upgrade, depending on the partition layout. ESX 2.5.5 servers with the default partition layout will not be able to upgrade to ESX/ESXi 4.0. ESX servers earlier than ESX 2.5.5 do not support an upgrade to ESX/ESXi 4.0.

After you have gone through all of the tasks listed in this section, you are ready to proceed with the upgrade of your environment from VI3 to VMware vSphere 4. Upgrading VirtualCenter 2.*x* to vCenter Server 4.0 is your first step.

Upgrade vCenter Server

The first step in the process of upgrading your environment from VI3 to VMware vSphere 4 is upgrading VirtualCenter Server 2.5 to vCenter Server 4.0. After VirtualCenter Server 2.5 is upgraded to vCenter Server 4.0, you have a variety of paths to take to get the ESX/ESXi hosts and virtual machines upgraded. You have to complete the upgrade to vCenter Server 4.0 before those options are available, though failing to upgrade VirtualCenter Server 2.5 to vCenter Server 4.0 first can result in downtime, a loss of connectivity, and the risk of potential data loss. Always be sure to upgrade VirtualCenter Server before upgrading any other components in the VMware vSphere environment.

In most cases, you'll want to upgrade VirtualCenter to vCenter Server on the same system, as described in the next section.

Upgrade to vCenter Server 4.0 on the Same System

In many cases, you'll perform the upgrade from VirtualCenter 2.*x* to vCenter Server 4.0 on the same physical system. You might consider this an in-place upgrade, because VirtualCenter 2.*x* will be upgraded in place to vCenter Server 4.0.

Before starting the VirtualCenter 2.*x* upgrade to vCenter Server 4.0, be sure the following tasks have been completed:

- You've made a backup of the VirtualCenter database.

- You have a backup copy of the VirtualCenter SSL certificates.

- You have the username and password that will be used for database access.

If these tasks have been successfully completed, you are ready to upgrade to vCenter Server 4.0.

To upgrade VirtualCenter 2.5 to vCenter Server 4.0, perform these steps:

1. Log in to the computer running VirtualCenter Server 2.5 as a user with administrative permissions.

2. Click Start ➤ Control Panel.

3. Open Administrative Tools, and then double-click Services.

4. Find the VMware VirtualCenter Server service and stop the service.

5. Insert the VMware vCenter media into the DVD drive. Autoplay will automatically launch the VMware vCenter Installer.

6. Click the link to install vCenter Server. This launches the installer for vCenter Server.

7. When prompted, select a language for the installer and click OK.

8. At the Welcome page for the vCenter Server installer, click Next.

9. Select I Agree To The Terms In The License Agreement and click Next.

10. Enter the license key for vCenter Server. If you do not yet have the license key, you can omit the license key to allow vCenter Server to run in evaluation mode. You can license vCenter Server later using vSphere Client. Click Next to continue.

11. Enter the database username and password for authentication to the database specified by the existing DSN. If you are using Windows NT authentication, you can leave the username and password blank. Click Next.

NOTE If you are using Windows NT authentication, the logged-on user during the installation process should be the same user that is used to access the database.

---

12. Select Yes I Want To Upgrade My vCenter Server Database to upgrade the database schema. This step is required in order to proceed with the upgrade.

13. Select I Have Taken A Backup Of The Existing vCenter Server Database And SSL Certificates and then click Next.

14. Specify the user account under which the vCenter Server service should run. If the database is using Windows NT authentication, this account should be the same account specified earlier in the wizard and the same account that has been configured for access to the database. Click Next to continue.

15. Accept the default port numbers and click Next.

16. Click Install to start the upgrade process.

It's also possible to perform an upgrade from VirtualCenter 2.*x* on one system to vCenter Server 4.0 on a different system. This approach is necessary if, during the upgrade, you want to move to a 64-bit platform (vCenter Server 4.0 supports 64-bit versions of Windows Server). This process is described in the next section.

Upgrade to vCenter Server 4.0 on a Different System

In this scenario, you upgrade VirtualCenter 2.*x* on one system to vCenter Server 4.0 on a different system. This allows you to switch to 64-bit for vCenter Server 4.0.

NOTE Although vCenter Server 4.0 supports 64-bit Windows Server versions, you must be sure to use a 32-bit DSN. Use the 32-bit ODBC Administrator application found at %WINDIR%\ SysWOW64\odbcad32.exe.

To upgrade to vCenter Server 4.0 on a different system, follow these steps:

1. Copy the SSL certificates from the source system (the system running VirtualCenter 2.*x*) to the destination system (the system that

will run vCenter Server 4.0). On a Windows Server 2003 system, the SSL certificates are located in `%ALLUSERSPROFILE%\Application Data\VMware\VMware VirtualCenter`. On a Windows Server 2008 system, the SSL certificates are located in `%ALLUSERSPROFILE%\ VMware\VMware VirtualCenter`.

2. Create a DSN that points to the existing database. If you are installing vCenter Server on a 64-bit system, the DSN must be 32 bit, as pointed out earlier.

3. On the destination system, run the vCenter Server installer and follow the steps outlined in the previous section to install vCenter Server 4.0.

Regardless of the method used, after the vCenter Server upgrade there are some postupgrade tasks that you need to perform. We'll describe these tasks next.

Perform Postupgrade Tasks

Once the upgrade to vCenter Server 4.0 is complete, there are a number of postupgrade tasks that administrators need to perform. These tasks include upgrading additional vCenter modules like vCenter Update Manager, vCenter Converter, or Guided Consolidation; upgrading vSphere Client; and verifying license settings. You'll learn how to perform these tasks in the next few sections.

Upgrade Additional vCenter Modules

Not only must you upgrade VirtualCenter 2.*x* to vCenter Server 4.0, but you must also upgrade the plug-ins that extend VirtualCenter's functionality. On the VMware vCenter installation media, VMware provides installers for three vCenter Server plug-ins:

- vCenter Update Manager (VUM)
- vCenter Converter
- Guided Consolidation

If you were using a previous version of one of these plug-ins with VirtualCenter 2.*x*, you'll also need to upgrade each of these to the version supplied on the VMware vCenter installer media. Refer to the *vSphere Upgrade Guide*, available from VMware's website at `http://www.vmware .com/support/pubs`, for more in-depth information on the upgrade process for each of these plug-ins.

Upgrade vSphere Client

Both ESX/ESXi and vCenter Server provide a simple web interface that makes it easy to download vSphere Client. Since at this point in the upgrade process you've only upgraded vCenter Server and not any of the ESX/ESXi hosts, you'll only be able to use vCenter Server's web interface to download and install vSphere Client.

NOTE It is possible to have both VMware vSphere Client as well as the older VMware Infrastructure Client installed on the same system at the same time. This might help ease the transition into the newer version of the software.

To download and install vSphere Client, follow these steps:

1. From the system onto which you want to install vSphere Client, open a web browser and navigate to the IP address or hostname of the vCenter Server computer.

2. Click the Download vSphere Client link.

3. Depending on the browser you use, you might be prompted to either save or run the file. If you are allowed to run the file, do so; otherwise, save the file, and then double-click it after it has finished downloading.

4. Click the Next button on the welcome page of the VMware vSphere Client 4.0 installation wizard.

5. Click the radio button I Accept The Terms In The License Agreement and then click Next.

6. Specify a username and organization name and then click Next.

7. Configure the destination folder and then click Next.

8. Click the Install button to begin the installation.

9. Click the Finish button to complete the installation.

At this point vSphere Client is now installed and you can use it to manage the new environment. If the previous version was left installed, you can use the VI Client to manage older systems.

In the event that you will have a mixed 3.*x*/4.0 environment for any length of time, you'll also want to be sure that vCenter Server 4.0's license settings are correct. The next section describes these settings.

Building a VMware vSphere Environment

PART I

> **TIP** If you already have the VI Client installed to manage your VI3 environment, you can use it to log in to vCenter Server 4.0 to upgrade to vSphere Client.

Verify License Settings

VMware vSphere 4.0 no longer needs or uses a license server, but older ESX/ESXi hosts still need a license server until they are upgraded to version 4.0. Depending on how the upgrade was handled, you might need to install a license server in order to service the older ESX/ESXi hosts.

Consider the following upgrade scenarios:

VirtualCenter with a local license server installed is upgraded to vCenter Server 4.0 on the same computer. In this scenario, the license server for the VI3 environment was installed on the VirtualCenter Server computer before the upgrade to vCenter Server 4.0 on the same computer. The license server is preserved and remains operational after the upgrade is complete. You only need to verify that vCenter Server is using the local license server for ESX/ESXi 3.x hosts.

VirtualCenter with a remote license server is upgraded to vCenter Server 4.0 on the same computer. The license server resides on a separate computer than the VirtualCenter Server computer, so it is unaffected by the upgrade to vCenter Server 4.0 and remains operational after the upgrade is complete. You just have to verify that vCenter Server 4.0 points ESX/ESXi 3.x hosts to the same remote license server.

VirtualCenter with a local license server installed is upgraded to vCenter Server 4.0 on a different computer. The installation routine for vCenter Server 4.0 does not install a license server, so the new computer running vCenter Server 4.0 will not have a functional license server running. If the old VirtualCenter Server computer is going to be retired, you must install a new license server into the environment and configure vCenter Server 4.0 to use that new license server for ESX/ESXi 3.x hosts.

VirtualCenter with a remote license server is upgraded to vCenter Server 4.0 on a different computer. The license server is unaffected by the vCenter Server 4.0 upgrade and remains fully functional. You only need to configure vCenter Server 4.0 to use the license server for ESX/ESXi 3.*x* hosts.

To verify that vCenter Server 4.0 is using the correct license server for ESX/ESXi 3.*x* hosts, follow these steps:

1. With vSphere Client running and connected to a vCenter Server instance, select Administration ➤ vCenter Server Settings.

2. Select Licensing on the left.

3. At the bottom of the dialog box, in the License Server section, enter the correct license server that vCenter Server should use, as shown in Figure 5.1.

4. Click OK to save the settings and return to vSphere Client.

Figure 5.1: Administrators should configure vCenter Server 4.0 to use the correct license server to provide licensing information to pre−vSphere ESX/ESXi hosts.

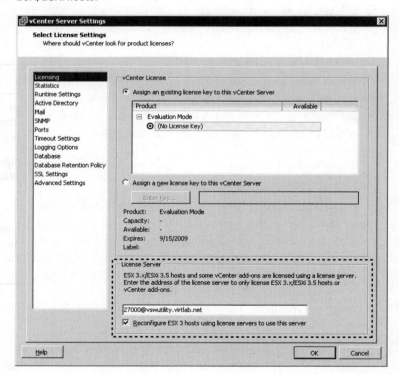

After completing these postupgrade tasks, vCenter Server 4.0 should be fully installed and fully operational in your environment. You're now ready to upgrade your ESX/ESXi hosts to version 4.0, as described in the next section.

Upgrade ESX/ESXi Hosts

Once you have upgraded vCenter Server to version 4.0, the process of upgrading the ESX/ESXi hosts to version 4.0 can start. You have three options for upgrading ESX/ESXi hosts:

- Use vCenter Update Manager (VUM).

- Perform a manual upgrade.

- Perform a fresh installation.

Each approach has its advantages and disadvantages. Table 5.1 compares the three approaches.

Table 5.1: Three Approaches to Upgrading Hosts

Method	Advantages	Disadvantages
Use vCenter Update Manager.	Uses VUM and is integrated into vCenter Server.	No support for custom Service Console partitions in ESX.
Perform a manual upgrade.	Administrator has full control over the upgrade process and preserves legacy configuration information.	Custom Service Console partitions are not migrated correctly.
Perform a fresh installation.	Ensures a clean and consistent configuration of the ESX/ESXi hosts.	Some reconfiguration might be necessary after the installation unless host profiles are used.

You must evaluate which option best meets your specific needs. For organizations that already leverage vCenter Update Manager, using VUM to upgrade the ESX/ESXi hosts makes a lot of sense. Organizations that plan to use host profiles may find that using the fresh installation approach makes the most sense. Organizations that do not use VUM or host profiles might find that performing a manual upgrade makes the most sense.

The next section describes the first of these three approaches: using vCenter Update Manager to upgrade ESX/ESXi hosts.

Upgrade ESX/ESXi Using vCenter Update Manager

vCenter Update Manager not only provides the ability to patch ESX/ESXi hosts and selected guest operating systems but can also assist in upgrading ESX/ESXi hosts to version 4.0. vCenter Update Manager will use a special type of baseline, a *host upgrade baseline*, to identify hosts that are not yet running ESX/ESXi 4.0 and specify how to upgrade the identified hosts to ESX/ESXi 4.0.

You must create the host upgrade baseline and then attach it to a container within vCenter Server, like a datacenter, folder, or cluster. After you have attached the baseline, a scan will identify those hosts that are not running ESX/ESXi 4.0, and initiating remediation will initiate the upgrade to ESX/ESXi 4.0 for the identified hosts.

NOTE Upgrading an ESX/ESXi 3.x host to ESX/ESXi 4.0 requires an existing Virtual Machine File System (VMFS) volume. Depending on how ESX/ESXi 3.x was installed, the host might not have a VMFS volume. This would force a fresh install instead of an upgrade.

The first step, though, is creating the host upgrade baseline by performing the following steps:

1. In vSphere Client, navigate to the Update Manager Administration area by using the navigation bar or by selecting View ➢ Solutions and Applications ➢ Update Manager.

2. Click the Baselines And Groups tab. Make sure the view is set to Hosts, not VMs/VAs. Use the small buttons just below the tab bar to set the correct view.

3. Select the Upgrade Baselines tab.

4. Right-click a blank area of the Upgrade Baselines list and select New Baseline. The New Baseline Wizard starts.

5. Supply a name for the baseline and an optional description, and note that vSphere Client has automatically selected the type as Host Upgrade. Click Next to continue.

6. Select the ESX upgrade ISO and the ESXi upgrade zip files. You can use the Browse button to find the files on the vCenter Server computer or another location accessible across the network.

7. Click Next to upload the files and continue; note that the file upload might take a few minutes to complete.

8. After the file uploads and file imports have completed, click Next.

9. The next screen asks about where to place the storage for the ESX Service Console. The Service Console (referred to here as the COS, or the Console OS) resides within a virtual machine disk file (VMDK file). The upgrade baseline needs to know where to place the VMDK for the COS during the upgrade process.

10. Select Automatically Select a Datastore on the Local Host and click Next.

11. If the upgrade process fails or if the host is unable to reconnect to vCenter Server, VUM offers the option of automatically rebooting the host and "rolling back" the upgrade. You can disable that option on the next screen by deselecting "Try to reboot the host and roll back the upgrade in case of failure." But for this exercise, leave this option selected and click Next to continue.

12. Review the summary of the options selected in the upgrade baseline. If anything is incorrect, use the Back button to go back and correct it. Otherwise, click Finish.

After you've created the host upgrade baseline, you must next attach the host upgrade baseline to one or more hosts, or to a container object like a data center, cluster, or folder. Let's look at attaching a baseline to a specific ESX/ESXi host. The process is much the same, if not identical, to the process for attaching a baseline to a datacenter, cluster, folder, or virtual machine.

Perform the following steps to attach the host upgrade baseline to an ESX/ESXi host:

1. Launch vSphere Client if it is not already running and connect to a vCenter Server instance.

NOTE You cannot manage, attach, or detach VUM baselines when vSphere Client connected directly to an ESX/ESXi host using vSphere Client. You must be connected to an instance of vCenter Server.

2. From the menu, select View ➤ Inventory ➤ Hosts And Clusters, or press the Ctrl+Shift+H keyboard shortcut.

3. In the inventory tree on the left, select the ESX/ESXi host to which you want to attach the host upgrade baseline.

4. From the right-hand pane, use the double-headed arrows to scroll through the list of tabs until you can see the Update Manager tab and then select it.

5. Click the Attach link in the upper right-hand corner; this link opens the Attach Baseline Or Group dialog box.

6. Select the host upgrade baseline that you want to attach to this ESX/ESXi host and then click Attach.

Next, you must scan the host for compliance with the attached baselines. On the Update Manager tab where you just attached the host upgrade baseline, there is a Scan link; click that link to initiate a scan. Be sure to select to scan for upgrades.

When the scan is complete, the results will show that the host is non-compliant (i.e., not running ESX/ESXi 4.0). To upgrade the host, use the Remediate button in the lower-right corner of the Update Manager tab. This launches the Remediate wizard.

To upgrade the host, follow these steps:

1. At the first screen, select the host upgrade baseline and then click Next.

2. Click the check box to accept the license terms and then click Next.

3. Review the settings specified in the host upgrade baseline. A blue hyperlink next to each setting allows you to modify the settings. To leave the settings as they were specified in the host upgrade baseline, simply click Next.

4. Specify a name, description, and a schedule for the upgrade and then click Next.

5. Review the settings and use the Back button to go back if any settings need to be changed. Click Finish when the settings are correct and you are ready to proceed with the upgrade.

vCenter Update Manager proceeds with the upgrade at the scheduled time (immediately is the default setting in the wizard). The upgrade will be an unattended upgrade, and at the end of the upgrade the ESX/ESXi host automatically reboots.

WARNING   When you are using host upgrade baselines to upgrade your ESX hosts, custom Service Console partitions are not honored. (ESXi does not have a user-accessible Service Console, so this doesn't apply.) While the old partitions are preserved (their contents are kept intact and mounted under the /esx3-installation directory), the new Service Console will have a single partition mounted at the root directory. If you want your ESX 4.0 hosts to have a custom partition scheme after the upgrade, you won't want to use vCenter Update Manager and host upgrade baselines.

As you can see, using vCenter Update Manager creates a streamlined upgrade process. When combined with using vCenter Update Manager to upgrade the VMware Tools and the virtual machine hardware, as described in the section titled "Perform Postupgrade Tasks," this makes for an automated upgrade experience. Administrators who had not considered using vCenter Update Manager should reconsider based on this upgrade functionality.

For organizations that choose not to deploy vCenter Update Manager, for whatever reason, their options for upgrading ESX/ESXi hosts are to perform a manual upgrade or to upgrade with a fresh installation. The next section discusses how to perform a manual upgrade.

Perform a Manual In-Place Upgrade

To perform a manual in-place upgrade, you must use the vSphere Host Update Utility, which is installed along with vSphere Client. Booting off the ESX 4.0 DVD won't allow you to perform an in-place upgrade; the DVD only performs fresh installations, as described in Chapter 2.

To perform a manual in-place upgrade, complete these steps:

1. Make sure the ESX/ESXi 3.x host is in maintenance mode. The vSphere Host Update Utility will not update the host if it is not in maintenance mode.

2. Launch the vSphere Host Update Utility.

3. If the host you wish to upgrade is not listed, select Host ➤ Add Host and specify the fully qualified hostname or IP address of the ESX/ESXi 3.x host.

4. Select the ESX/ESXi 3.*x* host in the list of hosts.

5. Click Upgrade Host. This launches the VMware ESX Upgrade wizard.

6. Specify the location of the ESX ISO image. Use the Browse button to find the ISO in the local system or on an accessible network location. Click Next after you've selected the upgrade package.

7. Select I Accept The Terms Of The License Agreement and click Next.

8. Make sure that the user credentials are correct and complete, and then click Next.

9. The wizard will go through a set of compatibility checks. After the compatibility checks are complete, the wizard prompts you to select the datastore where the Console OS VMDK should be stored. Select a datastore and click Next.

10. If the upgrade process fails or if the host is unable to reconnect to the network, the host will attempt to reboot the host and "roll back" the upgrade. You can disable that feature by deselecting the "Attempt to reboot the host and roll back the upgrade in case of failure" check box. Leave this option selected and click Next to continue.

11. Review the summary of the options selected in the upgrade baseline. If anything is incorrect, use the Back button to go back and correct it. Otherwise, click Finish.

NOTE   Don't forget that a VMFS volume is required when you are upgrading hosts to ESX/ESXi 4.0. Without a VMFS volume, a fresh install is required.

The vSphere Host Update Utility will copy across the ISO image, as shown in Figure 5.2, then reboot the host and perform the upgrade to version 4.0.

The vSphere Host Update Utility makes performing manual upgrades easy, but manual upgrades suffer from the same problem as using vCenter Update Manager: the custom Service Console partitions are not upgraded. For custom Service Console partitions, you're left with upgrading via a fresh installation.

Figure 5.2: The vSphere Host Update Utility copies the ISO image across
the network to the selected host for upgrade.

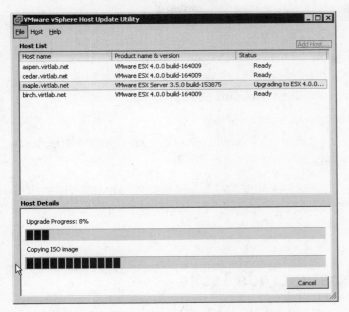

Upgrade with a Fresh ESX/ESXi Installation

Technically, this isn't an upgrade because you aren't preserving the
previous installation. However, this is a valid approach to getting your
hosts running ESX/ESXi 4.0. Because the ESX/ESXi hosts are typically
almost stateless—meaning that there is very little configuration data
actually stored on the host—rebuilding an ESX/ESXi host with a fresh
installation doesn't create a significant amount of work for you. Add in
the functionality provided by host profiles, which can automate virtually all the configuration of an ESX/ESXi host, and using this approach
becomes even more attractive. With host profiles, an administrator can
install ESX with a scripted installation file, join the host to vCenter
Server, apply a host profile, and that's it.

Chapter 2 provides complete information on how to install ESX and
ESXi. That information is equally applicable here, so we won't repeat
all the same information again. Refer to the installation information in
that chapter on how to install ESX and ESXi.

To upgrade your hosts with a fresh installation, the overall process would look something like this:

1. Upgrade vCenter Server to version 4.0. (You did this in the previous section of this chapter.)

2. Use VMotion to move all the virtual machines off a particular ESX/ESXi host.

3. Rebuild that specific host with ESX/ESXi 4.0.

4. Rejoin the host to vCenter Server.

5. Repeat steps 2 through 4 on the remaining hosts until all the hosts have been upgraded to ESX/ESXi 4.0.

After vCenter Server and all the ESX/ESXi hosts have been upgraded, you are ready to perform some important postupgrade tasks. The next section describes these tasks.

Perform Postupgrade Tasks

After vCenter Server and the ESX/ESXi hosts have been upgraded to version 4.0, there are some additional postupgrade tasks that a VMware vSphere administrator should perform.

Upgrade VMware Tools

As you probably already understand by now, the VMware Tools are an important component that should be installed in every guest operating system instance in your environment. After the ESX/ESXi hosts have been upgraded, the VMware Tools in all your guest operating system instances are now out of date and need to be updated to the latest version. This ensures that the guest operating systems are using the latest and most efficient drivers for operating in a virtualized environment.

Administrators can either upgrade VMware Tools manually, or use vCenter Update Manager to upgrade VMware Tools. The process of manually upgrading VMware Tools is described in Chapter 9, so this section will focus on using vCenter Update Manager to upgrade VMware Tools in your guest operating system instances.

vCenter Update Manager provides a prebuilt upgrade baseline named VMware Tools Upgrade to Match Host. This baseline cannot be modified or deleted, and it works by identifying virtual machines whose VMware Tools version does not match the ESX/ESXi host upon which the virtual machine is running. You can attach this baseline to groups of virtual machines and, after performing a scan, vCenter Update Manager will identify which virtual machines are running outdated versions of the VMware Tools. You can then remediate the baseline, which will upgrade the VMware Tools in the affected virtual machines. Most Windows versions require a reboot after upgrading the VMware Tools, so please be sure to plan accordingly.

Using vCenter Update Manager with the VMware Tools Upgrade to Match Host baseline is the equivalent of manually initiating an upgrade of the VMware Tools on each virtual machine independently. vCenter Update Manager helps automate the process.

Upgrade Virtual Machine Hardware

This task should only be completed after the VMware Tools have been upgraded to match the ESX/ESXi host version. Otherwise, new virtual hardware presented to the guest operating system instance inside the virtual machine may not work properly until the updated version of the VMware Tools is installed. By installing the latest version of the VMware Tools first, you ensure that any new virtual hardware presented to the guest operating system has the drivers necessary to work right away.

The process of manually upgrading the virtual machine hardware from version 4 (the version used by ESX/ESXi 3.x) to version 7 (the version used by VMware vSphere 4) is described in Chapter 9. You do not have to manually upgrade the virtual machine version, though; you also can use vCenter Update Manager to upgrade the virtual machine hardware version.

Like the VMware Tools, vCenter Update Manager comes with a prebuilt baseline named VM Hardware Upgrade to Match Host. When you attach this baseline, either directly or as part of a baseline group, to a number of virtual machines and then perform a scan, vCenter Update Manager will identify which virtual machines have outdated virtual machine hardware. You can then "remediate" these virtual machines. As part of the remediation, vCenter Server will shut down the virtual machines and perform a virtual machine upgrade.

NOTE The VM Hardware Upgrade to Match Host baseline can only remediate a virtual machine with an outdated virtual machine version when the virtual machine is powered off. If the virtual machine is powered on, no upgrades will occur. As soon as the virtual machine is powered down, any pending tasks will launch and become active.

PART II

Configuring Your vSphere Environment

IN THIS PART ▶

Configuring Your
vSphere Environment

PART II

6

Creating and Managing Virtual Networking

IN THIS CHAPTER, YOU WILL LEARN TO:

▶ **UNDERSTAND THE BASICS** (Pages 170–174)

- Work with Virtual Switches and Understand Network Services (Pages 170–171)
- Use NIC Teaming and Configure VLANs (Page 172)
- Use VLAN Tagging and View Networking Configuration and Network Adapter Information (Page 173)

▶ **NETWORK WITH VSWITCHES** (Pages 174–180)

- NIC Team the Service Console (Page 175)
- Assign Static IP Addresses for the Service Console (Page 176)
- Create a vSwitch for Virtual Machine Networking (Page 176)

▶ **NETWORK WITH VNETWORK DISTRIBUTED SWITCHES** (Pages 180–195)

- Configure a vNetwork Distributed Switch (Page 182)
- Add Additional Hosts and Adapters to a DVS (Page 184)
- Edit General and Advanced DVS Settings (Page 185)
- Manage Physical and Virtual Network Adapters (Page 185)
- Migrate Existing Virtual Adapters into DVS (Page 189)
- Add a dvPort Group and Edit a dvPort Group, Create a Private VLAN, and Migrate VMs to a DVS (Page 191–194)

▶ **UNDERSTAND ADVANCED NETWORKING** (Pages 195–201)

- Customize MAC Addresses (Page 195)
- Create a VMkernel Port for Software iSCSI (Page 196)
- Configure a Service Console Connection for Software iSCSI (Page 197)
- Troubleshoot Using the Command Line (Page 198)
- Enable Cisco Discovery Protocol and Enable IPv6 (Pages 199–200)

F our main resources combine to provide performance, stability, and flexibility in a virtualized environment: CPU, memory, storage, and networking. This chapter focuses on the fourth component: virtual networking. Networking ensures that the infrastructure is flexible in the way IP addressing is handled, provides stability because of the physical redundancy that can be built into the infrastructure, and aids in performance by making sure that adequate bandwidth is available for servers to use.

In this chapter, we are going to define the key building blocks of virtualization and demonstrate how to set them up. We will also explore best practices for setting up your environment.

Understand the Basics

In a physical infrastructure, routers and switches are separate from servers but are connected with network cables. In a virtual infrastructure, this is still the case, but there are virtual switches (vSwitches) inside a host that virtual machines connect to in order to communicate with the external world. In many cases, several network adapters connect a host with outside physical switches. Virtual switches are the core building blocks of virtual networking and combine with physical network adapters to separate, and sometimes combine, traffic to provide performance, redundancy, and isolation of networking for security purposes.

Let's explore a virtualized infrastructure, starting with vSwitches. Then we will move on to explore the network services that make up a vSwitch, learn how to physically set up redundancy on a vSwitch using NIC teaming, discover why VLANs are important to flexible networks, and demonstrate how to view networking configurations.

Work with Virtual Switches

Virtual switches are internal to an ESX/ESXi host and allow you to network traffic that is external to the host and traffic that never needs to leave the host (internal vs. external). If virtual machines require a lot of bandwidth to communicate with one another, think about placing those VMs on the same host and sharing the same vSwitch. Internal traffic (two VMs internal to a host) has a much higher bandwidth than bandwidth traffic that will move across physical switches and network cables (outside of a host to another host or physical server). An example is when several VMs need to communicate with a database that is also on the same host and vSwitch.

You can add multiple physical network adapters to a single vSwitch to achieve additional bandwidth, balance communication routes, and provide greater redundancy that wouldn't exist with just one adapter. By default there are 56 logical ports, and there's a maximum of 1,016 ports on a single ESX.

Isolation of virtual LANs (VLANs) can be defined by adding port groups or by creating multiple vSwitches. Network labels, although not defined as a security boundary, either allow or prohibit portability across hosts through VMotion. Two or more hosts that have the same network label and network may use VMotion to traverse the infrastructure.

Understand Network Services

A vSwitch can make three types of connections, as you can see in Figure 6.1:

Figure 6.1: Connection types

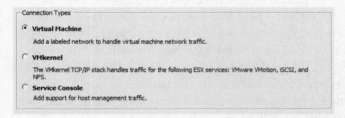

Virtual Machine   This connection type is the most frequently used as it is the backbone for virtual networking.

VMkernel   This connection type is used to handle VMotion, iSCSI, and NFS virtual networking.

Service Console   All communication from the physical world to the ESX goes through this type of switch, and this connection type is set up by default during a host installation.

Use NIC Teaming

The Service Console is a great place to employ a strategy of *NIC teaming* (however, NIC teaming is used on all three types of network services). This is when more than one physical network adapter is associated with a single vSwitch to form a team. This is often done on the Service Console to make sure that a single network failure does not disrupt an entire ESX host. A team can provide a failover path in the event of hardware failure or share the bandwidth load that exists between the vSwitch and the physical world.

Configure VLANs

VLANs are one of the most important aspects of virtual networking. This concept can enhance or diminish the capabilities of the virtual infrastructure. VLANs allow for a single physical LAN segment to be broken up into different broadcast domains. This strategy is most important to larger organizations that employ many different network segments for security and performance. If, for instance, an organization has 10 different VLANs, and if an ESX host needs access to those 10 VLANs, you can accomplish this in one of two ways:

- If you want your host to have access to all 10 of your VLANs, you can have 10 NICs and plug 10 network cables into the ESX; this isn't always possible or the best use of resources, as maintaining this spider web can create confusion. Additionally, if NIC teaming is to be used for redundancy, you will need a minimum of 20 network connections (2 at a minimum for each of the 10 VLANs). Furthermore, if every host needs this same networking, soon your datacenter will be nothing but cable management.

- Suppose VLAN tagging is used and each network cable is capable of carrying traffic from each network segment and is defined by port groups. In this example, fewer than 10 cables can be used. For example, you can use 6 network cables: 2 for the Service Console (which are NIC teamed), 2 for vSwitch #1 (which has 8 VLAN segments on it), and 2 for the last 2 VLAN segments—the DMZ and the internal backup network. Or the last 4 could be entirely dedicated to the 10 VLANs. As you can see, 6 cables are much easier to install and manage than a hypothetical 20 cables.

Use VLAN Tagging

VMware uses 802.1q for VLAN tagging, sometimes called *trunking*. This is a great way to set up a virtual infrastructure, as it allows for maximum flexibility with respect to networking. It is slightly more difficult to work with (compared to regular one-for-one networking), but the added benefits that it brings far outweigh that small amount of extra work. VLAN tagging is also a godsend when network adapter ports are limited—for example, some blade servers may have a limited number and you may want to separate the Service Console and VMotion while still maintaining two physical NICs for failover and load balancing.

View Networking Configuration and Network Adapter Information

Before we start working, you need to locate where this work will be done—in other words, how and where to begin. From vSphere Client, select the Host, select the Configuration tab, and finally select Networking (see Figure 6.2).

Figure 6.2: View networking information

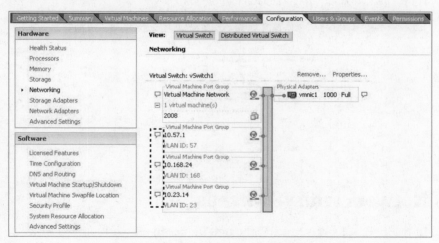

There is also another way to view information. Next to networking information are two types of icons that, if clicked, will display summary information for the object they represent. In basic networking, the icon looks similar to a small blue dialog box (Figure 6.2, on the left).

In the Distributed Virtual Switch view, the icon looks like a blue circle with the letter *i* in it (Figure 6.3, on the right).

Figure 6.3: Summary information

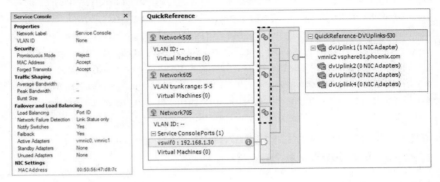

To view the network adapter information, from vSphere Client click Host, select the Configuration tab, and then click Network Adapters (see Figure 6.4).

Figure 6.4: View networking adapter information

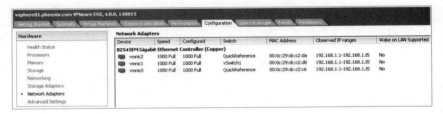

Network with vSwitches

In prior versions of VMware, the only choice in networking was to work with vSwitches. vSphere opens up the networking to use Cisco's Nexus 1000V and also maintains the familiar standard. What is nice about vSwitches is how easy they are to use and how functional they are. Let's dive into using vSwitches and set up the Service Console, assign a static IP, and create a vSwitch for virtual machine networking.

NIC Team the Service Console

The Service Console is one of the most important parts of an ESX host, and it is one of the main forms of communication with an ESX host. While virtual machines would continue to run and provide services without the Service Console, this would be similar to taking a cruise without a captain steering the ship. Therefore, it makes sense to put extra effort into safeguarding its operation. One of the ways to accomplish this is to assign the Service Console two physical NICs; this approach ensures that if one were to fail, communication with the host would not be lost. Enabling High Availability will keep vCenter from assuming that the host is down, creating what is referred to as a *split brain*, and trying to restart the VMs on another host while they are still running on the disconnected host. Let's take a look at how to team a network connection by adding an adapter and possibly adjusting which adapter is the primary.

1. From vSphere Client, select Host, click the Configuration tab, select Networking, and then click Properties (next to the vSwitch where the Service Console resides).

2. Click the Network Adapters tab, click Add (as shown in Figure 6.5), and select an available VMNIC (if none shows, there aren't any available). Then click Next (this screen has an option that lets you move the order of preference up or down; see Figure 6.6), click Next again, and finally click Finish.

Figure 6.5: Adding unclaimed adapters

Figure 6.6: Adjusting the top-level order on two adapters

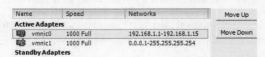

3. Click back to the Ports tab, highlight Service Console, click Edit (a warning will pop up that asks you to always be careful when editing the Service Console), and click Continue Modifying This Connection.

4. The Service Console Properties dialog box opens. Click the NIC Teaming tab, select the Load Balancing check box (as shown in Figure 6.7), click OK, and click Close.

Figure 6.7: Select the Load Balancing check box.

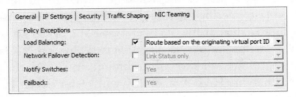

Assign Static IP Addresses for the Service Console

There are times when a DHCP address may have been used during multiple installations. If you need to change to static IPs, follow these steps:

1. From vSphere Client, select the Host, click the Configuration tab, click Networking, and then select Properties (next to the vSwitch where the Service Console resides).

   The default gateway for the Service Console can be edited in the next step or from the DNS And Routing tab; a default gateway for the VMkernel appears there as well.

2. Highlight the Service Console, click Edit (a warning dialog box will pop up asking you to always be careful when editing the Service Console), click Continue Modifying This Connection, click the IP Settings tab, and enter your information.

Create a vSwitch for Virtual Machine Networking

During installation you'll notice an option to create virtual machine networking that is combined with the Service Console. Many administrators choose to deselect this option and/or separate virtual machine networking from the Service Console. This isolation ensures that the ESX host is less likely to be open to attack if it is on the same network as other servers or, worse, end users.

In the following steps, we will create a vSwitch to separate the Service Console from virtual machine networking.

1. From vSphere Client, highlight the ESX, click the Configuration tab, and under Hardware, choose Networking.

2. In the top-right corner, click Add Networking to open a window where you can choose a connection type. This is where you can create a VMkernel switch (used for VMotion and IP storage); regardless of the connection type, the remaining steps are similar.

3. Choose Virtual Machine and click Next to reach a screen that will allow you to either create a new vSwitch or modify an existing one. Additionally, you have the option of choosing which physical NICs to associate with the vSwitch.

4. Make sure Create A Virtual Switch is selected, choose which VMNICs to use, and click Next (see Figure 6.8).

Figure 6.8: Creating a virtual vSwitch

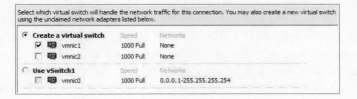

Network Labels

Network labels are nothing more than labels given to a network connection. They do not define any technical aspect of that connection, except for the ability to be portable (VMotion) across hosts. For example, if one connection is called "10.57.1" and on another host that same network connection is called "10.571" (missing the second dot), then there will be errors trying to VMotion across the hosts. Therefore, a simplified networking solution (when not utilizing vNetwork Distributed Switch [DVS]) ensures that the network labels are consistent.

Another strategy that many organizations utilize with naming strategies is to use a label that describes the IP network. This strategy accomplishes many things; first, it is easy to identify which network a virtual machine is part of based solely on the label. Second, if virtualization is used for disaster recovery solutions, the same naming strategy can be used when recovering virtual machines on replicated LUNs, and this will eliminate extra steps during a recovery period. IPs will not have to be looked up for each virtual machine, and/or the same labels can be utilized in a recovery destination and the virtual machine networking will work without any manual adjustment to networking.

Port Groups

Port groups are an extremely useful part of networking because they allow you to define VLANs. Imagine a virtual infrastructure that utilizes several different VLANs but does not take advantage of trunking. Each ESX may end up needing several network adapters in order to bring the different VLANs in the infrastructure. Or worse yet, only one IP network may be defined per cluster, with several clusters in the infrastructure. This setup can still be useful; however, it is limiting the whole idea of what makes virtual infrastructure so powerful to begin with. In this scenario, if virtual machines need to be moved to another cluster, their IP address must be changed, and this is sometimes a challenge with applications and often requires some amount of downtime. This may not occur often, but when the hardware in a cluster is at the end of its useful life, all the virtual machines will need to be migrated. Another challenge is what to do if a smaller cluster has a host hardware failure and additional capacity is needed. Again, this setup is not ideal in terms of flexibility.

Let's now imagine a different setup; in this example, trunking is deployed and all hosts in the infrastructure have access to the different IP networks through VLAN tagging. This means that any virtual machine can run from a network standpoint on any host in the infrastructure regardless of cluster boundaries. If a host fails on any cluster, virtual machines can be migrated to another host where there is excess capacity. Instead of running a few hosts at high CPU or memory levels, all resources in the infrastructure can be shared without networking boundaries.

With respect to port groups, enter a number between 1 and 4,094 as assigned by the network team. If 4,095 is assigned, the port group can see traffic on any VLAN. If 0 is entered, the port group can only see untagged traffic (non-VLAN).

When setting up a network label for VLAN tagging, you will need to enter a port group next to the VLAN ID (see Figure 6.9). If you are not using VLAN tagging, leave this field blank.

Figure 6.9: Network label and VLAN ID

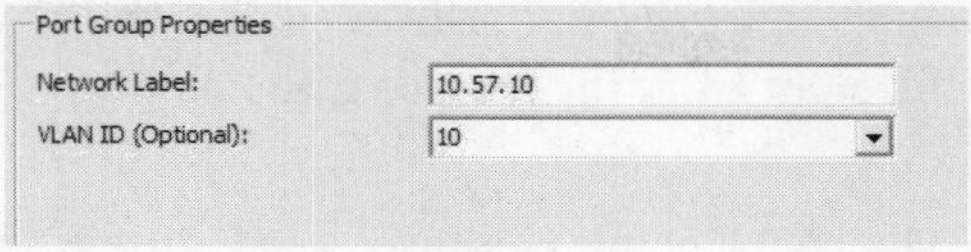

Port Group Properties	
Network Label:	10.57.10
VLAN ID (Optional):	10

Add a VMkernel and Enable VMotion

In order to add VMotion capabilities, a VMkernel connection type must be added and configured, VMotion must be enabled, and the connection must be configured. A VMkernel connection can be added to a Service Console vSwitch or a vSwitch can be added that is separate from all other networks. Many administrators choose to add a VMkernel connection to the Service Console vSwitch and simply designate a different IP network to keep the communication distinct from each other. In the following procedure, this tactic will be deployed.

1. From vSphere Client, choose Host, click the Configuration tab, click Networking, and select the properties of the Service Console switch.

2. Click the Add button in the bottom-left window and connection types will appear. Choose VMkernel and select Next.

3. Choose an appropriate network label; in this case, vmotion is simple, easy, and descriptive.

4. Select the Use This Port Group For VMotion check box (see Figure 6.10).

Figure 6.10: Enabling VMotion

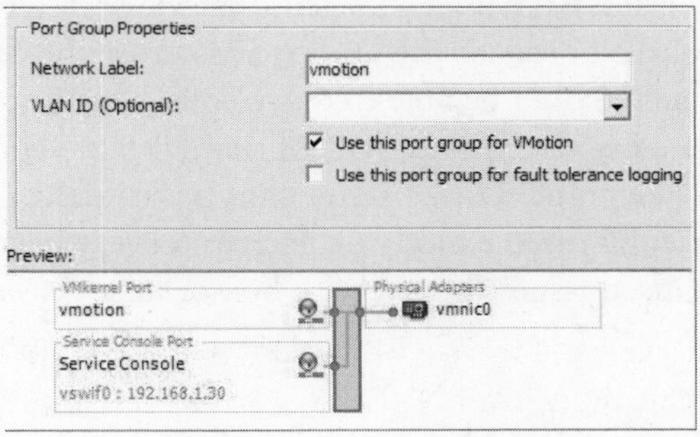

Port Group Properties	
Network Label:	vmotion
VLAN ID (Optional):	

☑ Use this port group for VMotion
☐ Use this port group for fault tolerance logging

Preview:

VMkernel Port
vmotion

Physical Adapters
vmnic0

Service Console Port
Service Console
vswif0 : 192.168.1.30

Configuring Your
vSphere Environment

PART II

5. Click Next.

6. Enter a static IP address and subnet mask. In this scenario, the static IP address will be different from the Service Console IP network.

7. Click Edit to enter the VMkernel Default Gateway (see Figure 6.11 for a closer look).

Figure 6.11: Configuring VMotion

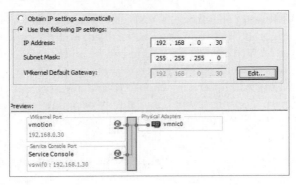

8. Click Next, click Finish, and then click Close.

Network with vNetwork Distributed Switches

A vNetwork Distributed Switch (DVS) is a single vSwitch that only spans across hosts the administrator chooses. If there is a cluster or a host(s) that doesn't need that particular vSwitch, that vSwitch will not show up on those hosts. And because the DVS spans across the config- ured hosts, a virtual machine will be able to move consistently across the virtual infrastructure because the settings of that DVS are config- ured at the datacenter viewpoint. This is significant because the old- style vSwitch had to be configured exactly on each and every host it was built on, which often caused issues if one check box or label was missed on any one host.

One of the great things about vNetwork Distributed Switching is their ability to migrate existing vSwitches and or connection types into a DVS and then centrally manage all networking through one interface. At first this is a lot to consume, but break it down into two pieces: the regular vSwitch (the old style) and the new DVS view. Most administrators are probably going to want to choose one view and stick with it. The easier of the two, although it takes more work, is the old standard of vSwitches on each host. It is easy to set up, but then you have to set it up exactly the same on each and every host without making mistakes. The more complex method is to use the new DVS and centrally manage everything.

The difference between the old standard of vSwitches and DVS is simple to illustrate. vSwitches are similar in nature to *sneakernet*; if you are not familiar with this term, imagine the early days of computers before they were all networked together. If you wanted to share information, you would have to copy that information and go to each computer and copy it there (wearing down your sneakers). Now visualize an administrator running to each ESX host to set up networking exactly like it is set up on every other host. Similar to this is not having a central database of usernames and passwords and having to enter that information on every server in the network without fat fingering a password; if there are only a few hosts in the environment, this may not be a big deal. However, if there are quite a few, it may be a good idea to bring in centralized management: DVS.

The following list breaks down the DVS into easily digestible pieces:

dvUplinks   Physical NICs plug into dvUplinks. These can be renamed or left to the default. When creating the DVS, choose the maximum number that any one host in the switch will have. If most of the hosts will only have two pNICs (physical NICs) but one will need four pNICs, then configure the DVS with four, and on some, there will be unused dvUplinks—which is no big deal.

Port Group   Defines port configuration options such as teaming and failover, VLAN options, traffic shaping, and security. There may be more than one port group on any one DVS, and virtual machines may occupy different port groups on the same DVS, depending on their needs or status in the organization.

Configure a vNetwork Distributed Switch

In this section we are going to create a DVS where one did not exist before. Let's take a look at how to accomplish this:

1. From vSphere Client, at the top-left click Home, then under Inventory click Networking (Figure 6.12). Make sure your data-store is highlighted, right-click it, and choose New vNetwork Distributed Switch (see Figure 6.13) to launch the Create vNet-work Distributed Switch Wizard.

Figure 6.12: Click Networking to begin.

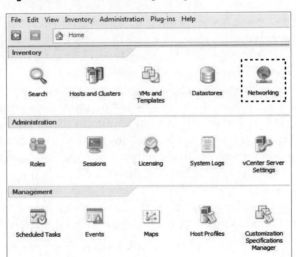

Figure 6.13: Creating a new DVS

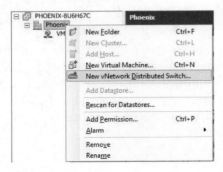

2. On the first screen (Figure 6.14), create a descriptive name and specify the number of NICs per host (dvUplink ports); then click Next.

Figure 6.14: Naming the DVS

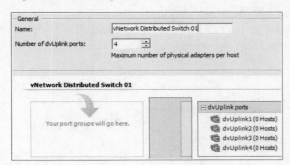

The next screen lets you add hosts and adapters to this DVS; in order to accomplish this, the NICs must be free. Note that additional hosts and adapters may be added at a later time. Take advantage of the View Details link to learn more about the physical NICs that are being added (hint: you may need to click the plus sign next to your hosts to see available NICs and their details).

3. Click Add Now (Figure 6.15) to add the hosts and adapters; then place a check mark beside the ones you want to add and click Next.

Figure 6.15: Adding hosts and adapters to your DVS

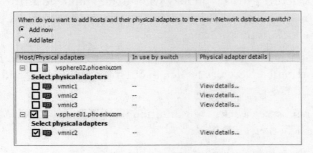

4. The next screen lets you create a default port group automatically (this is the default). If you leave this option selected, vSphere Client will create an early-binding port group with 128 ports.

When viewing networking on any host, you have two options: Virtual Switch or Distributed Virtual Switch (DVS). If the host is not part of a DVS, no options under the second button will appear. (To get an overall view of all hosts on a DVS, check the Networking section in Figure 6.12 under Datacenter.)

Review the setup (see Figure 6.16), and click Finish.

Figure 6.16: Reviewing the current setup

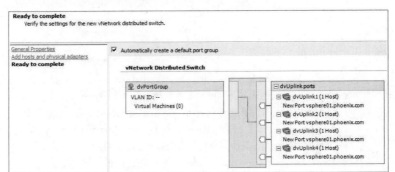

Add Additional Hosts and Adapters to a DVS

As your infrastructure grows, you may want to add more hosts to your DVS, and you may choose to add more adapters as well to address performance. Let's look at this process:

1. From vSphere Client, click Home, select Networking, highlight the vDistributed Network Switch in question, right-click, and select Add Host.

2. On the next screen, select any additional hosts and NICs (see Figure 6.17), then click Next.

3. Review the selection, and then click Finish.

Figure 6.17: Adding hosts and adapters to a DVS

Edit General and Advanced DVS Settings

General settings (see Figure 6.18) allow you to change the name and number of dvUplink ports. From vSphere Client, you click Home, click Networking, highlight the DVS switch, right-click, and select Edit Settings to access the General settings.

Click Advanced to access settings like MTU, CDP, and admin contact information.

Figure 6.18: Editing General and Advanced settings

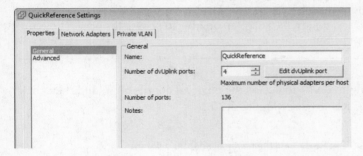

Manage Physical and Virtual Network Adapters

The DVS is new, and you may find yourself wondering how to manage the moving pieces. First, we'll look at managing the physical adapters, and then we'll move on to managing the virtual adapters.

Manage Physical Network Adapters

First let's look at the process of managing physical network adapters:

1. From vSphere Client, select Host, choose the Configuration tab, click Networking, and select the Distributed Virtual Switch

Configuring Your vSphere Environment

view (as shown in Figure 6.19). Then choose Manage Physical Adapters.

The resulting window lets you view the adapter and remove or add an adapter. Click either Remove or <Click to Add NIC> to open the next window.

Figure 6.19: Here you manage virtual and physical adapters.

> **WARNING** If you are adding a new adapter, it will remove that adapter from its current vSwitch. Be careful that the adapter being added is not currently serving virtual machines; also be aware of that adapter's ability to service the service console IP network. Always think through your steps when working with physical adapters, and have a backup plan on how to access the host if you loose remote connectivity.

2. Highlight a NIC to access the physical details on it, and then click Add or Remove (see Figure 6.20).

Figure 6.20: Reviewing the physical adapter's details

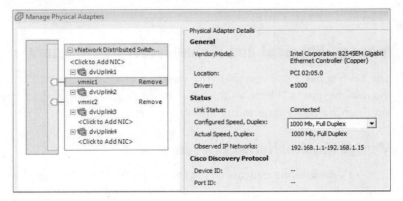

3. The Select A Physical Adapter window (see Figure 6.21) will have two choices: adapters that are currently managed by other vSwitches (avoid these) and vSwitches that are currently Unclaimed Adapters (choose these). Highlight the adapter you want to add, then click OK twice.

Figure 6.21: Choosing unclaimed physical adapters

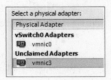

Managing Virtual Network Adapters

Now we will look at managing the virtual adapters:

1. From vSphere Client, select Host, choose the Configuration tab, click Networking, and select Distributed Virtual Switch view (as shown earlier in Figure 6.19). Then choose Manage Virtual Adapters.

   The Manage Virtual Adapters screen lets you add virtual network adapters or migrate existing network adapters from the vSwitch side.

2. There are two types of connections you can add: Service Console or VMkernel. In the top-left corner, click Add (as shown in Figure 6.22).

Figure 6.22: Managing virtual adapters

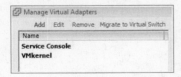

3. Select New Virtual Adapter and click Next.
4. Select VMkernel (refer to Figure 6.23), and then click Next.

Figure 6.23: New virtual adapter

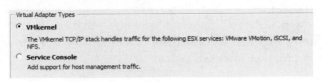

Creating a Service Console connection type is essentially the same process, except obviously you'd choose Service Console instead of VMkernel.

5. On the Connection Settings Screen, choose Port Group and then select the correct port. You can also use these options to enable VMotion or turn on fault tolerance logging (as shown in Figure 6.24).

Figure 6.24: Specifying the network connection

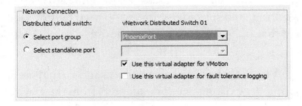

6. Enter the static IP settings (Figure 6.25), click Edit to define the VMkernel default gateway, and then click Next.

7. Review the settings, click Finish, and then click Close.

Figure 6.25: Defining a static IP

NOTE   If VMotion is enabled in this procedure, the default gateway will need to be added. This is often done in the DNS and Routing section (on the Configuration tab) under Software.

Migrate Existing Virtual Adapters into DVS

Why would you migrate existing virtual adapters into DVS? At the end of an upgrade process, you may find yourself with plenty of ESX hosts that are all configured the same way, in the old vSwitch style, and you want to take advantage of central management. Another possible scenario is when you want to get everything up and running in a format that is easier to understand and troubleshoot and, at a later time, make the move to DVS.

WARNING   Before proceeding with this process, make sure the current physical NIC associated with this DVS is capable of communicating on the same network that the Service Console is presently connected to. At the end of this procedure, the Service Console is going to switch to a different physical NIC. If by chance communication is lost, unplug the original pNIC and plug it into the pNIC that the DVS was plugged into. Then make your changes and start over. Keep in mind that in some cases this may not be easily accomplished, or perhaps not accomplished at all.

1. From vSphere Client, select Host, click the Configuration tab, select Networking, click Distributed Virtual Switch, and choose Manage Virtual Adapters.

2. In the top-left corner, click Add (in blue lettering).

3. Select Migrate Existing Virtual Adapters, as shown in Figure 6.26. Then click Next.

Figure 6.26: Migrating existing virtual adapters

Creation Type

○ **New virtual adapter**
  Add a new virtual adapter to the distributed virtual switch.

◉ **Migrate existing virtual adapters**
  Migrate virtual adapters to this distributed virtual switch. IP address, subnet mask, and default gateway will remain unchanged.

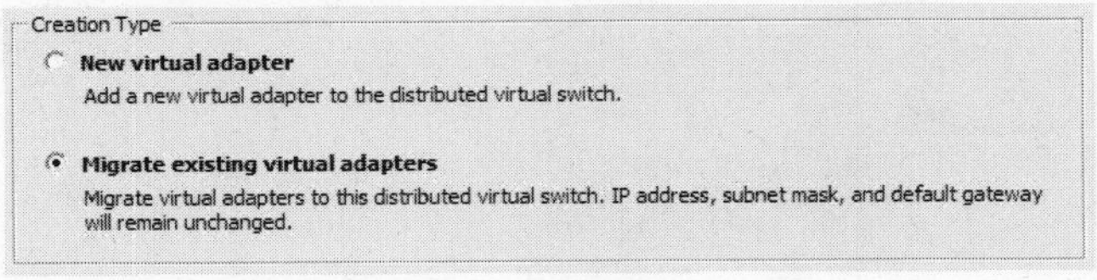

4. On the Network Connectivity screen, you'll see a list of virtual adapters to migrate. Select Service Console.

Typically this list won't be long since it is composed only of Service Console and VMkernel adapters. There is also the option of migrating another adapter from a different DVS. Also, use the Select By drop-down list and choose either Port Group or Distributed Virtual Port, as shown in Figure 6.27.

Figure 6.27: Choose Port Group or Distributed Virtual Port from the Select By drop-down list.

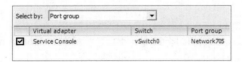

5. Click Select A Port Group to reveal the drop-down arrow and then select the port group to which this virtual adapter will be assigned. Then click Next.

6. When working with the Service Console, you'll be asked if you're sure you want to continue. Select Yes.

7. In the Ready To Complete screen, you will see a summary of the actions to be performed. Notice that the vswif0 (this is usually the first virtual switch and it usually contains the service console), along with the IP address of the Service Console of that host, has been added (see Figure 6.28). Click Finish, and then click Close.

Figure 6.28: Reviewing the migration details

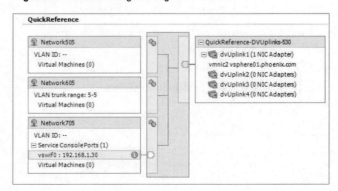

Notice that if the view in Networking is changed from Distributed Virtual Switch to Virtual Switch, there is no longer an entry for the Service Console. However, as long as the port group you chose was set up correctly, communication with the host is still ongoing without interruption. Also notice that the pNIC originally associated with the Service Console on the vSwitch has not moved into the DVS.

Once everything is working, you may want to go back and move the original pNIC into this DVS for load balancing and failover of the Service Console. For details, see the section "Manage Physical Network Adapters" earlier in this chapter.

Add a dvPort Group

A dvPort group can span many hosts and is used to ensure configuration consistency for VMs and virtual ports such as VMotion. Additionally, a dvPort group defines port configuration choices for each port on a DVS by configuring how a connection is made to the physical network.

1. From vSphere Client, select Home, select Networking, high-light the icon for DVS (in this case it is QuickReference; see Figure 6.29), right-click, and select New Port Group.

Figure 6.29: Adding a dvPort group

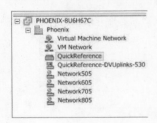

2. Enter the name, number of ports, and VLAN type (as shown in Figure 6.30), and then click Next.

   If VLAN Trunking is selected, an additional option is available for you to specify the VLAN Trunk Range.

3. Review the settings, and then click Finish.

Figure 6.30: Configuring VLAN trunking

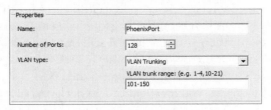

Edit a dvPort Group

The following steps illustrate how to edit dvPort groups:

1. From vSphere Client, select Home, select Networking, highlight the dvPort group, right-click, and select Edit Settings.

   In the next screen, you can modify the name, description, number of ports, and port binding (see Figure 6.31).

Figure 6.31: Editing a dvPort group

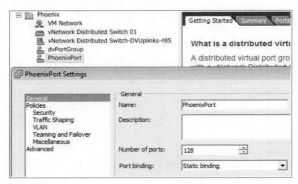

Here is a list of the port binding options and their purpose:

   Static Binding   Assign a port to a virtual machine when the VM is connected to a dvPort group.

   Dynamic Binding   Assign a port to a virtual machine on the first power-on while in the dvPort group.

   Ephemeral   Choose this option when there is no port binding.

2. Make your selections, and click OK.

Create a Private VLAN

With private VLANs, we can restrict communication between our VMs even when they are on the same VLAN or network segment. Let's take a look at how to accomplish this and create our first private VLAN:

1. From vSphere Client, select Home, select Networking, highlight the DVS you want to work with, right-click, and select Edit Settings.

2. Select the Private VLAN tab; under Primary Private VLAN ID, click where it says Enter A Private VLAN ID Here, and enter the VLAN ID number. Then click elsewhere in the window.

3. Highlight the VLAN ID just entered and it will show up under Secondary Private VLAN ID.

4. Enter the information in Enter A Private VLAN ID Here as before (as shown in Figure 6.32).

Figure 6.32: Creating a private VLAN

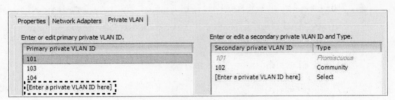

When you are creating private VLANs, you can create different types:

Promiscuous Port Communicates with all other private VLAN ports

Isolated Port Has Layer 2 separation from other ports within the same private VLAN, with the obvious exception of the promiscuous port

Community Port Communicates with other community ports and transmits traffic outside the group via the designated promiscuous port

5. Highlight the secondary private VLAN you just added and select the port type. When finished, click OK.

Migrate VMs to a DVS

There are two ways to migrate virtual machines into a DVS. The virtual machines network adapter settings can be changed to reflect the new settings, or you can use a VMware migration tool to move a group of virtual machines all at one time. This tool is granular enough to allow you to pick which virtual machines to move and which not to move until a later period, or even not at all. The following process demonstrates the migration tool:

1. From vSphere Client, click Home, select Networking, highlight Distributed Virtual Switch, right-click, and select Migrate Virtual Machine Networking.

2. From the Source Network drop-down list, choose the location of the existing virtual machines.

3. From the Destination Network drop-down list, choose the location where the virtual machines will be migrated to.

4. Click the Show Virtual Machines button.

5. Put a check mark next to the virtual machines that need to be moved and click OK (see Figure 6.33).

Figure 6.33: Migrating VMs to DVS

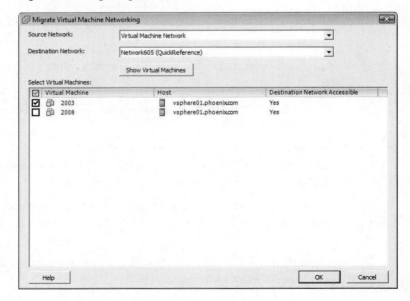

To migrate an individual virtual machine (without using the tool) into a DVS, edit the settings of the VM and simply change the network adapter settings (under Network Label) to reflect the location they will be migrated to.

Understand Advanced Networking

There are the day-to-day networking activities, and then there are the advanced networking topics. These are the things that sometimes come up to help us add more functionality, help us troubleshoot, or help us grow. Take, for example, the topic of customizing MAC addresses; this is clearly networking but not something that needs to be done on a regular basis. But it may help you provide a software-based key for some specific applications while avoiding a hardware key (think USB dongle). Let's take a look at this and other advanced networking topics.

Customize MAC Addresses

In what instances would you customize MAC addresses? There are more than a few applications out there that require some sort of license file to work, and some of them bind to the MAC address on the server. In some cases, it is possible to get a software vendor to give out a software-based license instead of a hardware-based USB key; but they will only do this for a vigilant and determined VMware administrator who won't take no for an answer. Virtual machines by default do not have static MAC addresses; therefore, if one is needed it must be assigned.

> **TIP** Do not change the MAC address unless it is absolutely necessary. Instead, let the software do what it does best and avoid unnecessary complexity.

The allowable range is from 00:50:56:00:00:00 to 00:50:56:3F:FF:FF. The last 3 bytes are configurable. Keep it simple; make the first static MAC address 00:50:56:00:00:01. Here's how:

1. From vSphere Client, select the virtual machine and click Edit Settings.

2. On the Hardware tab, highlight the network adapter. On the right there will be a MAC address that can be changed from Automatic to Manual.

   Unfortunately, the colons will need to be typed into the interface; it isn't intelligent in this respect.

3. Enter the desired MAC address, document it (so you have it for later reference), and click OK.

Create a VMkernel Port for Software iSCSI

Some installations will use Fibre Channel SAN, and others may choose to use iSCSI, which traverses the Ethernet. In this section we will look at the prerequisites for using iSCSI and then show you how to set it up.

NOTE   To create a VMkernel port for software iSCSI, you will need Gig network connections or better. Do not use network adapters less than this. They may still work, but performance will drag. Additionally, there must be a different IP address for both the VMkernel and the Service Console.

First we are going to create a VMkernel port, and then we will assign the Service Console to run there:

1. From vSphere Client, click Host, select the Configuration tab, click Networking, select the vSwitch view, and click Add Networking.

2. Select the VMkernel, and then click Next.

3. Choose Work With An Existing vSwitch or click Create A Virtual Switch.

   a. Put check marks next to the network adapters to be used with this switch.

   b. Choose an appropriate network label.

   c. Add the VLAN ID if one exists and click Next.

4. Enter the IP address information, and click the Edit button to set the default gateway for iSCSI (see Figure 6.34). Then click Next.

5. Finally, click Finish, Next, and then Finish.

Figure 6.34: iSCSI connection type

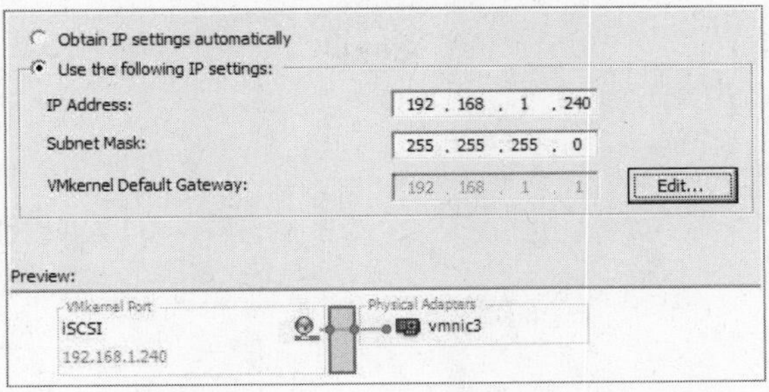

The VMkernel port has now been created. Our next step is to configure the Service Console connection to run on the same vSwitch as the VMkernel port (which is what we just completed in the previous steps).

Configure a Service Console Connection for Software iSCSI

Obviously if you are using iSCSI, all your connections need to be set up. In this section we will set up the Service Console:

1. Continuing from step 5 in the previous section, open the properties dialog box for the vSwitch and click the Ports tab; in the bottom left, click Add.

2. Select Service Console, and click Next.

3. Provide an appropriate network label, and then click Next.

NOTE   Host Configuration Protocol (HCP) is an option here; however, it is best to use static IP addresses to eliminate potential issues.

---

4. Enter an IP address and subnet mask, and click the Edit button to enter a default gateway (see Figure 6.35).

5. Click Next, and then click Finish.

Figure 6.35: Configuring a Service Console connection for iSCSI

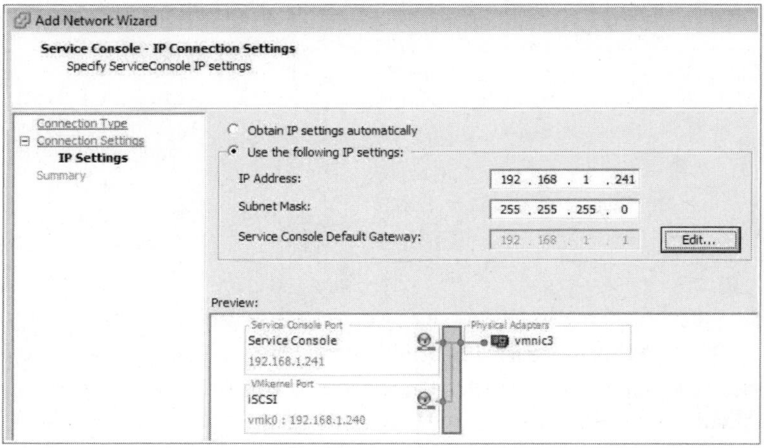

Troubleshoot Using the Command Line

Occasionally networking can be misconfigured, due to scripts not working properly, physical NICs being configured with the wrong network, or a whole host of other reasons. Being able to navigate via the command line while standing in front of the ESX host may be the only way to get the infrastructure back in tip-top shape. Table 6.1 presents some commands that are used to accomplish just that.

NOTE   If communication with an ESX host is not possible, step up to the Service Console and press Alt+F1.

Table 6.1: Handy Command-Line Tricks

Command	Description
esxcfg-vswif -1	Provides a list of the Service Console's current network interfaces. Make sure that vswif0 is defined and that the current IP address and netmask are accurate.

Table 6.1: Handy Command-Line Tricks *(continued)*

Command	Description
esxcfg-vswitch -1	Provides a list of the current vSwitch configurations. Ensure that the uplink adapter configured for the Service Console is connected to the correct physical network.
exscfg-nics -1	Provides a list of the network adapters. Check that the uplink adapter assigned to the Service Console is up and that the speed and duplex are both accurate.
esxcfg-nics -s <speed> <nic>	Changes the speed of a network adapter.
esxcfg-nics -d <duplex> <nic>	Changes the duplex of a network adapter.
esxcfg-vswif -I <new ip address> vswifX	Changes the service console's IP address.
esxcfg-vswif -n <new netmask> vswifX	Changes the service console's netmask.
esxcfg-vswitch -U <old vmnic> <service console vswitch>	Removes the uplink for the Service Console.
esxcfg-vswitch -L <new vmnic> <service console vswitch>	Changes the uplink for the Service Console. If there are long delays when using esxcfg-* commands, DNS might be misconfigured. The esxcfg-* commands require that DNS be configured so that localhost name resolution works properly. This requires that the /etc/hosts file contain an entry for the configured IP address and the 127.0.0.1 localhost address.

Enable Cisco Discovery Protocol

Cisco Discovery Protocol (CDP) allows an ESX to determine which Cisco switch port is connected to a given vSwitch and will allow properties of the Cisco switch to be viewed from vSphere Client. Obviously if Cisco hardware is not part of the organization, this procedure is not necessary or advised. Furthermore, this process requires logging directly into the ESX command-line interface.

PuTTy or SSH into the host, using the following code. Remember that the command line is case sensitive, and in the next step, the S in switch must be uppercase.

```
esxcfg-vswitch -b vSwitch0
```

The listen mode is the default. Possible outcomes are outlined in Table 6.2.

Table 6.2: Cisco Discovery Protocol Modes

Mode	Outcome
down	CDP is disabled.
listen	ESX listens for information but doesn't return information to Cisco.
advertise	ESX sends information but doesn't gather information about Cisco.
both	ESX listens and sends information.

To switch modes, enter the following command (see Figure 6.36). If the organization does not have Cisco hardware, change mode to down.

```
esxcfg-vswitch -B <mode> vSwitch0
```

Figure 6.36: Working with Cisco Discovery Protocol

```
root@vsphere01:~
login as: root
root@192.168.1.30's password:
Last login: Sun Apr 26 16:06:41 2009 from 192.168.1.3
[root@vsphere01 ~]# esxcfg-vswitch -b vSwitch0
listen
[root@vsphere01 ~]# esxcfg-vswitch -B advertise vSwitch0
[root@vsphere01 ~]# esxcfg-vswitch -b vSwitch0
advertise
[root@vsphere01 ~]#
```

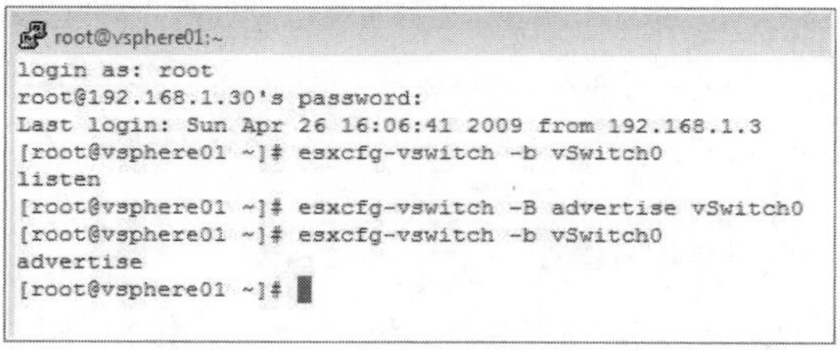

Enable IPv6

IPv6 is set to replace IPv4 because there are not enough IP addresses under the old method. You can run IPv6 in a mixed environment with

IPv4. It uses a 128-bit address and all features are capable of running under this protocol. Here's how to enable IPv6:

1. From vSphere Client, select Host; on the Configuration tab, choose Networking.

2. Choose Properties in the top-right corner of the next window.

3. Select Enable IPv6 Support On This Host and then click OK (see Figure 6.37).

4. Reboot the host to let the changes take effect.

Figure 6.37: Enabling IPv6

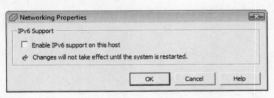

Configuring Your vSphere Environment

7

Configuring and Managing Storage

IN THIS CHAPTER, YOU WILL LEARN TO:

▶ **BECOME FAMILIAR WITH STORAGE CONCEPTS (Pages 204–209)**

▶ **IMPLEMENT STORAGE (Pages 209–242)**

V Mware ESX and ESXi natively provide virtualization of CPU, memory, network, and disk resources. The first three resources have to be utilized locally on the ESX/ESXi host. Disk resources can be utilized locally or remotely. The addition of remote storage is one of the foundations of where VMware ESX/ESXi leaves off and vSphere takes over.

Without the ability to leverage remote storage shared across two or more hosts, vSphere would be no more than a few tools to manage one or more hosts.

By using remotely shared storage attached to multiple hosts managed by vCenter Server, vSphere can leverage the combined complement of CPU, memory, network, and disk resources across a cluster.

To get started, you must become familiar with how storage works with vSphere, how to leverage it, and the steps required to use it.

Become Familiar with Storage Concepts

To best leverage the types of storage available, you must have a firm understanding of the various types of storage, and when and why they should be leveraged. For administrators designing a new vSphere implementation, this information can be crucial when they choose the appropriate storage system that meets the needs of the implementation, while also adhering to the financial constraints of the project.

Learn the Basics of Storage in vSphere

For vSphere to be able to run virtual machines they must reside on storage that the host can use. The storage can reside on local disks inside the host, through locally attached storage, or through remotely presented storage. Before we go into detail about local or remote storage, it is important that you understand how the storage is used for virtual machines.

Storage for guests is referred to as *datastores*. Datastores are logical containers that obscure the storage subsystem from the virtual machines. Datastores are typically formatted with the Virtual Machine File System (VMFS) format, which is an optimized, high-performance file system. Through the use of distributed locking for the virtual disk files, multiple virtual machines can be used on a single file system by one or more VMware ESX hosts simultaneously. This ensures that Storage Area Network (SAN) or Network Attached Storage (NAS) storage is safe and reliable for storing virtual machine configuration, disk, and swap files.

Because VMFS is designed to be a clustered file system, VMFS lets multiple hosts access one or more datastores concurrently. *On-disk locking* is the process of two or more hosts having access to a shared file system and not attempting to access files being accessed by another host. This process is used to prevent more than one host from attempting to power on, or operate, the same virtual machine.

VMFS datastores contain virtual machine configuration files, virtual machine disk files, virtual machine swap files, directories, symbolic links, raw device mappings, and the like. The VMFS maps these objects as *metadata*. The metadata is updated whenever files on the datastore are accessed or modified. This includes when guests are powered on or off, when guests are modified, and when any file attributes are modified. This metadata keeps all hosts with access to the datastore informed of the current status of any object on the datastore.

VMFS datastores can be configured through vSphere Client or through command-line options on storage systems that are recognized by the VMware ESX host. With a maximum supported size of 2 Terabytes (2TB)–512B per VMFS volume, datastores can be combined through the use of extents to create larger datastores, with a maximum combined size of 64TB. Additionally, if the storage system supports the ability to grow the storage amount, datastores can be increased without having to power off any running guests on the datastore.

When you are designing how storage is to be provided to vSphere hosts, keep in mind that it is difficult to determine peak-access times or optimize performance by looking at individual virtual machines. It is a best practice to run a mix of high and low utilization virtual machines across multiple hosts to provide an even balance of CPU and storage operations. In addition to evenly distributing the workload across datastores, remember the following:

- Only configure one VMFS datastore for each LUN presented to ESX or ESXi hosts.

- Choose a Redundant Array of Independent Disks (RAID) level that is appropriate for the type of workload the virtual machines will be running on the disk stored on the datastore. With regard to disk RAID levels, they should be configured in a similar fashion as if the virtual disks were running on a physical system.

Configuring Your vSphere Environment

PART II

- The following are the considerations for using a few large LUNs:
  - It's easy to create guests without having to continually provision space.
  - More space is available for snapshots and disk resizing.
  - You won't have as many datastores to manage.
- The following are the considerations for using more, smaller LUNs:
  - Space is optimized.
  - Many RAID levels are required for different virtualized workloads.
  - You plan to leverage disk shares and multipathing for greater flexibility.
  - You will achieve better performance.
  - You intend to use Microsoft Cluster Service, because each cluster disk resource must be in its own LUN.

Learn the Types of Supported Storage

VMware ESX supports two basic types of storage. *Local storage* is storage that is physically present in the host. This storage can either be physically housed in the host system or attached to the host using a storage controller connected to an external enclosure. *Remote storage* is storage that is not physically attached to the host and can include storage accessible to the host via a SAN or via a NAS device. Network attached storage is available using either the Internet Small Computer Systems (iSCSI) protocol or using the Network File System (NFS) protocol.

Initially VMware ESX only supported Small Computer Systems Interface (SCSI) disks and controllers for installation of ESX and local datastores. With later releases of ESX, Serial ATA (SATA) drives and controllers were supported, provided they appeared to the system as SCSI devices. vSphere has added support for different disk types. Table 7.1 displays the supported local disk types, provided the storage controller is on the Hardware Compatibility List (HCL).

Always refer to the current HCL reference documents at http://www .vmware.com/go/hcl.

Table 7.1: ESX Recognized Disk Types

Type	Installation and Booting	Virtual Machine Storage
SCSI	Yes	Yes
SATA	Yes	Yes
IDE	Yes	No
ATA	Yes	No

When you are working with local storage, the most important detail to remember is that the listed disk types are only supported if VMware ESX supports the appropriate driver for the physical controller. For example, an Intel ICH7 SATA controller was initially supported in ESX 3.5 but is no longer supported, while an Intel ICH9 SATA controller is supported in both ESX 3.5 and ESX 4.0. Even though a disk type is supported, it is completely dependent on the storage controller's access to the disks.

To leverage the abilities of VMware High Availability, VMotion, Storage VMotion, Distributed Resource Scheduling, and Fault Tolerance, VMware ESX must utilize storage that is shared among several VMware ESX hosts. For two or more hosts to share storage, that storage cannot be local to the ESX host, but rather must be remote. Initial releases of VMware ESX only supported Fibre Channel SAN storage for the purpose of providing shared storage. With the introduction of VMware Virtual Infrastructure 3 (VI3), iSCSI and NFS storage were added to the types of shared storage solutions supported. VMware ESX 4.0 retains the same types of remote storage that VI3 supported.

Remotely accessed storage is also certified by VMware based on criteria such as the storage controller, the protocol being used to access that storage, and the backend disks in the storage system. Using a broad term like "Fibre Channel Storage is supported" is not a valid statement. All three types of remote storage still have to be certified for proper support from VMware in the event of an issue. At the same time, just because storage is not on the HCL does not indicate it will not work properly. Additionally, when using the NFS protocol, storage may be supported, as long as the device providing the NFS storage is using the NFS v3 protocol.

Configuring Your
vSphere Environment

PART II

Learn the Benefits of Remote Storage

Using ESX and ESXi with remote storage can make storage more flexible, more efficient, and more reliable if implemented properly. Additional remote storage features can include failover and load-balancing technologies. Often a single storage system is used and therefore provides a central location for storage management.

Implementing vSphere with remote storage offers the following benefits:

- Data is often redundant with approved remote storage systems.

- Multiple paths can be configured to access the remote storage, removing a single point of failure for storage systems.

- ESX and ESXi hosts support multiple paths to storage systems automatically and provide available paths to any guests residing on the remote storage.

- Multiple paths and redundant storage systems make guest availability less prone to host failures.

- In the event of a host failure, guests are immediately available to be recovered on other hosts in the environment that have access to the same remote storage.

- Guests can be migrated from one host to another while still running VMware VMotion.

- Remote storage provides for the immediate recovery of guests after a host failure when used in conjunction with VMware High Availability.

- Remote storage allows for the use of VMware Distributed Resource Scheduler (DRS) to load balance guests across all hosts in a cluster.

- Remote storage allows guests uninterrupted operation when performing host maintenance, such as patching, upgrades, or host replacement, when used in conjunction with VMware VMotion and DRS.

All of these benefits of remote storage result from hosts sharing access to the remote storage by hosts in a vSphere environment coupled by the transportability and encapsulation of VMware guests. When guests are stored on shared storage, they can easily be moved from one host to another through hot or cold migrations. A *hot migration* is simply the process of migrating a guest from one host to another while the guest is still operating. This task can only be accomplished by purchasing a vSphere license that includes the VMware VMotion technology as well as some CPU compatibilities between hosts. A *cold migration* refers to the task of migrating suspended or powered-off guests from one host to another. When used with shared storage, cold migrations do not require adherence to any CPU compatibility requirements as long as the guest is powered off.

Some of the typical operations that can be performed when using shared storage include the following:

Zero or Minimal Guest Downtime   Zero downtime can be achieved by migrating guests from one host to another using VMotion or VMware DRS. Minimal downtime can be achieved by powering off or suspending guests, followed by migrating them to other hosts.

Guest Workload Balancing   Use VMware DRS to manually or automatically migrate guests from one host to another while maintaining an even level of host resource utilization.

Consolidated Storage   When hosts use centralized storage, all guests can be stored in the same location rather than on individual hosts. This allows for greater flexibility among hosts as well as a storage architecture that is more simplified than storing guests on individual hosts.

Disaster Recovery   Centralized storage provides for a central location to perform guest backups and restores. When vSphere is coupled with a storage system that incorporates replication, guests can be replicated to an alternate location for greater flexibility in recovering guests. Guests can then be restarted on hosts in the alternate location.

Implement Storage

As mentioned earlier, shared storage that is Fibre Channel, iSCSI, or NFS based is the core component of many of vSphere's enhanced features. Advanced features such as VMotion, High Availability, DRS, and Fault Tolerance would not be possible without shared storage. It is important to choose a Fibre Channel, iSCSI, or NFS solution that will meet the requirements of your vSphere environment. Knowing how to correctly configure the chosen storage can make the difference between having an optimal configuration and one that does not perform properly.

Configure Fibre Channel SAN Storage

Fibre Channel Storage was the first supported shared storage for VMware ESX and remains a viable shared storage solution with vSphere. There are many SAN storage vendors on the market. Before choosing any particular vendor and product offering, ensure it is on the HCL. The VMware HCL can be found here: www.vmware.com/go/hcl.

When implementing a SAN, keep the following in mind:

- Make sure the hardware and firmware versions are compatible with vSphere ESX and/or ESXi hosts.

- ESX and ESXi do not support Fibre Channel connected tape devices.

- Configure only one VMFS volume for a presented LUN.

- Only configure a diagnostic partition if using a diskless (SAN boot) configuration.

- Raw device mappings should be used for raw disk access (to leverage SAN hardware snapshotting) or for clustering a virtual machine with a physical machine.

- Guest-based multipathing software cannot be used to load-balance a single physical LUN.

- Choose the appropriate virtual SCSI controller for virtual machines.

- Virtual machine volume management software cannot mirror virtual disks. Windows dynamic disks are an exception but much be specially configured to operate properly.

- In Windows virtual machines, increase the SCSI Timeout value for better tolerance of I/O delays caused by path failover.

- Here are some LUN considerations:

  - LUN IDs must match for multipathing to work properly.

  - Provision LUNs to the appropriate host bus adapters (HBAs) before attaching ESX and ESXi hosts to the SAN. HBA failover is only possible if appropriate HBAs see the same LUNs.

  - Map LUNs to all hosts for greater flexibility using High Availability, DRS, Fault Tolerance, and VMotion.

- A situation where multiple hosts attempt to use different paths to access a datastore and cause the datastore to become unavailable can occur when VMotion or DRS is used with an active/passive SAN. This is called *path thrashing*. Ensure all systems have consistent paths to all SAN storage processors to prevent this.

- Here are some Fibre Channel HBA considerations:

  - When using multiple HBAs, use the same model and firmware revision.

  - A single HBA may be used for storage traffic, with a secondary HBA for failover. LUN traffic can be manually balanced across the HBAs for greater throughput on certain active/active SAN arrays. Set Path Policy to Fixed when using this configuration.

  - Set the timeout value for detecting a path failure in the HBA driver. For optimal performance, set this timeout to 30 seconds.

Fibre Channel storage can also be used for the ESX and ESXi installation. To use a Fibre Channel LUN to house the ESX or ESXi boot image, keep the following in mind:

- The HBA BIOS must be properly configured to access the SAN and presented LUNs.

- Because drivers scan the PCI bus in an ascending fashion, placing HBAs in the lowest slot number will allows drivers to detect them quickly.

- Whether using a single HBA in a nonredundant configuration, or dual HBAs in a redundant configuration, only a single path is available to hosts.

- Boot LUNs should only be accessible to the associated ESX or ESXi host that the LUN will be used by.

- When booting from an active/passive SAN, ensure the designated storage processor's World Wide Name (WWN) is active. If the storage processor is passive, the ESX or ESXi host will fail to boot.

- Connections from the ESX or ESXi host must be made through a SAN fabric. Connecting HBAs directly to storage or through arbitrated loop connections is not supported.

Configuring Your
vSphere Environment

PART II

Connect Fibre Channel Storage to an ESX or ESXi Host

In a typical configuration, Fibre Channel (FC) storage is used as a shared storage system for ESX and ESXi hosts. The vast majority of Fibre Channel storage implementations are configured in this manner. Because each Fibre Channel storage vendor has its own configuration parameters, a general installation guide cannot completely address all configuration steps for the available storage configurations available.

The basic process of connecting ESX and ESXi hosts to a FC SAN is as follows:

1. Connect FC cables from the ESX or ESXi host's HBAs to the FC fabric.

2. Configure the storage array.

3. In the FC fabric configuration, present the storage array to the fabric.

4. In the FC fabric configuration, present the ESX hosts' HBAs to the FC fabric.

5. Create LUNs and map them to ESX hosts through zoning.

   ESX hosts can now see the available LUNs when the HBAs are rescanned, as shown in Figure 7.1.

Figure 7.1: Fibre Channel devices displayed in vSphere Client

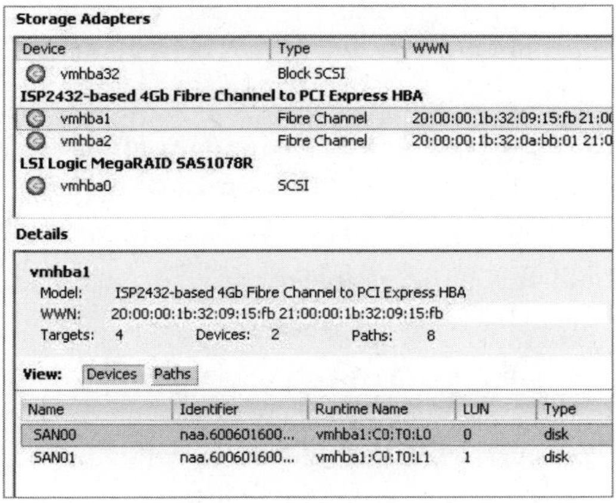

To configure and connect a specific vendor's storage system, consult the documentation specific to the storage system and VMware ESX.

Manage Fibre Channel Storage on an ESX or ESXi Host

To get started with configuring FC-based datastores, the ESX host must be aware of the LUNs that have been mapped to it. ESX hosts will automatically scan the HBAs on initial boot-up to determine which LUNs are being available. If SAN storage is attached to a host after it has booted, a simple HBA rescan is required.

The number of LUNs that are being presented to the HBAs will determine the amount of time it takes to rescan the HBAs. This does not typically take a long amount of time, but it can delay the boot time of an ESX or ESXi host. The fewer the number of LUN IDs to scan, the more quickly a host will scan and continue with the boot process.

Modify the LUN Scanning Parameters

The VMkernel scans for LUN IDs from 0 to 255, giving a total of 256 possible LUNs the host will recognize. Modifying the Disk.MaxLUN setting will improve the LUN discovery speed. The number of LUNs is not the only determining factor in the discovery speed, but it is a good place to start.

To change the maximum number of LUN IDs to scan, follow these steps:

1. From vSphere Client, select a host from Inventory.

2. Select the Configuration tab, and click Advanced Settings.

3. Select Disk from the list of options on the left of the Advanced Settings menu.

4. Scroll down to the Disk.MaxLUN setting.

5. Enter the largest LUN ID setting you want to scan to. If LUN IDs from 0 to 30 are mapped by the SAN, enter 30 and click OK.

Sparse LUN support is the ability to see multiple LUNs if they are not sequentially numbered. Figure 7.2 shows FC-attached disks that are mapped to an ESX host in a sparse configuration. An example is having LUN IDs of 0, 1, 3, and 6 mapped on the FC fabric. Without sparse LUN support, only LUN IDs 0 and 1 would be visible to hosts in the same zone. If LUN IDs are sequentially numbered, the discovery time can be shortened by disabling sparse LUN support. By default, ESX and ESXi have sparse LUN support enabled. Only disable sparse LUN support if LUNs are sequentially numbered.

Figure 7.2: Sparse LUN configuration

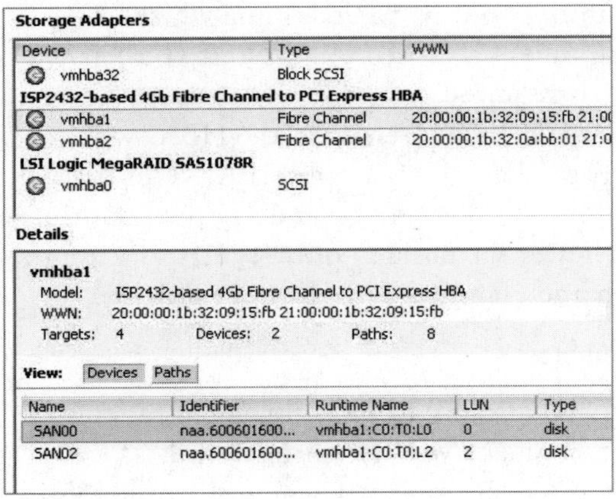

Take the following steps to disable Sparse LUN support:

1. From vSphere Client, select a host from Inventory.

2. Select the Configuration tab, and click Advanced Settings.

3. Select Disk from the list of options on the left of the Advanced Settings menu.

4. Scroll down to Disk.SupportSparseLUN, and set the value to 0.

5. Click OK.

Rescan Storage Adapters

Rescanning the storage adapters will scan the attached storage in an attempt to discover LUNs. After rescanning the storage adapters, any storage that is available to the host's HBAs will be visible in the Details panel on the Configuration tab under Storage Adapters in the Hardware panel.

In versions of ESX previous to 3.0, scanning the FC HBAs was performed through the Management User Interface (MUI). With the release of ESX 3.0, and subsequent releases, this is performed through the VI Client and vSphere Client.

1. In vSphere Client, select a host from Inventory and click the Configuration tab.

2. In the Hardware panel, select Storage Adapters.

3. On VMware ESX, to scan all adapters in the host, click Rescan above the Storage Adapters panel. To scan a single storage adapter, right-click on the storage adapter and choose Rescan. ESXi will always rescan all adapters in the host.

4. Because no datastores have been added, you only have to select the Scan For New Storage Devices check box.

5. To discover new datastores or update a datastore after its configuration has been changed, select Scan For New VMFS Volumes.

6. If new LUNs are discovered, they will appear in the details panel. Figure 7.3 displays LUNs discovered after performing a rescan operation.

Figure 7.3: LUNs discovered after a rescan

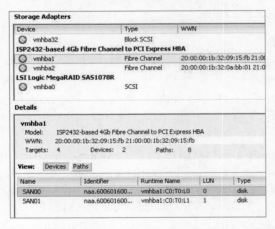

Before attempting to create FC-based datastores, it is important to ensure that the storage paths are properly configured. As mentioned previously, SANs typically operate in an active/passive or active/active configuration.

These configurations require some distinct path settings, depending on the configuration. It is best to follow the SAN manufacturer's recommendations when choosing the proper path configuration.

Review and Configure Device Paths

The following process will give you a better view of what paths are currently being used to communicate with attached storage:

1. From vSphere Client, select a host from Inventory.

2. Select the Configuration tab; then click Storage in the Hardware panel.

3. In the View panel, select Devices.

4. Click Manage Paths on the right side of the Device Details panel.

5. Notice the Path Selection Policy in the top section of the Manage Paths dialog box. Figure 7.4 shows one of the three default VMware-provided path policies.

Figure 7.4: Fixed path policy

6. Depending on the type of SAN system that the HBA is connected to, choose an appropriate path policy. The three default types are

Fixed   Uses a preferred path. If the path is unavailable, an alternate is chosen until the path is available again. Active/active SANs typically use the fixed policy.

Most Recently Used (MRU)   Uses any available path. If the current path becomes unavailable, an alternate is chosen. When the path is available again, the path is not moved back. Active/passive SANs typically use the MRU policy.

Round Robin   Uses an automatic pathing algorithm to determine the best path. Round Robin is designed to better load-balance storage paths and I/O performance.

Additionally, any third-party path policies will be displayed if they are installed on the host. Currently only EMC provides the ability to use additional path policies.

7. Click Close.

Create a New FC VMFS Datastore

To get a better view of what paths are currently being used to communicate to attached storage, take the following steps:

1. From vSphere Client, select a host from Inventory.

2. Select the Configuration tab; then click Storage in the Hardware panel.

3. In the View panel, select Datastores.

4. Click Add Storage on the right side of the Datastores panel. The Add Storage wizard opens.

5. Choose Disk/LUN as the storage type and click Next. The right panel will display storage devices found after the HBAs were scanned.

6. Select a storage device and click Next.

7. A review of the disk layout is displayed. Click Next.

8. Enter a descriptive datastore name and click Next.

9. Choose a maximum file size. This will determine the block size used on the datastore. The four options are

   - 256GB–512B, Block size: 1MB

   - 512GB–512B, Block size: 2MB

   - 1TB–512B, Block size: 4MB

   - 2TB–512B, Block size: 8MB

   A common practice is to simply use the 8MB block size, because it will accommodate any virtual disk size up to 2TB–512B, regardless of the datastore's physical size. It is a frequent mistake to create datastores using the 1MB or 2MB block size, only to have a requirement for a guest with a disk larger than the block size will allow. Datastore block sizes cannot be changed at a later time without reformatting the datastore.

   Choosing Maximize Capacity will use all the available space on the LUN. It is important to remember that it is a best practice to configure only one VMFS volume, or datastore, per LUN.

10. Click Next.

11. Click Finish to complete the datastore setup process.

Configure NPIV for Virtual Machines

N-Port ID Virtualization (NPIV) is the process of allowing Fibre Channel HBAs to register multiple World Wide Names (WWNs) and use multiple addresses. It is advantageous in the situation where a WWN can be assigned to a virtual machine.

Some of the benefits of using NPIV are as follows:

- Virtual and physical systems can have SAN storage managed in the same fashion.

- NPIV prioritizes and provides quality of service to ensure disk bandwidth.

Some of the limitations and requirements for NPIV to be used with guests include the following:

- The WWN of the physical HBAs must have access to all LUNs that are to be accessed by virtual machines running on that host.

- The physical HBA used must support NPIV. At this time, the following vendors have HBAs that support this:

    - QLogic—any 4GB HBA

    - Emulex—4GB HBAs that have NPIV-compatible firmware

- No more than four WWN pairs are generated per virtual machine.

- When a guest with NPIV is cloned, the NPIV settings are not copied to the clone.

- SAN switches used must be NPIV-aware.

- At the storage level, make sure that the NPIV LUN number and NPIV target ID match the physical LUN and Target ID when configuring an NPIV LUN for access at the storage level.

- vSphere Client must be used to configure or modify virtual machines with WWNs.

- Virtual machines must be powered off when adding or modifying NPIV settings.

- Virtual machines with NPIV enabled cannot be VMotioned or SVMotioned.

To add a WWN mapping to a virtual machine, take the following steps:

1. In vSphere Client, edit the guest to which you want to assign a WWN by right-clicking on the guest and choosing Edit The Virtual Machine Settings.

2. Click the Options tab and click Fibre Channel NPIVI, as shown in Figure 7.5.

Figure 7.5: Fibre Channel NPIV options

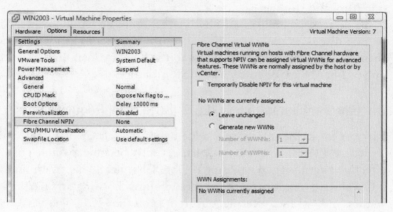

3. In the dialog box, select Generate new WWNs.

4. Click OK to close the guest configuration window.

5. Repeat steps 1 and 2 to record the WWNs that were generated, as you can see in Figure 7.6.

Figure 7.6: Generated WWNs

6. Record the WWNs, and give them to your SAN administrator to properly zone RDM LUNs that will be used by the guest.

7. To properly configure the guest WWN within your SAN zoning, refer to the appropriate SAN documentation provided by your SAN vendor.

Configure iSCSI SAN Storage

Before ESX/ESXi can work with a SAN, you must set up your iSCSI initiators and storage.

To do this, you must first observe certain basic requirements. This section discusses these requirements, provides recommendations, and then details how to provide access to the SAN by installing and setting up your hardware or software iSCSI initiators.

Become Familiar with ESX/ESXi iSCSI SAN Requirements

Support for iSCSI storage was added with the release of Virtual Infrastructure 3 (VI3). iSCSI storage has recently become a viable cost-effective alternative to traditional Fibre Channel SANs. With many iSCSI storage vendors on the market, before choosing any particular vendor and product offering, ensure it is on the HCL. The VMware HCL can be found here: www.vmware.com/go/hcl.

When implementing an iSCSI SAN, keep in mind the following:

- Make sure the hardware and firmware versions are compatible with vSphere ESX and or ESXi hosts.

- The network configuration for iSCSI initiators and the iSCSI storage system should reside on a network separate from host and guest IP traffic.

- ESX and ESXi do not support FC-connected tape devices.

- Configure only one VMFS volume for a presented LUN.

- Only configure a diagnostic partition if using a diskless (SAN boot) configuration.

- Raw device mappings should be used for raw disk access (to leverage SAN hardware snapshotting) or for clustering a virtual machine with a physical machine.

- Guest based multipathing software cannot be used to load-balance a single physical LUN.

- Choose the appropriate virtual SCSI controller for virtual machines.

- Virtual machine volume management software cannot mirror virtual disks. Windows dynamic disks are an exception but must be specially configured to operate properly.

- In Windows virtual machines, increase the SCSI Timeout value for better tolerance of I/O delays caused by path failover.

- Here are some LUN considerations:

  - LUN IDs must match for multipathing to work properly.

  - Provision LUNs to the appropriate HBAs before attaching ESX and ESXi hosts to the SAN. HBA failover is only possible if appropriate HBAs see the same LUNs.

  - Make LUNs available to all hosts for greater flexibility using High Availability, DRS, Fault Tolerance, and VMotion.

  - Path thrashing can occur when VMotion or DRS is used with an active/passive SAN, so ensure all systems have consistent paths to all SAN storage processors.

- Here are some iSCSI Initiator considerations:

  - Ensure Hardware iSCSI initiators are compatible with vSphere ESX and ESXi hosts.

  - Ensure the iSCSI target authentication scheme is compatible with the iSCSI initiator type.

- Here are some network considerations:

  - A best practice is to provide a dedicated network for iSCSI traffic between VMware hosts and iSCSI storage systems.

  - To use software iSCSI, VMkernel networking must be configured.

  - To use hardware iSCSI, the HBA has to have network parameters configured.

  - The storage system discovery address must be pingable using the vmkping command. The vmkping command originally initiated a ping using the VMKernel. In vSphere, vmkping and ping are interchangeable from ESX or ESXi hosts.

Configure Hardware iSCSI Initiators if Present

VMware ESX supports dedicated physical iSCSI adapters installed in the ESX or ESXi host, provided they are certified and on the HCL. These physical adapters handle the iSCSI traffic in the same fashion as Fibre Channel HBAs do for Fibre Channel SANs.

Modify iSCSI Name and IP Information

To get started, you must configure the hardware iSCSI initiator. When doing so, ensure that network settings are correct and that iSCSI names are formatted properly.

1. Log into either vCenter Server or an ESX/ESXi host using vSphere Client.

2. Select a host from the Inventory panel.

3. Select the Configuration tab.

4. Select Storage Adapters in the Hardware panel, as shown in Figure 7.7.

Figure 7.7: Storage adapters

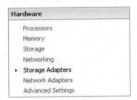

5. Configure the desired initiator by clicking Properties and then Configure.

6. At this point, either accept the default iSCSI name or enter a new name. Properly format the name to ensure compatibility with iSCSI storage systems.

7. Enter an iSCSI alias to be used to identify the hardware iSCSI initiator.

8. Change the IP address settings to be able to utilize the iSCSI storage network.

9. Click OK.

ISCSI name changes will only be valid for new iSCSI sessions. Any existing settings will remain until iSCSI logout and re-login.

Configure Software iSCSI Initiators

VMware ESX also has the ability to use iSCSI storage without the need for physical iSCSI adapters. The VMkernel has the ability to talk directly to iSCSI targets provided the software iSCSI initiator is enabled. To use the capability, you must complete some additional networking configuration.

The first requirement for VMware ESX to use the built-in software iSCSI initiator is to enable the iSCSI initiator:

1. Log into vCenter or an ESX host with vSphere Client.

2. Select a server from the Inventory panel.

3. Click the Configuration tab, and then click Storage Adapters in the Hardware panel.

4. Select the iSCSI initiator and click Properties.

5. Click Configure.

6. Select Enabled to enable the software iSCSI initiator.

7. The iSCSI name will be automatically populated. If desired, you can enter a new iSCSI name. It is important to format the iSCSI name properly to ensure compatibility with all iSCSI storage devices.

8. Click OK.

A VMkernel port and one or more physical adapters are required to use iSCSI storage via the software iSCSI initiator. The number of physical adapters you want to be used will dictate the network configuration:

- If only one physical adapter is used, the only networking requirement is to configure a VMkernel port mapped to the single physical adapter.

- If two or more physical adapters are used, each adapter must have a separate VMkernel port mapped to leverage iSCSI multipathing.

Configuring Your
vSphere Environment

PART II

Create a VMkernel Port for Software iSCSI

To get started, a single VMkernel port can be used for communication with iSCSI targets. To configure the VMkernel port:

1. Log into either the host or vCenter with vSphere Client.

2. Select the host from the Inventory panel.

3. Click the Configuration tab.

4. Click Networking.

5. Click Add Networking in the Virtual Switch view.

6. Select a VMkernel and click Next.

7. Select Create A Virtual Switch to create a new vSwitch, as shown in Figure 7.8.

Figure 7.8: Creating a virtual switch

8. If using a new vSwitch, select an adapter to use for iSCSI traffic.

9. Click Next.

10. Enter a network label in the Port Group Properties section that will designate this VMkernel port, as shown in Figure 7.9.

Figure 7.9: Labeling the VMkernel port

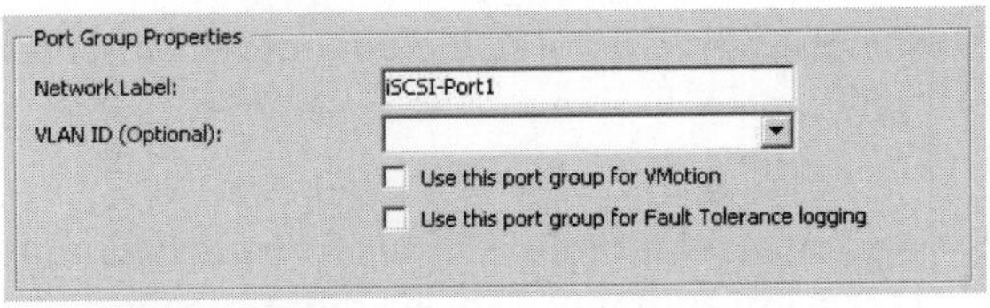

Port Group Properties	
Network Label:	iSCSI-Port1
VLAN ID (Optional):	

☐ Use this port group for VMotion
☐ Use this port group for Fault Tolerance logging

11. Click Next.

12. Specify the IP settings, as shown in Figure 7.10, and click Next.

Figure 7.10: Entering IP settings

13. Click Finish.

The network settings should appear similar to those in Figure 7.11.

Figure 7.11: Initial network settings

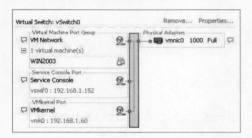

If only one physical adapter is going to be used for iSCSI traffic, configuration is complete. If more than one adapter is to be designated for iSCSI traffic, these steps may be repeated for the second adapter on a second virtual switch.

Configure Software iSCSI with Multipathing

Use this procedure if two or more network adapters are to be dedicated to iSCSI traffic and all the iSCSI network adapters are going to be connected to a single vSwitch. Each network adapter will be mapped to a single VMkernel port.

1. Log in to either the host or vCenter with vSphere Client.

2. Select the host from the Inventory panel.

3. Click the Configuration tab.

4. Click Networking.

5. Click Properties on the vSwitch being used for iSCSI.

Configuring Your vSphere Environment

6. Choose the Network Adapters tab, and add one or more unclaimed network adapters to the vSwitch, as shown in Figure 7.12.

Figure 7.12: Add Adapter Wizard

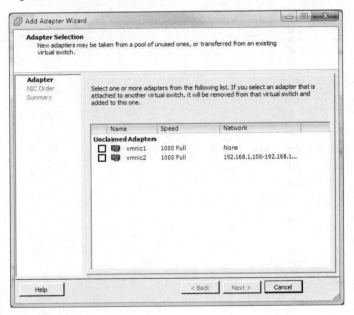

7. Click Next twice and then click Finish.

8. Ensure there is a VMkernel port for each physical adapter by viewing the Ports tab. If there are no distinct VMkernel ports for each network adapter, click Add, and proceed to add a VMkernel port as described in the "Create a VMkernel Port for Software iSCSI," section earlier in this chapter.

9. At this point, all network adapters are active for all ports on the vSwitch. To map each adapter to a distinct VMkernel port:

   a. Pick a VMkernel port, and click Edit.

   b. Select the NIC Teaming tab.

   c. Select Override vSwitch Failover Order.

   d. Ensure only one network adapter is listed as active and all others (if any) are listed as Unused, as shown in Figure 7.13.

Figure 7.13: Select Override vSwitch Failover Order.

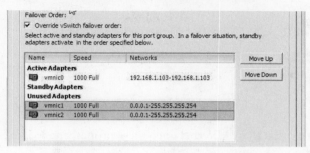

10. For each additional VMkernel port and network adapter, repeat these steps and choose adapters that are not assigned to other VMkernel ports. Figure 7.14 displays a configuration with two VMkernel ports using two network adapters.

Figure 7.14: iSCSI vSwitch

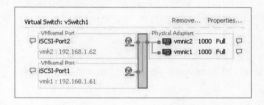

11. Identify the names of VMkernel iSCSI ports assigned to physical adapters. Figure 7.14 has iSCSI-Port1 listed as vmk1 and iSCSI-Port2 as vmk2.

12. From the ESX console, run the esxcli command to attach the VMkernel ports to the software iSCSI initiator:

```
esxcli swiscsi nic add -n <port_name> -d <vmhba>
```

Using the values from Figure 7.14, the commands would read as follows:

```
esxcli swiscsi nic add -n vmk1 -d vmhba33
esxcli swiscsi nic add -n vmk2 -d vmhba33
```

Configuring Your
vSphere Environment

PART II

This is shown in Figure 7.15.

Figure 7.15: Add VMkernel ports to the software iSCSI initiator.

```
root@esx40b:~
[root@esx40b ~]# esxcli swiscsi nic add -n vmk1  -d vmhba33
[root@esx40b ~]# esxcli swiscsi nic add -n vmk2  -d vmhba33
[root@esx40b ~]# █
```

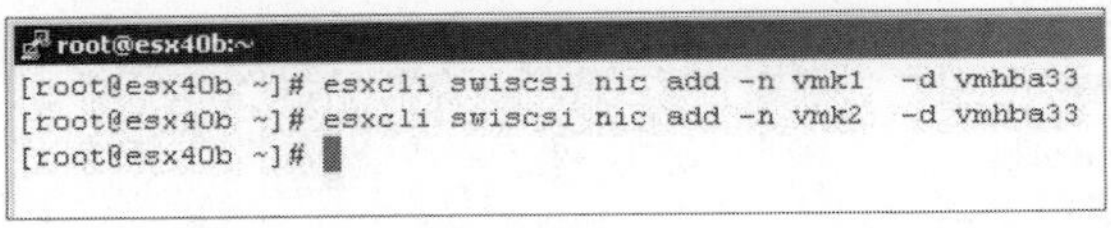

13. To verify that the VMkernel ports were properly added, execute the following command:

```
esxcli swiscsi nic list -d <vmhba>
```

14. In vSphere Client, click the Configuration tab and select Storage Adapters. Click Rescan to rescan the software iSCSI initiator.

If at a later time you want to remove a VMkernel port from being bound to the software iSCSI initiator, you must close any active iSCSI sessions between the host and any targets. The command to remove a VMkernel port from the software iSCSI initiator looks like this:

```
esxcli swiscsi nic remove -n <port_name> -d <vmhba>
```

15. The software iSCSI initiator is now configured with multipathing enabled.

Another important configuration to enable when using iSCSI storage is Jumbo Frames. Jumbo Frames are basically Ethernet frames that are larger than the standard 1,500 Maximum Transmission Units (MTU). Jumbo Frames can typically carry 9,000 bytes of data at a time, and therefore they allow for bigger chunks of data to be transferred across an Ethernet network. To use Jumbo Frames, ensure that all devices on the network support them. vSphere supports Jumbo Frames up to 9,000 bytes, or 9KB.

To configure Jumbo Frames on a vSwitch and VMkernel interface:

1. From the ESX console, use the following command to set the MTU size for the vSwitch:

```
esxcfg-vswitch -m <MTU> <vSwitch>
```

This sets the MTU for all uplinks on the vSwitch. The MTU value should be set to the largest MTU value among all the virtual network adapters connected to the vSwitch.

2. From the ESX console, use the following command to display vSwitches on the host and their respective configuration:

   ```
   esxcfg-vswitch -1
   ```

   See Figure 7.16.

Figure 7.16: Configuring Jumbo Frames on a vSwitch

```
[root@esx40b ~]# esxcfg-vswitch -m 9000 vSwitch1
[root@esx40b ~]# esxcfg-vswitch -1
Switch Name     Num Ports   Used Ports   Configured Ports   MTU    Uplinks
vSwitch0        32          4            32                 1500   vmnic0

   PortGroup Name      VLAN ID   Used Ports   Uplinks
   VM Network          0         0            vmnic0
   VMotion             0         1            vmnic0
   Service Console     0         1            vmnic0

Switch Name     Num Ports   Used Ports   Configured Ports   MTU    Uplinks
vSwitch1        64          5            64                 9000   vmnic2,vmnic1

   PortGroup Name      VLAN ID   Used Ports   Uplinks
   iSCSIPort2          0         1            vmnic2
   iSCSIPort1          0         1            vmnic1

[root@esx40b ~]#
```

3. From the ESX console, use the following command to delete the VMkernel port:

   ```
   esxcfg-vmknic -d <port group name>
   ```

4. From the ESX console, use the following command to read the VMkernel port with Jumbo Frame support:

   ```
   esxcfg-vmknic -a -i <ip address> -n <netmask>
   -m <MTU> <port group name>
   ```

5. Use the `esxcfg-vmknic -1` command to list the VMkernel interfaces and their configuration for Jumbo Frame support.

Configure iSCSI Targets for VMFS Datastores

Now that the iSCSI initiators have been configured, the next step is to configure ESX to see iSCSI targets for the purpose of remote storage. ISCSI targets must be discovered by ESX and ESXi. The two methods of discovery that are available to ESX and ESXi are Dynamic and Static. Each has a configuration tab in the properties of hardware and software iSCSI initiators. Before proceeding into the configuration, it is important to know the differences between Dynamic Discovery, also known as SendTargets, and Static Discovery.

Whenever an initiator contacts an iSCSI device, a SendTargets request is sent to the device and asks for a list of targets on the device. When devices are seen by ESX and ESXi, they are then listed on the Static Discovery tab. If static targets are removed from the Static Discovery tab, the next time a SendTargets request is sent, the target may reappear. When the host is using Static Discovery, iSCSI addresses do not have to be rescanned to see storage. No SendTargets request is sent to the specified iSCSI device or devices.

To set up Dynamic Discovery, take the following steps:

1. Log into vCenter or a specific host using vSphere Client.

2. Select a server from the Inventory panel.

3. Choose Storage Adapters in the Hardware panel on the Configuration tab.

4. Select an iSCSI initiator and click Properties.

5. Click the Dynamic Discovery tab, as shown in Figure 7.17.

Figure 7.17: Select the Dynamic Discovery tab.

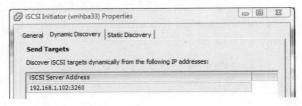

6. Click Add to add a new iSCSI device that will initiate the SendTargets communication, as shown in Figure 7.18.

Figure 7.18: Initiating the SendTargets communication

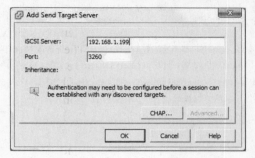

7. In the Add Send Targets Server dialog box, enter the IP address or iSCSI name of the iSCSI device and click OK.

   Once successful communication has occurred between the initiator and the iSCSI device, the iSCSI server address will be displayed on the Dynamic Discovery tab, as shown in Figure 7.19.

Figure 7.19: iSCSI Server addresses are listed.

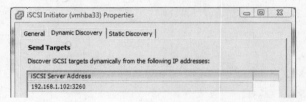

Additionally, any iSCSI storage targets discovered will appear in the Static Discovery tab. This is shown in Figure 7.20.

Figure 7.20: The discovered iSCSI targets are listed.

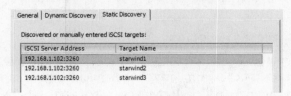

If an address, iSCSI name, or port is added incorrectly, the connection will fail. To modify the entry, it must be deleted and

re-added properly, as Dynamic Discovery targets cannot be modified. To remove a Dynamic Discovery server, select it, as shown in
Figure 7.19, and click Remove.

With iSCSI initiators, in addition to the Dynamic Discovery method,
you can also use Static Discovery, where you manually enter the IP
addresses and the iSCSI names of the targets to be contacted. To set up
Static Discovery, follow this procedure:

1. Log into vCenter or a specific host using vSphere Client.

2. Select a server from the Inventory panel.

3. Choose Storage Adapters from the Hardware panel on the
   Configuration tab.

4. Select an iSCSI initiator and click Properties.

5. Click the Static Discovery tab, as shown in Figure 7.20.

6. Click Add to add a new iSCSI target. The IP address or DNS name
   may be used in conjunction with the target device name, as shown
   in Figure 7.21.

Figure 7.21: Add Static Target Server

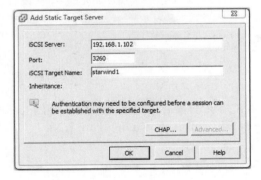

7. Click OK to add the Static target.

8. To remove a target, select the target and click Remove. Static
   Discovery targets behave similarly to Dynamic Discovery targets
   in that they cannot be edited. If changes are required, the Static
   target will have to be removed and a new target added.

Configure CHAP Authentication

Unlike the Fibre Channel protocol, the iSCSI protocol does not limit physical devices to physical ports. With iSCSI operating over standard Ethernet, any device could potentially communicate with any other device on the same network. To overcome the situation where data is not protected between devices, the iSCSI protocol will support authentication. VMware ESX and ESXi support Challenge Handshake Authentication Protocol (CHAP) for the purpose of securing iSCSI communications. CHAP authentication primarily uses a private value, known as a *CHAP secret*, to secure connections between iSCSI devices. This whole process can be simply described as password authentication. The hosts and the iSCSI targets must know the CHAP secret, or password, to be able to communicate with each other.

CHAP, which ESX/ESXi supports, uses a three-way handshake algorithm to verify the identity of your host and, if applicable, of the iSCSI target when the host and target establish a connection. The verification is based on a predefined private value, or CHAP secret, that the initiator and target share.

When VMware ESX 3.0 was released, CHAP authentication could only be accomplished at the adapter level. This proved to be difficult if many different iSCSI devices were available to be used and they did not share a common CHAP secret. This remains true in VMware ESX and ESXi 4.0 with hardware iSCSI initiators. Using the software iSCSI initiator, VMware ESX and ESXi 4.0 not only support CHAP authentication at the adapter level, but also at the level of each individual target. This addition provides VMware administrators with greater flexibility to communicate with many iSCSI targets that have one or more CHAP secret values. Table 7.2 displays the CHAP authentication levels supported by hardware and software iSCSI initiators.

Configuring Your vSphere Environment

PART II

Table 7.2: Adapter and Target Level CHAP Authentication

Initiator Type	Adapter Level CHAP	Target Level CHAP
Hardware	Yes	No
Software	Yes	Yes

VMware ESX and ESXi 4.0 provide some additional levels of security and flexibility when hosts use iSCSI targets. With CHAP authentication, the authorization is only from the host to the iSCSI target. Mutual CHAP authentication has been added in vSphere to provide for two-way authentication between hosts and iSCSI targets. Not only does the host have to authenticate against the iSCSI target, but the iSCSI target has to authenticate with the host for data to flow between them. This provides for a more secure solution than simple one-way CHAP.

Additionally, CHAP authentication can be configured with some variable security levels that alter the behavior of authentication in securing data communications. Table 7.3 displays the different CHAP security levels.

Table 7.3: CHAP Security Levels

CHAP Security Level	Behavior	Supported Initiators
Do Not Use CHAP	CHAP authentication is not used. This disables authentication.	Software Hardware
Do Not Use CHAP Unless Required By The Target	The host prefers to not use CHAP but will use CHAP authentication as an alternative.	Software
Use CHAP Unless Prohibited By The Target	The host prefers CHAP authentication but will use connections that do not have CHAP enabled.	Software Hardware
Use CHAP	CHAP authentication is required. There will be no successful connections without CHAP authentication.	Software

Ensure iSCSI targets that are being used have the appropriate settings when you configure CHAP settings. Additionally, when you configure iSCSI targets it is important to remember that the CHAP name and CHAP secret values are different for hardware and software iSCSI initiators:

Software iSCSI CHAP name has a 511-character limit and the CHAP secret has a 255-character limit.

Hardware iSCSI CHAP name has a 255-character limit and the CHAP secret has a 100-character limit.

When you are configuring CHAP authentication on iSCSI targets, plan accordingly to be able to accommodate software iSCSI initiators, hardware iSCSI initiators, or a combination of both.

To configure CHAP authentication for iSCSI targets:

1. Log into vCenter or an ESX host using vSphere Client.

2. Select a server from the Inventory panel.

3. Click Storage Adapters in the Hardware panel of the Configuration tab.

4. To configure a desired iSCSI initiator, select the initiator and click Properties.

5. On the General tab, click CHAP, as shown in Figure 7.22.

Figure 7.22: Select CHAP to configure CHAP authentication.

6. To configure one-way CHAP, do the following under CHAP:

    a. For software iSCSI initiators, select one of the following options:

      - Do Not Use CHAP Unless Required By The Target

      - Preferred

      - Required (Software iSCSI Only) (to be able to configure Mutual CHAP, you must select this option)

    b. Specify the CHAP name. Make sure that the name you specify matches the name configured on the storage side.

      - To set the CHAP name to the iSCSI adapter name, simply select Use Initiator Name.

      - To set the CHAP name to anything other than the iSCSI adapter name, deselect Use Initiator Name and enter a name in the Name field.

    c. Enter a one-way CHAP secret to be used as part of authentication. Be sure to use the same secret that you enter on the storage side.

Figure 7.23 shows a one-way CHAP configuration in the CHAP Credentials window.

Figure 7.23: One-way CHAP configuration

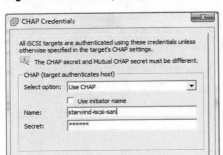

7. To configure Mutual CHAP, first configure one-way CHAP by following the directions in step 6. Be sure to select Required as an option for one-way CHAP. Then, specify the following under Mutual CHAP:

   a. Select Required.

   b. Specify the Mutual CHAP name.

   c. Enter the Mutual CHAP secret. Make sure to use different secrets for the one-way CHAP and Mutual CHAP.

   Figure 7.24 shows a Mutual CHAP configuration in the CHAP Credentials window.

Figure 7.24: Mutual CHAP configuration

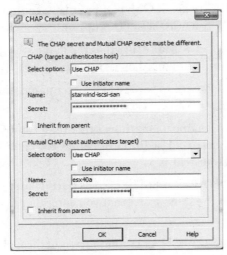

8. Click OK.

9. Rescan the adapter.

When CHAP and Mutual CHAP parameters are modified, they are only valid for new iSCSI connections. Any persistent connections will use the previous iSCSI credentials.

Set Up Per-Discovery and Per-Target CHAP Credentials

For software iSCSI, you can configure different CHAP credentials for each discovery address or static target:

1. Log into vCenter or an ESX host using vSphere Client.

2. Select a server from the Inventory panel.

3. Click Storage Adapters in the Hardware panel of the Configuration tab.

4. Select the software iSCSI initiator and click Properties.

5. Select the Dynamic Discovery tab to configure authentication at the iSCSI storage system level.

6. From the list of available targets, select a target and click Settings, and then click CHAP. Figure 7.25 displays the CHAP Credentials screen with the default settings inherited from the software iSCSI initiator.

Figure 7.25: The CHAP Credentials screen with the default settings inherited from the software iSCSI initiator

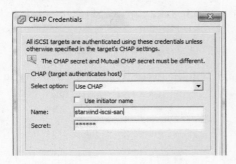

Configuring Your vSphere Environment

PART II

7. To configure one-way CHAP authentication, under CHAP:

   a. Deselect Inherit from parent.

   b. Select one of the following options:

      ▪ Do Not Use CHAP Unless Required By The Client

      ▪ Use CHAP Unless Prohibited By The Target

      ▪ Use CHAP (required if using Mutual CHAP)

   c. Specify the CHAP name. This will use the iSCSI adapter name if the Use Initiator Name box is checked. Deselect this check box to use any other name.

   d. Enter the CHAP secret for authentication. This must match the secret value on the storage side.

8. Mutual CHAP is configured only after CHAP is configured in the previous step. Specify the following under Mutual CHAP:

   a. Deselect Inherit From Parent.

   b. Select Use CHAP.

   c. Enter the Mutual CHAP name.

   d. Enter a Mutual CHAP secret. This secret value cannot be the same as the CHAP secret.

9. Click OK.

Static Discovery targets can also be configured with independent CHAP and Mutual CHAP values by performing the following steps:

1. Click the Static Discovery tab, select an iSCSI target, and click Settings.

2. Click CHAP.

3. Perform steps 6 through 9 in the preceding list for each Static Discovery target that will be using CHAP or Mutual CHAP authentication.

4. Rescan the adapter.

As before, if any CHAP or Mutual CHAP values change, they will be used for new iSCSI sessions. For existing sessions, new settings will not be used until the session is closed and reopened.

Create a New iSCSI VMFS Datastore

To add an iSCSI datastore, take the following steps:

1. From vSphere Client, choose a host from Inventory.

2. Select the Configuration tab, and then select Storage in the Hardware panel.

3. In the View panel, select Datastores.

4. Click Add Storage from the right side of the Datastores panel. The Add Storage wizard will open.

5. Choose Disk/LUN as the storage type and click Next. The right panel will display storage devices found after the HBAs were scanned.

6. Select a storage device and click Next. A review of the disk layout is displayed.

7. Click Next.

8. Enter a descriptive datastore name and click Next.

9. Choose a maximum file size. This will determine the block size used on the datastore. The four options are

   - 256GB–512B, Block size: 1MB

   - 512GB–512B, Block size: 2MB

   - 1TB–512B, Block size: 4MB

   - 2TB–512B, Block size: 8MB

   A common practice is to simply use the 8MB block size, because it will accommodate any virtual disk size up to 2TB–512B, regardless of the datastore's physical size. It is a frequent mistake to create datastores using the 1MB or 2MB block size, only to have a requirement for a guest with a disk larger than the block size will allow. Datastore block sizes cannot be changed at a later time without reformatting the datastore.

   Choosing Maximize capacity will use all of the available space on the LUN. It is important to remember that it is a best practice to configure only one VMFS volume, or datastore, per LUN.

10. Click Next.

11. Click Finish to complete the datastore setup process.

Configure NFS Storage

The Network File System (NFS) protocol is another remote storage option that is supported by vSphere. As with iSCSI, NFS storage is accessed via an Ethernet network. The same configuration that is used to connect software iSCSI initiators to iSCSI storage can be used to connect to NFS storage. Keep in mind that NFS storage is actually not a VMFS datastore, but rather a remotely mounted NFS export. Storage multipathing is not available with NFS storage.

Configure NFS Storage with ESX and ESXI

NFS-based storage has been around for approximately 25 years and several different versions have been released over that time. VSphere currently supports version 3, or NFSv3. Any device that provides storage using NFSv3 should work with vSphere, but to be certain, ensure the device is on the HCL. The VMware HCL can be found here: `http://www.vmware.com/go/hcl`.

When implementing NFS storage, keep in mind the following:

- Make sure the hardware and firmware versions are compatible with vSphere ESX and or ESXi hosts.

- Storage vendor documentation should be consulted for additional NFS device configuration and host configurations.

- Eight NFS datastores are supported by default.

- A maximum of 64 NFS datastores can be mounted to an ESX or ESXi host.

- As with iSCSI storage, it is best to have a dedicated Ethernet network for NFS storage, separate from host and guest IP traffic.

- Choose the appropriate virtual SCSI controller for virtual machines.

- Virtual machine volume management software cannot mirror virtual disks. Windows dynamic disks are an exception but must be specially configured to operate properly.

- In Windows virtual machines, increase the SCSI Timeout value parameter for better tolerance of I/O delays caused by path failover.

Create a VMkernel Port to Connect to NFS Storage

The procedure for creating a VMkernel port to connect to NFS storage is identical to the steps for creating one for software iSCSI. For the step-by-step instructions, please refer to the earlier section "Create a VMkernel Port for Software iSCSI."

Another important configuration to enable when using NFS storage is Jumbo Frames. Jumbo Frames support for NFS storage is new in vSphere; VI3 did not support Jumbo Frames with NFS. Jumbo Frames also are covered in detail in the section "Create a VMkernel Port for Software iSCSI."

VSphere supports a maximum of eight NFS datastores with a default installation. With the maximum number of supported NFS datastores at 64, before attaching the first NFS datastore, it is a good practice to modify the NFS.MaxVolumes parameter. To change the maximum number of NFS volumes from 8 to 64, follow this procedure:

1. Log in to either the host or vCenter with vSphere Client.
2. Select the host from the Inventory panel.
3. Click the Configuration tab.
4. Click Advanced Settings.
5. Click NFS in the left panel of Advanced Settings.
6. Scroll until the NFS.MaxVolumes setting is visible.
7. Change the value from 8 to 64, as shown in Figure 7.26.

Figure 7.26: Change the NFS.MaxVolumes setting to 64.

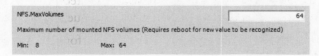

NFS.MaxVolumes   64

Maximum number of mounted NFS volumes (Requires reboot for new value to be recognized)

Min: 8   Max: 64

8. Click OK.
9. Reboot the ESX or ESXi host.

Configuring Your vSphere Environment

PART II

Attach a NFS Mount as a Datastore

NFS datastores are different from both FC and iSCSI VMFS volumes. The file system that the ESX or ESXi host uses is not a VMFS formatted file system. Also, there is no way to configure the amount of space that the host sees from vSphere Client. The space available to the host is configured on the NFS device. You no longer have to be concerned about block size or maximum virtual disk file size based on block size.

Follow these steps to add an NFS mount as a datastore:

1. From vSphere Client, choose a host from Inventory.

2. Select the Configuration tab, and then select Storage from the Hardware panel.

3. In the View panel, select Datastores.

4. Click Add Storage on the right side of the Datastores panel.

5. The Add Storage wizard will open. Choose Network File System as the storage type and click Next.

6. As shown in Figure 7.27, enter the fully qualified domain name (FQDN) or IP address of the NFS storage device.

7. Enter the name of the NFS export.

8. Enter the name of the datastore.

Figure 7.27: Mounting an NFS export

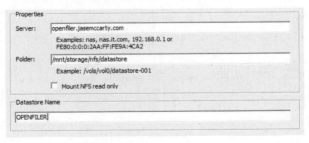

9. Click Next. A review of the NFS mount configuration is displayed.

10. Click Finish to complete the datastore setup process.

8

High Availability and Business Continuity

Configuring Your vSphere Environment

PART II

Information technology (IT) professionals in organizations of all sizes and types seek to minimize downtime, planned or unplanned. Downtime means lost productivity, and lost productivity means lost money. In some organizations, the amount of money lost due to downtime can be quite significant. VMware vSphere provides a number of features that help reduce or eliminate downtime, both planned and unplanned.

Minimize Planned Downtime

There are a variety of reasons why planned downtime might be necessary. Perhaps you, as a system administrator, need to perform hardware maintenance on a physical server. Perhaps a storage array needs to be upgraded or replaced. In either case, VMware vSphere offers two key features that help you minimize the amount of planned downtime that is required. VMotion and Storage VMotion allow you to reduce or eliminate the planned downtime required in many instances. In this section, we'll review both VMotion (live migration of virtual machines) and Storage VMotion (live migration of virtual machine storage).

Configure and Use VMotion

VMotion is the live migration of running virtual machines from one physical ESX/ESXi host to a second physical ESX/ESXi host, without any downtime or without any interruption in service. Generally, you can use VMotion to move virtual machines without your end users even knowing that a live migration occurred. This enables you to easily change the location of running virtual machines on the fly in response to changing business needs. If you need to take a physical ESX/ESXi host down in the middle of the day for emergency hardware maintenance, you can use VMotion to move all the virtual machines on that host to another host and then take the first ESX/ESXi host down for maintenance. When the maintenance is complete, you can use VMotion to bring the virtual machines back again. All of this occurs without any downtime or any interruption of service to the applications running within the virtual machines.

> **NOTE** VMotion is a core component of VMware vSphere and is leveraged in a number of different ways. VMware Distributed Resource Scheduler (DRS) uses VMotion as the mechanism whereby it balances workload distribution across a cluster of ESX/ESXi hosts. Maintenance mode uses VMotion to vacate an ESX/ESXi host so that the host can be taken offline for maintenance. VMware Fault Tolerance (FT), discussed later in this chapter, uses a form of VMotion to create the secondary VM.

Configure an ESX/ESXi Host for VMotion

VMotion has several prerequisites that the ESX/ESXi hosts must meet before you can use VMotion to migrate a running virtual machine:

- The source and destination ESX/ESXi hosts must use the same processor family (Intel or AMD) and generation (Xeon 55xx, AMD 83xx). Migrations between different versions of the same processor family—for example, between a Xeon 55xx and a Xeon 54xx—are possible only when using Enhanced VMotion Compatibility (EVC).

- The source and destination ESX/ESXi hosts must have identically configured virtual machine port groups or must participate in the same vNetwork Distributed Switch.

- The ESX/ESXi hosts must be managed by the same vCenter Server instance.

- The source and destination ESX/ESXi hosts must have Gigabit Ethernet or better connectivity within the same Layer 2 broadcast domain.

Once all the other requirements have been met, the final step in configuring VMotion on an ESX/ESXi host is to create a VMkernel port and enable it for VMotion. This VMkernel port must have Gigabit Ethernet or better connectivity to the physical network.

The procedure for creating a VMkernel port is different if you are using a vNetwork Standard Switch or a vNetwork Distributed Switch.

To create a VMkernel port on a vNetwork Standard Switch and enable it for VMotion, use these steps:

1. Select the ESX/ESXi host on which you want to create the VMkernel port and click the Configuration tab.

Configuring Your vSphere Environment

PART II

2. Click the Networking link.

3. Select the Virtual Switch button to view the vNetwork Standard Switch configuration for the selected ESX/ESXi host.

4. Click the Add Networking link. This opens the Add Network wizard.

5. Select the VMkernel radio button, and then click Next.

6. Select the radio button to either create a new virtual switch or use an existing virtual switch, as appropriate for your environment. If you are creating a new virtual switch, you must also select the network interface cards (NIC) that will serve as uplinks for the new virtual switch. Click Next when you are ready to proceed.

7. Supply a name for the VMkernel port and a VLAN ID, if necessary.

8. Select the check box Use This Port Group For VMotion, and then click Next.

9. If you want to use Dynamic Host Configuration Protocol (DHCP), select the Obtain IP Settings Automatically radio button. Otherwise, select the Use The Following IP Settings radio button and then enter the IP address, subnet mask, and VMkernel default gateway. Click Next when you are finished.

10. Review the configuration and, if it is correct, click the Finish button to finish the wizard. Otherwise, use the Back button to go back and make the necessary changes.

To create a VMkernel port on a vNetwork Distributed Switch and enable it for VMotion, follow these steps:

1. Select the ESX/ESXi host on which you want to create the VMkernel port, and then click the Configuration tab. Note that this host must already be a member of the vNetwork Distributed Switch.

2. Click the Networking link.

3. Select the Distributed Virtual Switch button to view the vNetwork Distributed Switch configuration for the selected ESX/ESXi host.

4. Click the Manage Virtual Adapters link.

5. In the Manage Virtual Adapters dialog box, click the Add link. This opens the Add Virtual Adapter wizard.

6. Select the New Virtual Adapter radio button, and then click Next.

7. Select the VMkernel radio button and click Next.

8. With the Select Port Group radio button selected, choose an existing port group to host the new VMkernel port. If you don't already have a port group for the VMkernel port, you must cancel this process, create the port group, and then restart these steps.

9. Be sure to select the Use This Virtual Adapter For VMotion check box.

10. Once you've selected a port group and selected the Use This Virtual Adapter For VMotion check box, click Next.

11. If you want to use Dynamic Host Configuration Protocol (DHCP), select the Obtain IP Settings Automatically radio button. Otherwise, select the Use The Following IP Settings radio button and then enter the IP address, subnet mask, and VMkernel default gateway. Click Next when you are finished.

12. Review the configuration and, if it is correct, click the Finish button to finish the wizard. Otherwise, use the Back button to go back and make the necessary changes.

After you've created the VMkernel port and enabled it for VMotion, you are ready to migrate a running virtual machine, assuming you've ensured that the ESX/ESXi hosts meet the other requirements listed earlier.

Use VMotion to Migrate a Virtual Machine

In the same way that the ESX/ESXi hosts have requirements in order to use VMotion, virtual machines must also meet certain requirements in order for VMotion to work. The requirements for a running virtual machine to migrate using VMotion are as follows:

- The virtual machine must reside on shared storage that is accessible to both the source and destination ESX/ESXi hosts. This includes the virtual machine's disk, configuration, log, and non-volatile random access memory (NVRAM) files.

- The virtual machine must not be connected to any device physically available to only one ESX/ESXi host, such as a floppy drive, CD/DVD drive, serial port, parallel port, or raw disk storage. This includes a physical mode Raw Device Mapping (RDM).

NOTE   Raw Device Mappings (RDMs) can operate in virtual mode or in physical mode. Physical mode RDMs have more restrictions than virtual mode RDMs but might be necessary in some situations. For more detailed information, consult the VMware vSphere documentation.

- The virtual machine must not be connected to an internal-only virtual switch (that is, a virtual switch without any connectivity to the physical network).

- The virtual machine must not have its CPU affinity set to a specific CPU.

Once you have verified that a virtual machine meets these requirements, you are ready to actually migrate a virtual machine using VMotion. To do so, perform these steps:

1. Right-click the virtual machine you wish to migrate and from the context menu, select Migrate. This starts the Migrate Virtual Machine wizard.

2. Select the Change Host radio button, and then click Next.

3. Select the destination host or cluster to which this virtual machine should be migrated. If vCenter Server detects an incompatibility, the details will be displayed in the lower portion of the Migrate Virtual Machine wizard and the Next button will be grayed out, as shown in Figure 8.1. You will need to correct the reported compatibility issues before you can proceed. If no compatibility issues are listed, click Next to continue.

4. If multiple resource pools exist on the destination ESX/ESXi host or cluster, you must select the desired destination resource pool, and then click Next. This step will not appear if the destination host or cluster does not have more than one resource pool.

5. Select the Reserve CPU For Optimal VMotion Performance (Recommended) radio button to set aside guaranteed CPU resources for the live migration. Otherwise, as the text indicates on the Migrate Virtual Machine wizard, the duration of the VMotion operation might be extended. Click Next.

Figure 8.1: The Migrate Virtual Machine wizard won't allow a VMotion operation to continue if compatibility issues are detected.

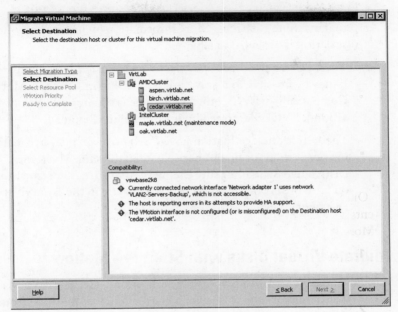

6. Review the settings and, if everything is correct, click Finish. Otherwise, click the Back button to go back and change the settings as needed.

vSphere Client's Tasks pane will show the progress of the VMotion migration. If the migration fails, you will need to troubleshoot the failure.

Troubleshooting VMotion

Some common configurations problems that users see with VMotion are as follows:

- The ESX/ESXi hosts do not have a VMkernel NIC enabled for VMotion. You'll need to create a VMkernel NIC and enable it for VMotion, as explained earlier in the section titled "Configure an ESX/ESXi Host for VMotion."

- The virtual machine has a virtual device backed by a physical resource (like a CD/DVD or floppy drive, serial port, or parallel port). All such devices must be marked as Disconnected in the virtual machine's settings. More information on how to correct this situation is provided in Chapter 9.

- The CPUs on the source and destination host are not compatible. It may be possible to resolve this issue using Enhanced VMotion Compatibility (EVC); otherwise, there is no supported workaround. EVC is described in more detail in Chapter 1.

- The source and destination ESX/ESXi hosts do not have matching port groups or do not participate in the same vNetwork Distributed Switch. Ensure that network settings are consistent on both hosts or that both hosts participate in the same vNetwork Distributed Switch.

Migrate Virtual Disks with Storage VMotion

Similar in nature to VMotion, Storage VMotion is a technology that allows you to migrate the storage of a running virtual machine from one storage location to a second storage location with no downtime. This gives you a powerful tool for balancing storage workloads, migrating to new storage solutions, or responding to changing storage requirements.

Unlike VMotion, Storage VMotion does not require any specific configuration on each ESX/ESXi host, other than connectivity to the source and destination datastores. Also unlike VMotion, you can use Storage VMotion with VMs on local storage. Because the ESX/ESXi host must have connectivity to both the source and destination datastores, you can't perform a local-to-local migration of storage using Storage VMotion, but you can perform local-to-shared or shared-to-local storage migrations.

To migrate a running virtual machine using Storage VMotion, follow these steps:

1. Right-click the running virtual machine whose storage you want to relocate and select Migrate.

2. In the Migrate Virtual Machine wizard, select Change Datastore and click Next.

3. If there are multiple resource pools on the ESX/ESXi host, select the destination resource pool. If you want the resource pool to remain unchanged, select the same resource pool in which the VM is currently located. Click Next.

4. Select the destination datastore. If vCenter Server detects a compatibility error, that error will be displayed at the bottom of the dialog box. You will need to cancel the wizard, correct the error, and then restart the process. Click Next to continue.

5. Select the Same Format As Source radio button to preserve the format of the virtual machine's virtual disk files. Otherwise, select Thin Provisioned Format or Thick Format as appropriate. Click Next.

6. Review the configuration and, if everything is correct, click Finish. Otherwise, use the Back button to go back and make the necessary changes.

The Tasks pane of vSphere Client displays the progress of the Storage VMotion operation. Depending on the size of the disks being migrated, the process may be lengthy. There is no downtime during the actual disk migration process, although virtual machine performance may be negatively impacted.

Troubleshooting Storage VMotion

The most common problem with Storage VMotion involves VM snapshots. A VM may not have an active snapshot in order for you to migrate the storage using Storage VMotion. All snapshots must be committed and removed before Storage VMotion can migrate the storage. If the snapshots cannot be committed, you have the option of using VMware Converter, as outlined in Chapter 9, to perform a virtual-to-virtual migration to commit the snapshots.

Protect Against Host Failure

Downtime isn't always planned, and a key part of ensuring high availability and business continuity is protecting against unplanned downtime as well. The two primary causes of unplanned downtime are host failure (where an ESX/ESXi host fails for some reason) and VM failure (where the guest operating system within a virtual machine fails for some reason). In this section we'll discuss how to protect against host failure; in the next section you'll learn how to guard against VM failure.

VMware vSphere provides two features that are intended to help you protect against the failure of an ESX/ESXi host:

- VMware High Availability (HA) uses a heartbeat to detect the failure of an ESX/ESXi host and restarts virtual machines when it detects a host failure.

- VMware Fault Tolerance (FT) uses VMware's vLockstep technology to keep two virtual machines mirrored in real time. If the host where the primary VM is running fails, the secondary VM takes over almost instantaneously.

Because VMware FT builds on top of VMware HA—in fact, VMware FT requires VMware HA to be enabled before it can be enabled—we'll discuss VMware HA first.

Set Up VMware High Availability

VMware High Availability (HA) provides functionality to automatically restart virtual machines in the event of a physical host failure. VMware HA accomplishes this through the use of an agent that runs on each ESX/ESXi host; this agent communicates with the agent on other hosts within a VMware HA-enabled cluster. When the agent detects that a host has failed, the VMs on that host are automatically restarted on an available host in the cluster. As the vSphere administrator, you have the ability to configure key parameters such as failover capacity and VM restart priority.

Because VMware HA requires communication between the ESX/ESXi hosts, there are a couple of prerequisites you should verify before enabling VMware HA:

- VMware HA is very sensitive to name resolution issues. Be sure that Domain Name System (DNS) name resolution is working correctly on all ESX/ESXi hosts in the cluster. Each ESX/ESXi host should be able to resolve both the short name and the fully qualified domain name (FQDN) for all the other ESX/ESXi hosts in the cluster.

- VMware HA is also sensitive to network failures. You should ensure that the management interfaces on your ESX/ESXi hosts have adequate network redundancy. vCenter Server will warn you if an ESX/ESXi host does not have management network redundancy, as you can see in Figure 8.2.

Figure 8.2: vCenter Server will warn you if ESX/ESXi hosts do not have sufficient management network redundancy.

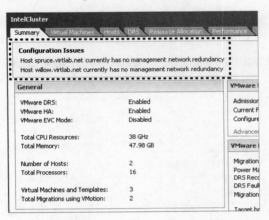

Configuring Your
vSphere Environment

PART II

Enabling VMware HA on a Cluster

After you've verified the prerequisites and you're ready to enable VMware HA on an existing cluster of ESX/ESXi hosts, follow these steps:

1. Right-click the cluster and select Edit Settings.

2. Select the Turn On VMware HA check box.

3. Click OK to apply the settings.

When you click OK, vCenter Server will start configuring the VMware HA agent on each ESX/ESXi host. The Tasks pane in vSphere Client will show you the progress of configuring VMware HA on each host in the cluster.

After VMware HA has been enabled on a cluster, there are additional settings you can adjust, including admission control and admission control policy. These are discussed next.

Configuring VMware HA Failover and Capacity Settings

For the most part, VMware HA is self-configuring. When you enable VMware HA as described previously, vCenter Server configures each of the hosts, and the hosts will begin sending and receiving heartbeats. There are a couple of settings, however, that you might need to adjust for your specific environment. Figure 8.3 shows the settings dialog box for a VMware HA–enabled cluster.

Figure 8.3: Admission Control and Admission Control Policy are two additional settings you might need to configure for VMware HA.

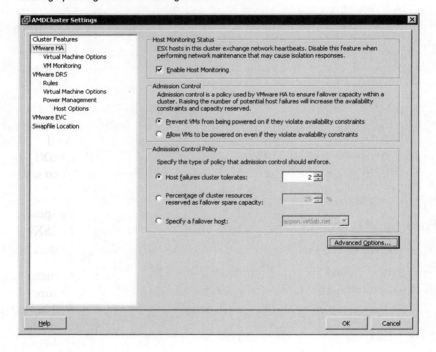

As you can see in Figure 8.3, Admission Control has two possible settings:

Prevent VMs From Being Powered On If They Violate Availability Constraints With this setting, vCenter Server will prevent the user from powering on more VMs than the VMware HA–enabled cluster can handle based on the configured failover capacity. This ensures that the cluster is always capable of handling the VMs running on the hosts in the cluster, even during times of degraded capacity.

Allow VMs To Be Powered On Even If They Violate Availability Constraints   When Admission Control is set to Allow VMs To Be Powered On Even If They Violate Availability Constraints, vCenter Server will not prevent the user from starting more VMs than the cluster can handle based on the configured failover capacity. In times of degraded capacity due to one or more ESX/ESXi host failures, some VMs might not have enough resources to run.

The Admission Control setting is affected by the Admission Control Policy, which controls the failover capacity for the VMware HA-enabled cluster. There are three possible ways to specify failover capacity for the cluster, as you can see in Figure 8.3:

- The Host Failures Cluster Tolerates option allows you to specify the number of EX/ESXi host failures the cluster should be able to handle. In a cluster of four ESX/ESXi hosts, setting this value to 2 basically means that the cluster should plan for a maximum of 50 percent capacity on the cluster.

- The Percentage Of Cluster Resources Reserved As Failover Spare Capacity option allows you to specify a percentage of overall capacity that should be reserved. In a cluster of four ESX/ESXi hosts, setting this value to 25 percent is roughly analogous to setting the host failures setting to 1.

- The Specify A Failover Host option allows you to specify a specific host that should be used as failover in the event of an ESX/ESXi host failure.

You might need to adjust these settings based on your environment. For example, if you have a four-node cluster and you want to be sure that you do not run more virtual machines than could be handled in the event of one of those nodes failing, you would set Admission Control to Prevent VMs From Being Powered On and set Admission Control Policy to Host Failures Cluster Tolerates to 1.

You can also set virtual machine restart priority and the default isolation response action; we describe these options in the next section.

Setting VM Restart Priority and Isolation Response

VMware HA also provides you with the option of configuring the VM restart priority. This value can be set on a cluster-wide basis, as well as on a per-VM basis; together, this allows you to grant a higher priority to more important workloads and force less important workloads to use a lower priority when restarting. Figure 8.4 shows the user interface for setting both the cluster-wide VM restart priority as well as the per-VM restart priority.

Figure 8.4: You can configure VM restart priority on a cluster-wide basis as well as on a per-VM basis.

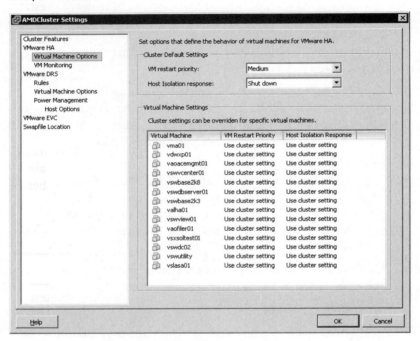

In addition to VM restart priority, you can also set the host isolation response on a cluster-wide basis as well as on a per-VM basis. The *host isolation response* is what happens when an ESX/ESXi host in a VMware HA–enabled cluster loses connectivity to all the rest of the hosts in the cluster. In this instance, the ESX/ESXi host must determine the answer to this question: am I isolated from the network, or did the rest of the cluster go offline?

The answer to this question is determined by attempting to get a response to a ping to the default isolation address. The default isolation address is, by default, set the same as the default gateway for the ESX/ESXi host's management interfaces. If the ESX/ESXi host receives a response from the isolation address, then it knows that it is not isolated from the network and that the rest of the cluster must be offline. If the ESX/ESXi host does not receive a response, it will determine that it is isolated and then trigger the isolation response. The default isolation response is to shut down the virtual machines on the host; this is so that other hosts in the cluster can start up the virtual machines. You may want to change the isolation response either for the entire cluster or on a per-VM basis; this is accomplished in the same way as the VM restart priority, as shown in Figure 8.4.

So far we've described the majority of the configuration that you might need to perform for VMware HA. However, in some instances you may need to set some advanced options. We'll explore these options next.

Setting Advanced Options for VMware HA

In many cases, most users will never need to bother with the Advanced Options button (shown earlier, in Figure 8.3). However, in some cases, you might have a need to set a specific value here. Table 8.1 describes a few of the most commonly used values.

Table 8.1: Commonly Used VMware HA Advanced Options

Advanced Option	Description
das.usedefaultisolationaddress	Value is set to True or False; instructs ESX/ESXi whether to use the default isolation address (the default gateway for the management interfaces).
das.isolationaddress[x]	Value is an IP address. [x] can be a value from 1 to 10. Specifies the IP address(es) that an ESX/ESXi host should use to determine if it is isolated.
das.failuredetectiontime	Value is in milliseconds. Specifies the amount of time for an isolation response action.
das.failuredetectioninterval	Value is in milliseconds. Specifies the heartbeat interval among ESX/ESXi hosts in a VMware HA–enabled cluster.

After setting any of these values, you must right-click on the ESX/ESXi hosts in the cluster and select Reconfigure For HA for the new setting to take effect.

Troubleshooting VMware HA

Far and away, the most common problem with VMware HA revolves around name resolution. Misconfigured DNS settings, such as different domain names within the cluster, will cause VMware HA to fail to configure correctly. It is imperative that you ensure that every ESX/ESXi host is able to resolve the name of every other ESX/ESXi host in the cluster before you attempt to enable VMware HA.

Some other common problems with VMware HA include the following:

- The management interface's default gateway does not respond to ping requests. In this case, VMware HA won't function correctly because hosts will not be able to determine whether they are isolated. Use the das.usedefaultisolationaddress and das.isolationaddress advanced settings to specify a different isolation address.

- The network architecture during a failure may cause isolation response events. In some cases, convergence after a network failure may exceed the default interval that ESX/ESXi hosts use to determine host failures. You can increase the default intervals and failure detection times as described in the section "Setting Advanced Options for VMware HA," earlier in this chapter.

Set Up VMware Fault Tolerance

One of the most anticipated new features within VMware vSphere is VMware Fault Tolerance. VMware FT utilizes VMware's new vLockstep technology to keep two virtual machines—a primary VM and a secondary VM—in perfect lockstep with each other. These mirrored VMs run on two different physical hosts. If either of these physical hosts fails, the virtual machine will continue running on the other host, ensuring a seamless failover with no downtime in the event of a host failure.

Because VMware FT builds on top of VMware HA, the two features work together to protect the VM workload in all different host failure scenarios. Consider these three examples:

- In the event of the failure of the ESX/ESXi host on which the primary (protected) VM is running, the secondary VM becomes the new primary and takes over seamlessly. VMware FT creates a new secondary VM on another ESX/ESXi host.

- In the event of the failure of the ESX/ESXi host on which the secondary VM is running, the primary VM continues running without any interruption. VMware FT creates a new secondary VM on another ESX/ESXi host.

- In the event both of the ESX/ESXi hosts involved fail, VMware HA will restart the primary VM on a new ESX/ESXi host. VMware FT will then create a new secondary VM on another ESX/ESXi host.

Examining VMware FT Requirements

VMware FT does have some configuration requirements that you must satisfy before you can enable VMware FT on a specific virtual machine. Requirements to support VMware FT exist at the cluster, host, and virtual machine levels:

- VMware HA must be enabled on the cluster. Host monitoring should also be enabled for the cluster.

- Host certificate checking must be enabled on all hosts that you will use for VMware FT. Host certificate checking is enabled by default.

- All hosts must have a VMotion and a Fault Tolerance Logging NIC configured.

- At least two hosts must have CPUs from the same compatible CPU group. Maximum flexibility is possible when all the hosts in the cluster have compatible CPUs.

- All hosts must run the same ESX/ESXi version and patch level.

- All hosts must have access to virtual machine networks and datastores.

ESX/ESXi hosts have the following requirements to use VMware FT:

- Hosts must have a CPU that supports VMware FT.

NOTE   VMware Knowledge Base article 1008027, available from VMware's website at http://kb.vmware.com/kb/1008027, contains information on the CPU types supported by VMware FT.

- The ESX/ESXi host must have Hardware Virtualization enabled in the BIOS. Some hardware manufacturers ship servers with Hardware Virtualization disabled.

- The hardware vendor should certify the host as FT-capable. You can refer to the VMware Hardware Compatibility List (HCL), available at www.vmware.com/resources/compatibility/search.php, for hardware compatibility information.

- As mentioned earlier, each ESX/ESXi host must have both a VMotion and a Fault Tolerance Logging NIC configured.

Finally, VMware FT has the following requirements for virtual machines that are to be protected:

- Virtual machines must be stored on shared storage.

- Virtual machines cannot use physical mode RDMs. Virtual mode RDMs are acceptable.

- Virtual machine disk (VMDK) files must be Thick Provisioned with the Cluster Features option enabled.

- Virtual machines must not have a snapshot. Snapshots must be committed before you can enable VMware FT.

- Virtual machines must have only a single virtual CPU (vCPU). VMs with multiple vCPUs cannot have VMware FT enabled.

- Virtual machines cannot have CD/DVD or floppy drives that are backed by a physical device.

- Virtual machines cannot be configured to use paravirtualization.

- Virtual machines cannot have USB or sound devices.

- Virtual machines cannot use N_Port ID Virtualization (NPIV); this topic is discussed in Chapter 7.

- Virtual machines cannot use NIC passthrough.

- Virtual machines cannot use the paravirtualized SCSI (PVSCSI) or VMXNET3 network devices. Chapter 9 provides more information on the PVSCSI and VMXNET3 devices.

In addition, VMware FT will disable certain other features once it is active. Extended Page Tables/Rapid Virtualization Indexing (EPT/RVI), Distributed Resource Scheduler (DRS), and device hot-plugging are all disabled or turned off after VMware FT is enabled for a virtual machine.

Configuring an ESX/ESXi Host for VMware FT

Assuming that you have enabled VMware HA, the first step in configuring VMware FT is configuring a Fault Tolerance Logging NIC. As with a VMotion NIC, the procedure for configuring a Fault Tolerance Logging NIC varies depending on whether you are using a vNetwork Standard Switch or a vNetwork Distributed Switch.

Perform these steps to configure a Fault Tolerance Logging NIC with a vNetwork Standard Switch:

1. Select an ESX/ESXi host in the cluster and click the Configuration tab.

2. Click the Networking link.

3. Select the Virtual Switch button to view the vNetwork Standard Switch configuration for the selected ESX/ESXi host.

4. Click the Add Networking link. This opens the Add Network wizard.

5. Select the VMkernel radio button, and then click Next.

6. Select the radio button to either create a new virtual switch or use an existing virtual switch, as appropriate for your environment. If you are creating a new virtual switch, you must also select the NICs that will serve as uplinks for the new virtual switch. Click Next when you are ready to proceed.

7. Supply a name for the VMkernel port and a VLAN ID, if necessary.

8. Select the Use This Port Group For Fault Tolerance Logging check box, and then click Next.

9. If you want to use Dynamic Host Configuration Protocol (DHCP), select the Obtain IP Settings Automatically radio button. Otherwise, select the Use The Following IP Settings radio button and then enter the IP address, subnet mask, and VMkernel default gateway. Click Next when you are finished.

10. Review the configuration and, if it is correct, click the Finish button to finish the wizard. Otherwise, use the Back button to go back and make the necessary changes.

To create a VMkernel port on a vNetwork Distributed Switch and enable it for Fault Tolerance Logging, follow these steps:

1. Select the ESX/ESXi host on which you want to create the VMkernel port, and then click the Configuration tab. Note that this host must already be a member of the vNetwork Distributed Switch.

2. Click the Networking link.

3. Select the Distributed Virtual Switch button to view the vNetwork Distributed Switch configuration for the selected ESX/ESXi host.

4. Click the Manage Virtual Adapters link.

5. In the Manage Virtual Adapters dialog box, click the Add link. This opens the Add Virtual Adapter wizard.

6. Select the New Virtual Adapter radio button, and then click Next.

7. Select the VMkernel radio button and click Next.

8. With the Select Port Group radio button selected, choose an existing port group to host the new VMkernel port. If you don't already have a port group for the VMkernel port, you must cancel this process, create the port group, and then restart these steps.

9. Be sure to select the Use This Virtual Adapter For Fault Tolerance Logging check box.

10. Once you've selected a port group and selected the Use This Virtual Adapter For VMotion check box, click Next.

11. If you want to use Dynamic Host Configuration Protocol (DHCP), select the Obtain IP Settings Automatically radio button. Otherwise, select the Use The Following IP Settings radio button

and then enter the IP address, subnet mask, and VMkernel default gateway. Click Next when you are finished.

12. Review the configuration and, if it is correct, click the Finish button to finish the wizard. Otherwise, use the Back button to go back and make the necessary changes.

After you have ensured that all the requirements are met, you are ready to enable VMware FT for a virtual machine.

Enabling VMware FT for a Virtual Machine

VMware FT is enabled on a per–virtual machine basis. This provides you with flexibility in choosing which virtual machines should be protected using VMware FT, and it allows you to mix protected and unprotected VMs within the same cluster and on the same ESX/ESXi hosts.

Perform the following steps to enable VMware FT for a specific virtual machine:

1. Many guest operating systems must be powered off in order to enable VMware FT. VMware KB article 1008027, referenced earlier, provides information on which guest operating systems must be powered off on which hardware platforms in order to enable VMware FT. If necessary, power down the virtual machine by right-clicking on a virtual machine and selecting Power ➤ Shut Down Guest.

2. Once the virtual machine is powered down (if necessary), right-click the virtual machine and select Fault Tolerance ➤ Turn On Fault Tolerance.

3. In the Turn On Fault Tolerance dialog box, click Yes to confirm the operation. The dialog box informs you that the VM disk may need to be converted, that the Distributed Resource Scheduler (DRS) automation level will be set to disabled, and that a memory reservation will be put into place as part of the process of enabling VMware FT.

vCenter Server will create the secondary VM on a second ESX/ESXi host and then synchronize it with the primary VM. You can use the Fault Tolerance area of the VM summary screen, shown in Figure 8.5, to check on the status of a VM's protection.

Configuring Your
vSphere Environment

PART II

Figure 8.5: The Fault Tolerance area of the VM's Summary tab in vCenter Server provides additional information on the status of a VM's protection.

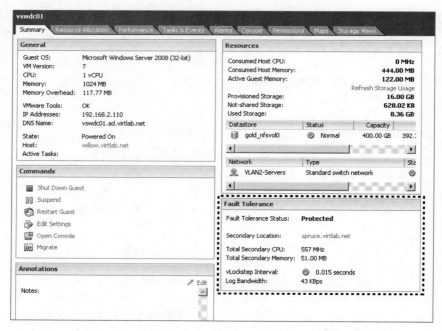

In the event you need to disable VMware FT, follow these steps.

1. Right-click the virtual machine that currently has VMware FT enabled and select Fault Tolerance ➤ Turn Off Fault Tolerance.

2. Click Yes in the Turn Off Fault Tolerance dialog box to confirm the operation.

vCenter Server will unregister and destroy the secondary VM and disable VMware FT for the selected VM. As pointed out in the confirmation dialog box, vCenter Server will also return the DRS automation level to the cluster default. Note that the memory reservation set by VMware FT remains, and if the disks were converted to Thick Provisioned that conversion is not reversed.

Troubleshooting VMware FT

The most common problems with VMware FT relate to incorrect configuration of either the ESX/ESXi hosts or the virtual machines. Here are some common configuration problems:

- The server's CPU is not supported for VMware FT.

- Hardware virtualization extensions are not enabled in the server's BIOS.

- The virtual machine is using a physical mode RDM or a virtual device backed by a physical resource (like a CD/DVD or floppy drive).

- The virtual machine is using NPIV.

- The virtual machine has an active snapshot.

- The virtual machine is using the paravirtualized SCSI (PVSCSI) or VMXNET3 devices. These devices are not supported with VMware FT.

Guard Against VM Failure

In addition to ESX/ESXi host failure, the failure of the guest operating system within a virtual machine is another source of unplanned downtime. VMware vSphere provides a couple of tools for helping with this potential problem. First, vSphere can monitor virtual machines for failure, and restart them if it detects a failure; this feature is called *VM Monitoring*. Second, vSphere provides a framework, called the *VMware Consolidated Backup framework*, which backup vendors can use to perform backups of virtual machines. These backups can help you protect against data loss within virtual machines.

First we'll look at VM Monitoring.

Enable VM Monitoring

VM Monitoring is an extension of VMware HA and requires that VMware HA is already enabled. Using the heartbeats from the VMware Tools, VM Monitoring will watch the status of virtual machines. VM

Monitoring also watches the I/Os from virtual machines. When the heartbeats and the I/Os stop—presumably due to a failure of the guest operating system within the VM—VM Monitoring will restart the VM automatically. You can control the sensitivity of VM Monitoring as well as enable or disable VM Monitoring on a per-VM basis within a cluster.

To enable VM Monitoring, follow these steps:

1. Right-click the VMware HA–enabled cluster and select Edit Settings.

2. From the list on the left, select VM Monitoring.

3. Click the Enable VM Monitoring check box.

Now you can customize the sensitivity to the heartbeats from the virtual machines using the settings in the Default Cluster Settings area of the dialog box. Table 8.2 summarizes the predefined sensitivity settings.

Table 8.2: VM Monitoring Predefined Sensitivity Settings

Slider Bar Setting	Predefined Values
Low	2-minute interval to receive a VM heartbeat Restarts the VM a maximum of 3 times every 7 days
Medium	60-second interval to receive a VM heartbeat Restarts the VM a maximum of 3 times every 24 hours
High	30-second interval to receive a VM heartbeat Restarts the VM a maximum of 3 times every hour

If these predefined settings aren't sufficient, enable the Custom check box and you can set the Failure Interval, Minimum Uptime, Maximum Per-VM Resets, and Maximum Resets Time Window settings directly, as shown in Figure 8.6.

As mentioned earlier, you can customize, even disable, VM Monitoring on a per-VM basis within the cluster. In the Virtual Machine Settings area of the dialog box—refer to Figure 8.6—you can select one of the predefined values (Low, Medium, High), a custom value, or even disable VM Monitoring entirely for that VM. This allows you to have a great deal of control over which VMs should be monitored. In addition, it allows you to disable VM Monitoring for VMs that do not have the VMware Tools installed. Keep in mind that installing the VMware Tools is always recommended, however.

Figure 8.6: You can set custom values for VM Monitoring to meet the needs of your environments.

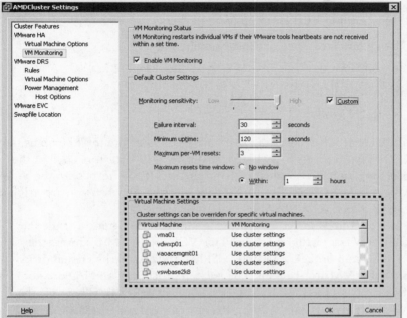

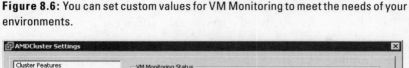

While VM Monitoring is helpful, it does not protect against data loss within a virtual machine. For that, you'll need a backup solution. One component of a backup solution is often VMware Consolidated Backup, which we'll discuss next.

Install and Use VMware Consolidated Backup

VMware Consolidated Backup (VCB) is a framework that third-party backup vendors can use to integrate their backup products with VMware vSphere. Although VMware vSphere ships with VCB 1.5 Update 1, all the future development of VCB has been transitioned to VCB's replacement, called the vStorage APIs for Data Protection (VADP). Future backup solutions should leverage these application programming interfaces (APIs) instead of using VCB.

For the near term following vSphere's release, though, VCB is the only real solution available to integrate third-party backup products into VMware vSphere. Until the widespread availability of VADP and backup solutions written for VADP, you need to know how to install VCB and use it with your third-party backup software.

Understanding VCB Backup Modes

VCB can operate in one of three backup modes:

- SAN Mode
- Hot-Add Mode
- LAN Mode

In *SAN Mode*, VCB uses a separate physical computer, known as the VCB proxy, to access SAN LUNs hosting VMFS datastores. All of the processing and I/O is offloaded from the ESX/ESXi hosts onto the VCB proxy computer. However, SAN Mode works only when you are using a Fibre Channel or iSCSI SAN.

In *Hot-Add Mode*, a VCB proxy is still required, but this time the VCB proxy is a virtual machine. This VCB proxy VM performs the actual backup process by using SCSI hot-add to add the virtual disks from other VMs for backup. The backup processing and I/O are not offloaded from the ESX/ESXi hosts, but backup traffic is kept off the LAN. This type of backup supports any form of supported storage, including Network Attached Storage (NAS) or local storage.

In *LAN Mode*, the VCB proxy uses an over-the-network protocol to access the virtual disks of other VMs for backup. This mode supports any type of supported storage. Backup processing and I/O are not offloaded from the ESX/ESXi hosts, and the LAN is used as the transport for moving the backup data.

Depending on which of these modes you wish to use, you must perform different steps to configure your environment and install VCB. The next few sections provide more information on the steps required to install VCB.

Configuring Windows for VCB

Before installing VCB, you must disable Windows Server's automount functionality. All versions of Windows, except the Enterprise and the Datacenter editions of Windows Server 2003 and Windows Server 2008, automatically assign drive letters to visible volumes. To prevent corruption of your VMFS volumes, you must disable this functionality.

This step is necessary for the VCB proxy regardless of the backup mode you choose to use.

WARNING   Be sure to disable automatic drive letter assignment *before* presenting VMFS LUNs to the VCB proxy server. Otherwise, you run the risk of corrupting your VMFS volumes and losing data.

To disable automatic drive letter assignment on the server that will serve as the VCB proxy, follow these steps:

1. Log in as a user with administrative privileges.

2. Open a command prompt and enter this command:

   diskpart

3. At the DISKPART> prompt, enter this command:

   automount disable

4. To clear any previously assigned drive letters, enter this command:

   automount scrub

5. Exit DiskPart by typing exit and pressing Enter.

After you have disabled automatic drive letter assignment, you are ready to proceed with configuring the storage area network, if necessary.

Configuring the Storage Area Network for VCB

If you want to use VCB to perform SAN mode backups, you must use a physical server for the VCB proxy server. This physical server must have Fibre Channel host bus adapters (HBAs) or iSCSI connectivity to the SAN, and you must configure the SAN so that the VCB proxy has access to the LUNs hosting VMFS datastores. The VCB proxy cannot back up virtual machines stored on VMFS datastores to which it does not have direct access.

Typically, this step involves zoning the SAN fabric (for a Fibre Channel SAN) and presenting the LUNs to the VCB proxy based on the Fibre Channel World Wide Name (WWN) or iSCSI Qualified Name (IQN).

Configuring Your
vSphere Environment

PART II

Once you have verified that the VCB proxy can "see" the same set of LUNs to which the ESX/ESXi hosts have access, you are ready to proceed with verifying network connectivity between the VCB proxy and other elements of the virtual infrastructure.

Note that this step—configuring the SAN—is not required if you are using VCB for hot-add or LAN mode backups.

Verifying Network Connectivity

The machine, physical or virtual, that will serve as the VCB proxy must have network connectivity to vCenter Server over TCP port 443. In addition, the VCB proxy must have network connectivity to your ESX/ESXi hosts over TCP port 902. You will need to verify that this connectivity exists.

This connectivity is required regardless of the backup mode in which VCB will operate.

Installing VCB

After you have disabled automatic drive letter assignment, configured the SAN (where necessary), and verified network connectivity to vCenter Server and the ESX/ESXi hosts, you are ready to install VCB.

Perform these steps to install the VCB framework on the computer that will serve as the VCB proxy:

1. Log in to the VCB proxy as a user with administrative privileges.

TIP The VMware VCB installation package is found on the VMware vCenter Installer DVD in the \VCB folder. You can also download VCB from the VMware website at www.vmware.com/downloads. The filename of the installation package on the DVD media for the General Availability (GA) release of VMware vSphere 4 is VMware-vcb-150805.exe, but newer versions might be available from VMware's website.

---

2. Double-click the VMware-vcb-XXXXXX.exe executable package.

3. Click Next to start the VMware Consolidated Backup Framework installation wizard.

4. Select the I Accept The Terms In The License Agreement radio button and click Next.

5. Click Next to accept the default installation location.

6. Click Install to start the actual installation process.

7. If you are prompted with a security alert while installing a device driver, click Yes to allow the driver to be installed.

8. Click Finish to complete the installation.

Congratulations! You've successfully configured the VCB proxy and your SAN and have installed the VCB framework. You're now ready to use VCB with your third-party backup product.

Using VCB with Your Third-Party Backup Product

VCB integrates with a number of third-party backup products. Some of these third-party backup products require you to install an additional piece of software, called an *integration module*, on the VCB proxy in order to work with the backup software. Some third-party backup products do not require an additional integration module.

Because each third-party backup product has its own unique requirements to integrate with VCB and its own unique procedures for backing up virtual machines with VCB, we can't provide any more detailed information on how to back up your virtual machines with VCB. Instead, we refer you to the documentation for your specific third-party backup solution to find complete details on integrating VCB into your backup strategy.

Configuring Your
vSphere Environment

PART II

9

Managing Virtual Machines

IN THIS CHAPTER, YOU WILL LEARN TO:

▶ **CREATE VIRTUAL MACHINES (Pages 274–285)**
- Create a New Virtual Machine (Page 274)
- Clone an Existing Virtual Machine (Page 278)
- Deploy a Virtual Machine from a Template (Page 281)
- Create a Template (Page 281)

▶ **MODIFY VIRTUAL MACHINES (Pages 285–294)**
- Reconfigure the Hardware of a Virtual Machine (Page 286)
- Add Hardware to a Virtual Machine (Page 289)
- Remove Hardware from a Virtual Machine (Page 293)

▶ **MANAGE VIRTUAL MACHINE HARDWARE VERSIONS (Pages 294–297)**
- Determine the Virtual Machine Hardware Version (Page 295)
- Upgrade Virtual Machine Hardware (Page 296)

▶ **PERFORM OTHER VIRTUAL MACHINE MANAGEMENT TASKS (Pages 297–303)**
- Change the Virtual Machine Power State (Page 297)
- Work with Virtual Machine Snapshots (Page 298)
- Install or Upgrade the VMware Tools (Page 302)

While installing VMware vSphere 4 from scratch (or upgrading VMware Infrastructure 3 to VMware vSphere 4) is important, managing virtual machines is perhaps even more important. After all, managing virtual machines is where most VMware vSphere administrators will spend their time. Naturally, vSphere 4 provides a full set of virtual machine management features to help you with these tasks.

Create Virtual Machines

Creating virtual machines is an essential and fundamental task for any vSphere administrator. Fortunately, the very nature of virtualization with VMware vSphere—such as the ability to quickly and easily create or modify virtual machines—means that making a mistake when creating a virtual machine is usually not a big deal. Still, it's important for you to understand the various ways of creating virtual machines, why each method is useful, and when to use each method.

For a vSphere administrator just getting started with VMware vSphere, the first step will generally be to create a new virtual machine from scratch. That process is described in the next section.

Create a New Virtual Machine

To streamline the creation of a new virtual machine, vCenter Server provides a wizard to walk you through the process. To invoke this wizard, right-click on a datacenter, cluster, host, or resource pool and select New Virtual Machine. This will invoke the Create New Virtual Machine wizard.

To create a new virtual machine after invoking the Create New Virtual Machine wizard, follow these steps:

1. At the first screen in the Create New Virtual Machine wizard, select Custom in order to see all the configuration options for a new virtual machine. Click Next.

2. Specify a name for the new virtual machine and select a location for the virtual machine in the inventory. The Inventory Location box shows the contents of the VMs And Templates inventory view within vCenter Server. Click Next.

3. Depending on the object selected when the wizard was invoked, the next screen prompts you to select a location where the virtual machine will run.

   - If you right-clicked on a datacenter to invoke the wizard, select a host or cluster on which to run this virtual machine.

   - If you right-clicked on a cluster to invoke the wizard and that cluster is configured for manual automation with VMware Distributed Resource Scheduler (DRS), the wizard prompts you to select a specific host within the cluster. This is also true when you right-click on a resource pool hosted in a cluster set for manual automation.

TIP   For clusters whose DRS automation level is set to Fully Automated, the user does not have to select a host on which to run the virtual machine. The placement of the virtual machine onto a host in the cluster happens automatically; this is called *intelligent placement*.

   - If the cluster has multiple resource pools, you are prompted to select the resource pool in which the virtual machine should reside. This is also true for parent resource pools with multiple child pools.

   Once you have selected the appropriate location for the new virtual machine, click Next.

4. Select the datastore where the virtual machine's virtual machine disk (VMDK) files should reside. After you have selected the desired datastore, click Next.

5. Select Virtual Machine Version 4 if the VMware environment also includes hosts running earlier versions of ESX/ESXi. You should also select Virtual Machine Version 4 if the virtual machine needs to be compatible with VMware Server 1.0. Otherwise, select Version 7. Click Next to continue.

6. Use the radio buttons to select the correct guest operating system family, and then use the drop-down list to select the specific version of that guest operating system. For example, if the guest will run 64-bit Windows Server 2008, select the Microsoft Windows radio button and choose Windows Server 2008 (64-Bit) from the drop-down list. Click Next to continue.

7. Choose the number of virtual CPUs (vCPUs) this virtual machine should have. Click Next to continue.

TIP Don't overprovision virtual machines. Assign only the resources that the virtual machine will need. It's easy to go back later and assign additional vCPUs or memory, should the applications within the virtual machine need those additional resources.

---

8. Select the amount of memory to be assigned to the virtual machine. Note that the slider bar provides some reference points, such as the minimum recommended amount, the default recommended amount, and the maximum recommended amount. After selecting the amount of memory to assign to the VM, click Next.

9. Choose how many virtual network interface cards (NICs) to assign to the virtual machine. For each NIC, select the appropriate adapter type, as shown in Figure 9.1. The E1000 adapter is the default for many guest operating systems and is supported by drivers supplied with many guest operating systems. Click Next to continue.

Figure 9.1: Each virtual network interface card must have a specific adapter type selected. The E1000 adapter type is compatible out of the box for many guest operating systems.

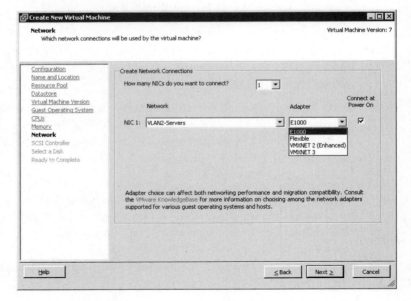

10. Select the appropriate SCSI controller for the guest operating system. Newer guest operating systems will support the LSI Logic SAS controller; otherwise, select the LSI Logic Parallel controller. Click Next to continue.

NOTE   The VMware Paravirtual controller is not supported for use with boot disks.

---

11. Select Create A New Virtual Disk, and then click Next.

12. Specify a size for the new virtual disk; then specify whether the disk should be thin provisioned or be configured to support features such as VMware Fault Tolerance. Note that thin provisioning and Fault Tolerance are mutually incompatible.

13. If the virtual disk should be stored in a different datastore than the virtual machine configuration files, select Specify A Datastore and choose the datastore where the virtual disk should be located. Otherwise, the default selection of Store With The Virtual Machine is fine. Click Next to proceed.

14. You can change the SCSI ID of the virtual disk in the Virtual Device Node section, but this is rarely changed during virtual machine creation. The default is SCSI 0:0.

15. You can also select to make the virtual disk an independent disk, which precludes the use of virtual machine snapshots. If a disk is configured to be an independent disk, you must select Persistent or Nonpersistent, which controls how changes to the virtual disk are managed. Click Next to continue.

16. Review the configuration listed. If everything is correct, click Finish to complete the creation of the new virtual machine. Otherwise, use the Back button to go back through the wizard and change settings where necessary.

The new virtual machine will appear in vSphere Client in the appropriate location. In the Hosts And Clusters inventory view, the virtual machine will appear in the cluster, host, or resource pool where it will run; in the VMs and Templates inventory view, it will appear in the datacenter or folder where it is stored.

Configuring Your
vSphere Environment

PART II

Creating new virtual machines from scratch is fine, but what if you need to create a new virtual machine that is the same as an existing virtual machine? In this instance, you have the option of using vCenter Server's cloning functionality, as described in the next section.

Clone an Existing Virtual Machine

vCenter Server offers you the ability to clone existing virtual machines in order to create new virtual machines. This ability makes it very easy for you to quickly create a number of virtual machines whose configuration is exactly the same. During the cloning process, vCenter Server clones not only the virtual machine configuration, but also the virtual machine's virtual hard disks. This makes the clone truly an exact copy of the original.

In many cases, though, you won't want exact copies of the original. Consider a virtual machine that already has an instance of Windows Server 2008 installed. Cloning that virtual machine to create an exact copy would also create an exact copy of the guest operating system, which would then create problems with duplicate IP addresses and duplicate network names. To work around this issue, vCenter Server lets you customize the cloned virtual machine and the guest operating system inside the cloned virtual machine.

NOTE Customizing the cloned virtual machine or the guest OS inside the cloned virtual machine isn't absolutely required. What if you wanted to use vCenter Server's cloning functionality to create a backup of a virtual machine? In that case, customization would defeat the purpose of using cloning.

Note that in order to customize virtual machines with a Windows-based guest operating system, you have to install Sysprep onto the vCenter Server computer. Specific instructions for how this is accomplished are provided in the document titled *ESX and vCenter Server Installation Guide*, publicly available in PDF from VMware's website at www.vmware.com/pdf/vsphere4/r40/vsp_40_esx_vc_installation_guide.pdf.

To clone an existing virtual machine, follow these steps:

1. In vSphere Client, navigate to either Hosts And Clusters inventory view or VMs And Templates inventory view.

2. Right-click the virtual machine that should serve as the original for the clone, and select Clone from the context menu. This launches the Clone Virtual Machine wizard.

NOTE   It is possible to clone running virtual machines, but generally you should only clone virtual machines that are powered off.

3. Specify a name for the cloned virtual machine and select a location in the inventory for the virtual machine to be placed. Click Next to continue.

4. Select the host or cluster on which the virtual machine should run. Click Next.

5. If you selected a cluster that either does not have VMware DRS enabled or has VMware DRS configured for manual automation, the wizard prompts you to select a specific host within the cluster. Select a host and click Next.

6. If multiple resource pools are available on the selected cluster or host, choose the correct resource pool and click Next.

7. Select the datastore where the virtual machine should be stored and click Next.

TIP   If the cloned virtual machine's virtual disk files should be stored separately from the virtual machine configuration files, use the Advanced button to specify different locations.

8. Select the format—Same Format As Source, Thin Provisioned Format, or Thick Format—for the cloned virtual machine's virtual disks. Click Next to continue.

9. If you want to leave the cloned virtual machine exactly the same as the original, select Do Not Customize. Otherwise, select Customize Using The Customization Wizard and click Next. If you have previously created a customization specification, select Customize Using An Existing Customization Specification.

NOTE   Steps 10 through 20 assume you are cloning a virtual machine with a Windows-based guest operating system. The steps are different for other guest operating systems.

10. Provide a name and organization, and then click Next.

11. Select Use The Virtual Machine Name and click Next.

12. Supply the product key for the Windows guest OS and select the correct server license mode. Click Next to continue.

13. Enter and confirm the password for the Administrator account, and then click Next.

14. Select a time zone and click Next.

15. If there are commands you want to run during the Sysprep process, enter them here; otherwise, just click Next.

16. Specify the network settings. It's generally best to select Typical Settings. Click Next to continue.

17. Specify whether the cloned virtual machine should join a workgroup or a domain, and supply credentials if joining a domain. Click Next.

18. Leave Generate A New Security ID (SID) selected and click Next.

19. If you would like to save the answers supplied so far in vSphere Client Windows Guest Customization wizard, supply a name and a description, and then click Next. Otherwise, uncheck Save This Customization Specification For Later Use.

20. Click Finish to complete the guest customization (not the cloning process).

21. Review the settings. If everything looks correct, click Finish to start the cloning process. Otherwise, use the Back button to go back and change settings as necessary.

vCenter Server will clone the virtual machine; you can track the progress of the cloning operation via the Tasks pane of vSphere Client. If you select Power On This Virtual Machine After Creation on the final screen of the Clone Virtual Machine wizard, vCenter Server will automatically power on the cloned VM and perform the customization. Otherwise, the customization will occur the first time the VM is powered on.

TIP Cloning virtual machines is most powerful and most useful when you clone virtual machines that already have the guest operating system installed. Use cloning and customization specifications to provide quick and easy cloning of virtual machines and entire guest operating systems.

In addition to cloning existing virtual machines, vCenter Server can deploy virtual machines by cloning them from a special object known as a *template*.

Deploy a Virtual Machine from a Template

vCenter Server can not only clone existing virtual machines but can also create new virtual machines by cloning a template. The next section, "Create a Template," provides more information on exactly what templates are and how they are created and managed. Once you have created a template, you can deploy new virtual machines based on that template easily and quickly in much the same fashion as cloning virtual machines. All the same benefits apply—the new virtual machine deployed from a template has the same hardware configuration, the same data on the virtual disks, the same identity, and so forth. vCenter Server can perform customization on the guest operating system just as when you clone existing virtual machines. Aside from the fact that this involves a template, the process is identical.

To deploy a virtual machine from a template, simply right-click the template and select Deploy Virtual Machine From This Template. This launches the Deploy Template wizard. The Deploy Template wizard follows the same steps outlined in the earlier section "Clone an Existing Virtual Machine," so refer back to those steps for more detailed information.

> **NOTE** Templates are only visible in the VMs And Templates inventory view.

Using templates instead of existing virtual machines to deploy new virtual machines does have some advantages, as discussed in the next section.

Create a Template

Since vCenter Server offers you the ability to clone virtual machines, why would you need a template? As with virtual machines, you can clone templates to create new virtual machines. Unlike virtual machines, templates cannot be powered on, and the configuration of a template cannot be modified. If you want to ensure that the base configuration being cloned is not modified or tampered with, marking the base virtual machine as a template will achieve that goal.

There are two ways to create a template:

- Convert an existing virtual machine to a template
- Clone an existing virtual machine to a template

Both of these operations are visible on the context menu of an existing virtual machine. While they accomplish the same task—creating a template—the process these two operations follow is very different, each with its own advantages and disadvantages. Converting an existing virtual machine to a template is the fastest, so that's the approach discussed first.

Convert an Existing Virtual Machine to a Template

To convert an existing virtual machine to a template, you only need to right-click a virtual machine and select Template ➢ Convert To Template. Figure 9.2 shows the option to convert a virtual machine to a template. That's all there is to it—just select the menu option, and the selected virtual machine will be marked as a template.

Figure 9.2: When a virtual machine is converted to a template, it will disappear from the Hosts And Clusters view and appear in the VMs And Templates view.

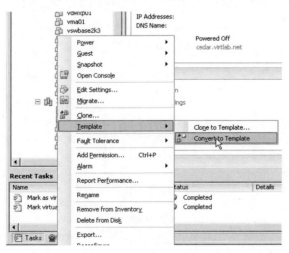

While it is marked as a template, the virtual machine's configuration cannot be modified, and the virtual machine cannot be powered on. Otherwise, the virtual machine's virtual disks are left intact and unchanged.

Because the virtual machine and its disks are left unchanged, you can also convert from a template back to a virtual machine. This is extremely useful because it allows you to convert a template to a VM, make configuration changes or install patches, and then convert it back to a template again.

To convert a template back into a virtual machine, follow these steps:

1. In vSphere Client, navigate to the VMs And Templates inventory view.

2. Right-click the template that should be converted back to a virtual machine and select Convert To Virtual Machine. This opens the Convert Template To Virtual Machine wizard.

3. Select a host or cluster to run the virtual machine and click Next.

4. If the cluster does not have VMware DRS enabled or VMware DRS is configured for manual automation, select a specific host within the cluster and select Next.

5. If the cluster has multiple resource pools, select a resource pool and click Next.

6. Review the settings. If everything is correct, click Finish; otherwise, use the Back button to go back and change settings as needed.

When you convert a template back into a virtual machine, the template will disappear from the VMs And Templates view and the virtual machine will appear in both the VMs and Templates view as well as the Hosts And Clusters view.

In the event—for whatever reason—you do not want to convert an existing virtual machine into a template, vCenter Server can also clone a VM into a template. This functionality is discussed in the next section.

Clone an Existing Virtual Machine to a Template

There may be situations in which you can't (or don't) want to convert a virtual machine into a template. In these cases, you can still take advantage of the benefits of templates by simply cloning the virtual machine to a new template. Thus, the existing virtual machine is left intact and untouched, but you gain the benefit of an unchangeable template for deploying new virtual machines.

To clone an existing virtual machine into a template, follow these steps:

1. In vSphere Client, navigate to either the Hosts And Clusters inventory view or the VMs And Templates inventory view.

2. Right-click the virtual machine that should be cloned to a template and select Template ➢ Clone To Template. This starts the Clone Virtual Machine To Template wizard.

3. Specify a name for the new template and select a location in the inventory. Keep in mind that the inventory view shown is the VMs And Templates inventory view.

4. Select a host or cluster on which to store this template, and then click Next.

5. If you selected a cluster that does not have VMware DRS enabled or has VMware DRS enabled but configured for manual automation, select a specific host within the cluster and select Next.

6. Select a datastore in which to store the template's files, and then click Next.

7. Choose a disk format—Same Format As Source, Thin Provisioned Format, or Thick Format—and click Next.

8. Review the settings. If everything is correct, click Finish to start the cloning process; otherwise, use the Back button to go back and change settings as necessary.

vCenter Server will clone the selected virtual machine into a new template according to the settings specified in the Clone Virtual Machine To Template wizard. Note that there was not an option for customizing the template; that's because the guest OS customization will take place when new virtual machines are deployed from this template. There is no need to perform customization when creating a template.

Along with creating templates to use for deploying new virtual machines, you have a number of other methods for creating virtual machines. This variety gives you a great deal of flexibility to use the method best suited for the need at hand.

Of course, creating virtual machines isn't the sum of what you need to do when it comes to virtual machines. Many times you have to modify virtual machines after they've been created. The next section covers modifying virtual machines.

Modify Virtual Machines

Knowing how to create virtual machines is certainly quite useful, but you also need to know how to modify existing virtual machines. There are many different reasons why an existing virtual machine might need to be modified:

- The application or applications within the virtual machine need more memory than was initially allocated to the virtual machine.

- You have to attach a virtual CD-ROM device to the virtual machine to install software or software updates.

- The virtual machine needs to be attached to a different network segment.

The procedure for many of these tasks is going to look similar. Aside from two specific instances, which are described in the next section, making any of these changes requires you to open the Virtual Machine Properties dialog box by right-clicking the virtual machine and selecting Edit Settings. Figure 9.3 shows the properties dialog box for a virtual machine.

Figure 9.3: The Virtual Machine Properties dialog box is the central point for modifying virtual machines.

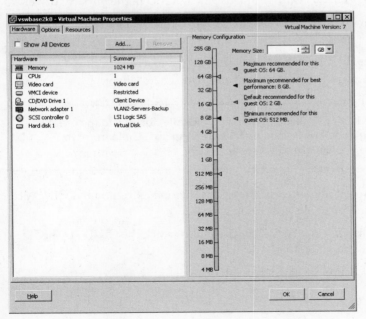

Sidebar: Configuring Your vSphere Environment

PART II

Reconfigure the Hardware of a Virtual Machine

Reconfiguring a virtual machine's hardware is a fairly broad task that could involve changing the amount of memory assigned to a VM; connecting or disconnecting a floppy drive, CD/DVD drive, or network card; or changing the disk controller type. This section describes how to perform three very common tasks:

- Attach or detach a CD/DVD drive
- Connect or disconnect a network interface card
- Change the network to which a network interface card connects

Attach or Detach a CD/DVD Drive

Working with virtual CD/DVD drives on virtual machines is an extremely common task. You will often need to gain access to a CD/DVD in order to install software or add components to the guest operating system. But where, exactly, is the CD/DVD drive for a virtual machine? That's a good question!

You have three options for getting access to a CD/DVD drive in a virtual machine:

- Map the CD/DVD drive in the virtual machine to the ESX/ESXi host's CD/DVD drive and use a CD/DVD in the physical drive.
- Map the CD/DVD drive in the virtual machine to an ISO file that is an image of the physical CD/DVD.
- Map the CD/DVD drive in the virtual machine to the CD/DVD drive on the client system running vSphere Client.

TIP Using ISO files provides the most flexibility and the greatest performance, but it does require creating an ISO file from the physical CD/DVD in some cases.

In all three situations, the process is the same. To mount a CD/DVD into a virtual machine, follow these steps:

1. Right-click the virtual machine into which the CD/DVD should be mounted and select Edit Settings.

2. Make sure the Hardware tab is selected.

3. From the list of hardware on the left, select CD/DVD Drive 1.

4. The next step depends on what method is used to map the CD/DVD into the virtual machine:

   - To map the CD/DVD to the physical CD/DVD in the system running vSphere Client, select the Client Device radio button. Note that the Connected and Connect At Power On options under Device Status will be disabled.

   - To map the CD/DVD to the physical CD/DVD in the ESX/ESXi host, select the Host Device radio button and then choose the correct host device from the drop-down list. Generally, /dev/scd0 is a valid option. If the VM is running, check the Connected check box to immediately connect the CD/DVD drive; otherwise, select Connect At Power On to have the CD/DVD drive connected when the VM powers on the next time.

   - To map the CD/DVD to an ISO image, select Datastore ISO File and then use the Browse button to navigate to an ISO image stored on a reachable datastore. To connect the CD/DVD drive immediately, select Connected; otherwise, select Connect At Power On to have the CD/DVD drive connected when the VM is next powered on.

5. Click OK to save the changes and return to vSphere Client.

VMware also provides a handy toolbar button to help streamline this task, as shown in Figure 9.4. This toolbar button provides easy access to the same options outlined previously.

Figure 9.4: This toolbar button provides quick access to connect or disconnect a CD/DVD drive.

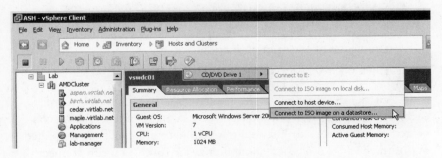

Configuring Your vSphere Environment

PART II

If you need to simply connect or disconnect a CD/DVD, just open the Virtual Machine Properties dialog box, select the CD/DVD drive, and then simply select the Connected check box. This toggles the connection state of the CD/DVD drive.

To boot a virtual machine from a CD/DVD, configure the drive as described previously and select Connect At Power On. The CD/DVD drive in the virtual machine will be connected when the VM is powered on and the VM will—if the CD/DVD is bootable—boot from the CD/DVD drive.

TIP   Best practices state that vSphere administrators should not leave CD/DVD drives connected in virtual machines. Remember to disconnect CD/DVD drives in virtual machines when they are not being used.

Connect or Disconnect a Network Interface Card

Connecting or disconnecting the virtual network interface card (NIC) in a virtual machine is analogous to inserting or removing the network cable from the back of a physical system. When the virtual NIC is connected, it's as if the virtual network cable is plugged in; when the virtual NIC is disconnected, the virtual network cable is unplugged.

To connect or disconnect a virtual NIC, follow these steps:

1. Open the Virtual Machine Properties dialog box by right-clicking on a virtual machine and selecting Edit Settings.

2. Select the Hardware tab.

3. From the list of hardware on the left, select the desired network interface card.

4. Select the Connected check box to toggle the value.

5. To ensure that the NIC starts up as connected, make sure the Connect At Power On option is checked.

6. Click OK to return to vSphere Client.

If a virtual machine has multiple virtual network interface cards, each of the virtual network interface cards can be independently connected or disconnected. Just as a physical network cable can be pulled out of the back of a physical computer at any time, you can connect or disconnect a virtual NIC at any time, whether the virtual machine is powered on or powered off.

Change the Network to Which a Network Interface Card Connects

In addition to connecting or disconnecting the virtual NIC, you may also need to change the network to which the virtual NIC connects. This process is similar to connecting or disconnecting the virtual NIC.

To change the network to which a virtual NIC connects, follow these steps:

1. Right-click the virtual machine whose virtual NIC should be changed and select Edit Settings.

2. Select the Hardware tab, and then select the virtual NIC from the list of hardware on the left.

3. From the Network Label drop-down list, select the desired network to which this virtual NIC should connect.

4. Click OK to save the changes and return to vSphere Client.

Although this changes the connection for that virtual NIC, you must still perform any necessary reconfiguration within the guest operating system. The reconfiguration within the guest operating system would include things like changing the assigned IP address, subnet mask, and default gateway.

The creation and configuration of the virtual networks to which the NICs connect is described in more detail in Chapter 6.

While it's not possible to describe all the various configuration tasks that you can perform on a virtual machine, these three examples provide an idea of how to reconfigure the hardware for a virtual machine. Most, if not all, of the other configuration tasks are performed in much the same manner as what we described earlier.

Related to reconfiguring hardware is adding hardware to a virtual machine. This process is described in the next section.

Add Hardware to a Virtual Machine

There may be instances where you need to do more than just reconfigure a virtual machine; you may have to add hardware. Perhaps the

Configuring Your vSphere Environment

PART II

applications running within the virtual machine need more memory, or perhaps the guest operating system is consistently using all the CPU cycles being given to it. Maybe more disk space is needed. In any case, you can quickly and easily add hardware to the virtual machine to address the need.

Only certain types of hardware can be added while a virtual machine is running. These include USB controllers, network adapters, virtual hard disks, and other SCSI devices. To add other types of hardware, you must first shut down the virtual machine.

NOTE   VMware vSphere does support a feature called *hot add*, where other types of hardware can be added while the guest operating system in a virtual machine is running. This feature is only supported for Windows Server 2008 and must be enabled before you can use it. Ironically, the virtual machine must be powered off in order to enable hot add.

As with reconfiguring virtual machine hardware, adding hardware to a virtual machine is generally similar regardless of the type of virtual hardware being added. The next few sections describe how to add a network adapter, a virtual disk, memory, or an additional CPU to a virtual machine.

Add a Network Adapter to a Virtual Machine

Network adapters, referred to as Ethernet adapters in vSphere Client user interface, can be added to a virtual machine when the virtual machine is running as well as when the virtual machine is powered off.

To add a network adapter to a virtual machine, follow these steps:

1. Right-click the virtual machine and select Edit Settings. This opens the Virtual Machine Properties dialog box.

2. Click Add. This opens the Add Hardware wizard.

3. Select Ethernet Adapter, and then click Next.

4. Under Adapter Type, select the type of network adapter to add to the virtual machine.

5. Under Network Connection, select Named Network With Specified Label; then use the drop-down to select the correct port group or distributed virtual port group.

6. Under Device Status, leave Connect At Power On selected. Click Next.

7. Review the settings. If everything is correct, click Finish. Otherwise, use the Back button to go back and change settings as needed.

8. In the Virtual Machine Properties dialog box, the new network adapter will be listed with a status of Adding. Click OK to commit the changes and return to vSphere Client.

Once the task in the Tasks pane completes, you must take steps in the guest operating system to recognize the new hardware (if the virtual machine is running). In Windows, for example, you should open Device Manager and scan for new hardware. This will allow the guest operating system to detect the new hardware and will give you the opportunity to configure the hardware appropriately.

Add a Virtual Hard Disk to a Virtual Machine

Like network adapters, virtual disks can be added to a virtual machine when the virtual machine is powered off or when it is powered on.

To add a virtual hard disk to a virtual machine, perform these steps:

1. Right-click the virtual machine and select Edit Settings. This opens the Virtual Machine Properties dialog box.

2. Click Add. This opens the Add Hardware wizard.

3. Select Hard Disk, and then click Next.

4. Select Create A New Virtual Disk, and then click Next.

TIP Administrators who simply need to add an existing virtual disk to a virtual machine can select the Use An Existing Virtual Disk option.

---

5. Under Capacity, specify a size for the new virtual disk.

6. Under Disk Provisioning, select options to use thin provisioning or to support Fault Tolerance. These options are mutually exclusive.

7. Under Location, leave the default option of Store With The Virtual Machine selected. Click Next.

8. Leave the Virtual Device Node at the default setting, unless you need the new virtual disk to have a separate SCSI controller. If a separate SCSI controller is needed, set the Virtual Device Node to SCSI (1:0). Be aware that you cannot add a new virtual disk to a new SCSI controller while the VM is running; you must power off the VM if you need a new SCSI controller added.

NOTE VMware's high-performance paravirtualized SCSI (PVSCSI) controller is not supported for boot disks. Therefore, setting the Virtual Device Node to SCSI (1:0) is the only way to add a second SCSI controller and take advantage of PVSCSI's performance benefits.

---

9. Under Mode, select whether the disk will be an independent disk and, if it is an independent disk, whether it will be a persistent disk or a nonpersistent disk. Click Next.

10. Click Finish if the settings are correct; otherwise, go back using the Back button and change settings as needed.

11. The new virtual disk (and new SCSI controller, if one is being added) will be listed in the Virtual Machine Properties dialog box with a status of Adding. Click OK to commit the changes and return to vSphere Client.

As with adding a new network adapter, you must perform some additional configuration within the guest operating system after vSphere Client has completed the addition of the new virtual disk. In Windows, for example, you must run the Disk Management console and select Action ➢ Rescan Disks. The new virtual disk should then appear and can be formatted as desired.

Add Memory to a Virtual Machine

Unlike network adapters and virtual disks, memory can only be added to a virtual machine when the virtual machine is powered off (although recall from earlier that there is limited support for hot-adding memory in specific configurations).

To add memory to a virtual machine, perform these steps:

1. Ensure that the virtual machine to which memory should be added is powered off. Shut down the virtual machine first, if necessary.

2. Right-click the virtual machine and select Edit Settings.

3. From the list of hardware on the left, select Memory.

4. Use the slider bar or the Memory Size box to specify the new memory setting for the virtual machine.

5. Click OK to commit the changes and return to vSphere Client.

Generally, no additional work is necessary in order for the guest operating system to recognize the additional memory when the virtual machine is booted after making this change.

TIP   If you previously specified a Memory Limit on the Resources tab, be sure to adjust that limit or the benefits of the additional memory won't be realized.

Add a CPU to a Virtual Machine

Like memory, virtual machines need to be powered off in order to add a virtual CPU (vCPU) to a virtual machine.

To add a vCPU to a virtual machine follow these steps:

1. Power off the virtual machine if it is not already powered off.

2. Right-click the virtual machine and select Edit Settings.

3. From the list of hardware on the left, select CPUs.

4. Chose the desired number of processors from the Number Of Virtual Processors drop-down box.

5. Click OK to save the changes and return to vSphere Client.

Depending on the guest operating system in the virtual machine, additional work might or might not be required in order to take advantage of the additional vCPU. Refer to the documentation for the particular guest operating system to know for sure.

Just like hardware must sometimes be added to a virtual machine, hardware must sometimes be removed from a virtual machine as well. Removing hardware is discussed in the next section.

Remove Hardware from a Virtual Machine

In general, the virtual machine needs to be powered off in order to remove hardware from the virtual machine. There are some exceptions, like network adapters and virtual disks, but otherwise the virtual machine should be powered off.

Once a virtual machine is powered off, opening the Virtual Machine Properties dialog box—by right-clicking on the virtual machine and selecting Edit Settings—allows you to remove hardware using the Remove button at the top of the window. Clearly, removing some types of virtual hardware will have a significant impact; if you remove the only virtual disk for a virtual machine, for example, it won't be able to boot.

There are few intricacies to removing some types of hardware:

- You can't remove SCSI controllers directly. Instead, you must remove all the virtual disks or SCSI devices attached to those controllers, and vSphere will remove the controllers automatically.

- You can't "remove" memory. Instead, you need to lower the amount of memory assigned to the virtual machine using the slider. The same goes for vCPUs.

- The video card cannot be removed.

Aside from these exceptions, removing hardware is usually as straightforward as selecting the hardware item and clicking the Remove button. The item will be marked in strikethrough text with a status of Removed. Once you click OK to commit the changes, the hardware will be removed from the virtual machine.

You should now have a solid understanding of how to control the hardware of a virtual machine. The next section discusses another aspect of virtual machine hardware: the virtual machine version.

Manage Virtual Machine Hardware Versions

As VMware's virtualization products have evolved, so too have the capabilities of the virtual machines running on them. As VMware has introduced new versions of some of their products, VMware has also introduced a new virtual machine hardware version. With the release of VMware vSphere, VMware adds support for version 7 of the virtual machine hardware in their server virtualization product suite; this virtual hardware version provides support for the new functionality offered by VMware vSphere.

NOTE   Virtual machine hardware version 7 was actually first introduced in VMware Workstation 6.5.

As discussed in the section "Create Virtual Machines," vCenter Server prompts you to select either version 7 or an earlier version, version 4, that is compatible with previous versions of VMware's products. In most cases, you won't need to worry too much about virtual machine hardware versions. There are really only two instances in which the virtual machine hardware version becomes important:

- After an upgrade from VMware Infrastructure 3 to VMware vSphere 4
- When maintaining a mixed environment running both VMware Infrastructure 3 and VMware vSphere 4

NOTE   The virtual machine hardware version is also important when you are importing and exporting virtual machines to or from other VMware virtualization platforms. In those cases, however, the import or export process—typically handled by VMware Converter—takes care of the virtual machine hardware version.

In these situations, the two tasks that you need to know how to perform are determining the virtual machine hardware version and upgrading the virtual machine hardware. These tasks are described in the following sections.

Determine the Virtual Machine Hardware Version

You will need to know how to determine the virtual machine hardware version of a particular virtual machine. vCenter Server provides an easy and straightforward way of determining the current virtual machine hardware version.

To view the current hardware version for a virtual machine, simply right-click the virtual machine and select Edit Settings. In the upper-right corner of the dialog box the current hardware version is displayed, as shown in Figure 9.5.

TIP   The hardware version is also found in the virtual machine's configuration (VMX) file as the virtualHW.version directive.

Configuring Your vSphere Environment

PART II

Figure 9.5: vCenter Server displays the hardware version for virtual machines.

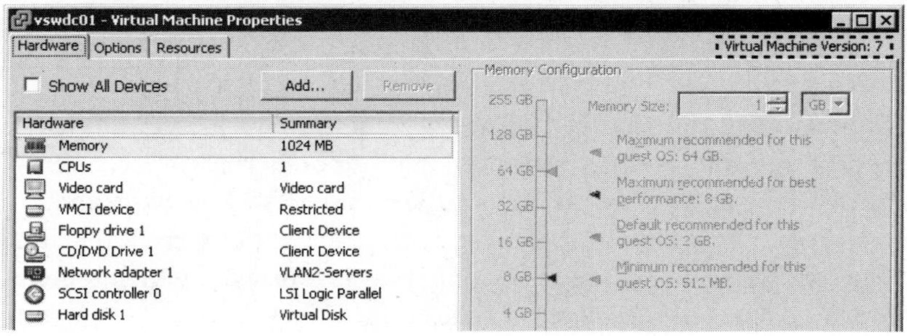

Why is knowing the hardware version of a virtual machine important? Some features of VMware vSphere are not supported with Virtual Machine Version 4, including:

- Incremental backups when using VMware Data Recovery, VMware's new backup product

- Support for hot-plug virtual hardware

- VMware Fault Tolerance

- New high-performance network (VMXNET3) and storage (PVSCSI) devices

- Support for more than four virtual CPUs (vCPUs)

If a virtual machine has not been created as Virtual Machine Version 7 or has not been upgraded to Virtual Machine Version 7, that virtual machine cannot take advantage of these new features. Fortunately, there is a virtual machine hardware upgrade process that allows you to convert Version 4 VMs to Version 7 VMs, and that process is described in the next section.

Upgrade Virtual Machine Hardware

If you need to use a new feature of VMware vSphere that requires Virtual Machine Version 7, you can upgrade the virtual machine to the new version.

WARNING Before upgrading the virtual machine hardware, you should install the latest version of the VMwareTools, as described later in this chapter in the section "Install or Upgrade the VMware Tools."

To upgrade a virtual machine to Version 7, follow these steps:

1. Shut down the virtual machine. The virtual machine version cannot be upgraded when the virtual machine is powered on.

2. Right-click the virtual machine and select Upgrade Virtual Hardware.

3. Click Yes in the Confirm Virtual Machine Upgrade dialog box.

4. If the virtual machine is not running the latest version of the VMware Tools, a question will appear on the Summary tab of the virtual machine informing you that the virtual machine's network device will lose its configuration if you proceed with the upgrade. This message does not appear if the latest version of the VMware Tools is installed in the virtual machine.

Upon next boot, the guest operating system in the virtual machine might detect new hardware as a result of the virtual machine version upgrade, and in some cases might indicate that a reboot is necessary in order to work properly. Once such reboots have been completed, the virtual machine is ready to take advantage of VMware vSphere–specific features, like VMware Fault Tolerance.

In addition to creating virtual machines, managing and modifying virtual machines, and upgrading virtual machine versions, there are a number of other virtual machine management tasks with which you should be familiar. The next section discusses these additional management tasks.

Perform Other Virtual Machine Management Tasks

vCenter Server also provides a range of other virtual machine–related management tasks that you might be called upon to perform. These tasks are described in this section.

Change the Virtual Machine Power State

Turning on a physical server is easy—just push the power button. But where is the power button for a virtual server? And are there different options for managing the power state of a virtual machine?

Indeed there are different options for managing a VM's power state, and they are found on the context menu for a virtual machine, on the Power submenu:

Power On   As the name implies, this option applies power to the virtual machine.

Power Off   This option removes power from the virtual machine. It can be considered the equivalent of pulling the power plug out of the back of the virtual machine—the guest operating system is not shut down in an orderly fashion.

Suspend   This option suspends the virtual machine. The virtual machine can be resumed quickly and will not require a cold boot; instead, the VM resumes right where it left off when it was suspended. Depending on the Power Management setting on the Options tab of the virtual machine properties, this option might or might not use the guest operating system's suspend functionality.

Reset   Resets the virtual machine, as if the hardware reset button had been pushed. The guest operating system does not perform an orderly shutdown and restart, so there is a possibility of data loss or data corruption.

Shut Down Guest   This option is only available when the virtual machine is running the VMware Tools. This option initiates an orderly shutdown of the guest operating system and then turns off the power to the virtual machine.

Restart Guest   Also relying on the presence of the VMware Tools, this option initiates a restart of the guest operating system.

In general, you should use the Shut Down Guest option to initiate orderly shutdowns of the guest operating system. Otherwise, you run the risk of data corruption, file system damage, application failure, and potential data loss.

Work with Virtual Machine Snapshots

VMware vSphere's snapshots feature is a great way of providing an extra layer of protection when you need the ability to "roll back" to a previous virtual machine state. For example, you can take a snapshot of a virtual machine before upgrading the software in the virtual machine. If a problem occurs with the upgrade, you can revert to the snapshot and be back where you were before starting the upgrade. It is truly quite a powerful ability.

However, snapshots are not backups, and should not be used as backups. The files associated with snapshots will grow in size over time and can, in certain instances, fill your datastores. Full datastores will then cause all sorts of other problems. You should plan on using snapshots to provide the short-term ability to undo changes within a virtual machine, such as a guest operating system upgrade, installation of a patch or service pack, or application upgrade.

Working with snapshots involves three basic tasks:

- Taking (or creating) a snapshot

- Deleting a snapshot

- Reverting to a snapshot

These tasks are described in the next three sections.

Taking a Snapshot

To take a snapshot of a virtual machine, follow these steps:

1. Right-click a virtual machine and select Snapshot ➤ Take Snapshot. This opens the Take Virtual Machine Snapshot dialog box.

2. Supply a name for this snapshot.

3. Enter a description of the snapshot. Ideally, this description should provide an idea of the state of the virtual machine at the time of the snapshot.

4. To include the virtual machine's memory in the snapshot, leave the Snapshot The Virtual Machine's Memory option selected.

5. Select Quiesce Guest File System (Needs VMware Tools Installed) if the file system of the guest operating system should be quiesced before the snapshot is taken. This can help improve the consistency of the snapshot by flushing data to the virtual disks before the snapshot is taken.

6. Click OK to take the snapshot.

The Tasks pane in vSphere Client shows the progress of the snapshot creation. Depending on the amount of memory assigned to the virtual machine, the snapshot creation may take a few moments.

Once the snapshot is in place, additional files are created in the virtual machine's datastore, as shown in Figure 9.6.

Figure 9.6: Snapshots create additional files in the virtual machine's datastore.

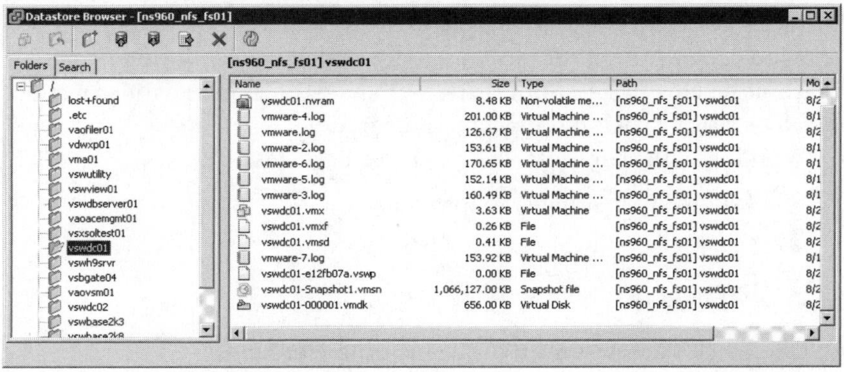

As additional snapshots are taken, additional files are created for each snapshot. To remove these files safely, you must delete the snapshot, as described in the next section.

TIP   Snapshots can grow very large over time—up to the size of the virtual machine's virtual disks plus a small amount. If free space in the datastore is a concern, do not allow snapshot files to remain for a very long time. Otherwise, the datastore could fill up and cause a number of other problems.

Deleting a Snapshot

You can delete snapshots from within the Snapshot Manager dialog box. To access the Snapshot Manager dialog box, click the toolbar button or right-click the virtual machine and select Snapshots ➤ Snapshot Manager.

In the Snapshot Manager dialog box—the title bar reads "Snapshots for *VirtualMachineName*"—simply select the snapshot to delete and click Delete. A dialog box will appear asking for confirmation, and then the snapshot is deleted. Depending on the size of the snapshot, the deletion may take some time. A task in the Tasks pane helps you gauge the progress of the operation.

So what happens to the changes stored in the snapshot when the snapshot is deleted? The answer to that question depends on whether the snapshot you are deleting is the active snapshot.

Figure 9.7 shows the Snapshot Manager dialog box. As you can see, this virtual machine has two snapshots. The snapshot named Snapshot Number 1 is active, as indicated by the fact that the "You are here" marker is after this snapshot (so changes made while this snapshot is active will be written to this snapshot). The snapshot named Snapshot Number 2 is not active. When you delete an active snapshot, the changes are committed to the base disk. When you delete an inactive snapshot, the changes are discarded and cannot be recovered.

Figure 9.7: Deleting a snapshot has different results depending on whether or not the snapshot is active.

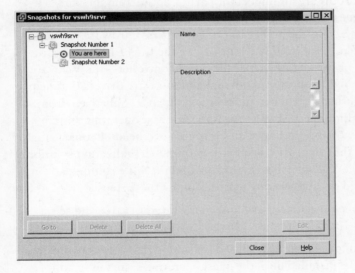

Moving back and forth between snapshots is done using to Go To button, which is described in more detail in the next section.

Reverting to a Snapshot

Reverting to a snapshot is also done from within the Snapshot Manager dialog box. Select the snapshot to which to revert and click Go To. A dialog box appears, informing you that the current state of the virtual machine will be lost unless it has been saved in a snapshot. Click Yes to proceed with reverting to the selected snapshot.

Keep in mind that any changes made to a virtual machine after a snapshot is taken are lost when you revert to an earlier snapshot. Refer back to Figure 9.7. If the "You are here" marker was after Snapshot Number 2 and you chose to revert to Snapshot Number 1, all changes made after Snapshot Number 2 was taken would be lost and could not be recovered.

Besides snapshots, another task that you must handle is making sure that the VMware Tools are installed and kept up-to-date on all the virtual machines in the environment. The next section discusses installing and upgrading the VMware Tools.

Install or Upgrade the VMware Tools

The VMware Tools are an important part of optimizing the performance of guest operating systems in virtual machines. Although VMware vSphere has the ability to present generic hardware to guest operating systems in virtual machines—like the Intel E1000 network interface card or the LSI Logic parallel SCSI controller—the VMware Tools contain highly optimized, virtualization-aware drivers that help the guest operating system run more efficiently in a vSphere environment. By installing the VMware Tools in the guest operating system, you can reduce the performance and resource overhead of your virtual machines and thus improve the efficiency of the virtualization solution.

To install the VMware Tools into a virtual machine running a Windows-based guest operating system, follow these steps:

1. Right-click the virtual machine in the inventory tree and select Guest ➤ Install/Upgrade VMware Tools.

2. A warning message is displayed indicating that the VMware Tools cannot be installed until the guest operating system is installed. Click OK.

3. An AutoPlay dialog box appears, prompting you for action. Select the option Run Setup.exe. If the VMware Tools installation process does not begin automatically, open Windows Explorer and double-click the CD/DVD drive icon. The VMware Tools installation should then launch.

4. Click Next on the VMware Tools installation wizard welcome page.

5. Select the appropriate setup type for the VMware Tools installation and click Next. The Typical radio button will suffice for most

situations. The Complete installation option installs more features than are used by the current product, while the Custom installation option allows for the greatest level of feature customization.

6. Click Install.

7. Once the installation is complete, click Finish.

8. Click Yes to restart the virtual machine immediately or click No to manually restart the virtual machine at a later time.

NOTE Instructions for installing the VMware Tools into other guest operating systems are not included here because of the differences that occur between the various guest operating systems. Refer to Scott Lowe's *Mastering VMware vSphere 4* (Sybex, 2009) for more information on how to install the VMware Tools into other guest operating systems.

Once the VMware Tools are installed, upgrades to the VMware Tools are only necessary when the ESX/ESXi hosts are patched or upgraded. Virtual machines running a Windows-based guest operating system can upgrade VMware Tools in an unattended fashion. When you choose Guest ➤ Install/Upgrade VMware Tools, the VMware Tools will install and then the virtual machine will reboot automatically. For other guest operating systems, upgrading the VMware Tools is generally the same as installing the VMware Tools.

Note that the presence of the VMware Tools running in the guest operating system is a prerequisite for a number of features within VMware vSphere. VM Monitoring, for example, relies on the VMware Tools. The Power ➤ Shut Down Guest command relies on the VMware Tools. The information displayed in vCenter Server on the Summary tab of a virtual machine relies, to a certain extent, on the VMware Tools. You are strongly encouraged to make installing the VMware Tools a mandatory part of every virtual machine build.

NOTE Another virtual machine management task includes enabling or disabling VMware Fault Tolerance (FT). VMware FT is enabled or disabled on a per-VM basis and allows you to provide High Availability to virtual machines. This feature, as well as how to enable or disable it, is described in detail in Chapter 8.

Configuring Your vSphere Environment

PART II

10

Importing and Exporting Virtual Machines

Virtualized infrastructures built using VMware vSphere exist to run virtual machines (VMs). In addition to creating those virtual machines from scratch, administrators also have the option of importing machines into the environment. These VMs can also, should the need arise, be exported out of the environment. This chapter discusses how to import and export virtual machines.

Understand the Migration Process

Migrating systems, whether they are physical systems or virtual systems, into a VMware vSphere environment is a key task that virtually every vSphere administrator will need to perform at some point in his or her career. While VMware has gone to great lengths to make this migration process as easy as possible, it is still important for vSphere administrators to understand the types of migrations that are possible and the components that are involved in these migrations.

Understand the Types of Migrations

When it comes to importing or exporting virtual machines, there are two basic types of migrations you will encounter:

- Physical-to-virtual (P2V) migrations
- Virtual-to-virtual (V2V) migrations

A *physical-to-virtual (P2V) migration* involves importing an instance of an operating system running on a physical system into VMware vSphere and placing that operating system instance onto a corresponding virtual machine. Because this procedure is what brings existing workloads into your virtualization installation, it's a key task for establishing or expanding your VMware vSphere environment.

A *virtual-to-virtual (V2V) migration* involves importing or exporting virtual machines. You might perform a V2V migration to import virtual machines from a competing virtualization solution, or even a different VMware platform. Similarly, you might perform a V2V migration to export an existing VMware vSphere virtual machine to run on a different VMware platform. Finally, you might even use a V2V migration to reconfigure an existing virtual machine, as you'll see later in this chapter.

NOTE There is also a third type of migration, but it is rarely used: a virtual-to-physical (V2P) migration. VMware doesn't provide any tools for performing a V2P, so administrators who need to perform a V2P migration will have to find and acquire third-party tools.

Within these two basic types of migrations, there are two different ways of performing the actual migration. You can perform:

- A *hot migration*, in which the source system (physical or virtual) is running and active while the migration is being performed.

- A *cold migration*, in which the source system (physical or virtual) is shut down and inactive while the migration is being performed.

Physical-to-virtual migrations might be either hot or cold migrations, but most virtual-to-virtual migrations will be cold migrations.

In addition to understanding the types of migrations you might perform as a VMware vSphere administrator, you must also understand the various components involved in performing these migrations. Depending upon the type of migration, different components might be involved.

Review the Components in a Migration

To import virtual machines into or export virtual machines out of a VMware vSphere environment, a number of components are required.

vCenter Converter

VMware vCenter Converter is central to all the different types of migrations you might perform. You would typically install vCenter Converter on the same system as VMware vCenter Server, although you can install it on a separate computer that has access to vCenter Server. VMware designed vCenter Converter to operate in conjunction with vCenter Server, so vCenter Converter requires a running instance of vCenter Server in order to function.

NOTE vCenter Converter communicates with vCenter Server over TCP port 443, which is the port for Hypertext Transfer Protocol (HTTP) over Secure Sockets Layer (SSL).

Configuring Your
vSphere Environment

PART II

vCenter Converter Plug-In

Because VMware designed vCenter Converter to integrate fully with vCenter Server, vCenter Converter also requires vSphere Client. vCenter Converter uses a vSphere Client plug-in to integrate with vSphere Client so that all vCenter Converter operations are triggered and managed from within vSphere Client. As with all other vSphere Client plug-ins, you must install this plug-in separately for every instance of vSphere Client running in your environment.

vCenter Converter Agent

To perform a hot migration, vCenter Converter uses a piece of software on the source system (physical or virtual) called the vCenter Converter Agent. This software installs on the source system and assists in the process of migrating the source system while the operating system instance on that source system is still running.

vCenter Converter Boot CD

In the event that performing a hot migration is not an option, you can use the vCenter Converter Boot CD to boot the source system and perform a cold migration. Some older operating system versions and some applications might be incompatible with hot migrations, so performing a cold migration would be the only way to get these source systems into your VMware vSphere environment.

Now that you have an idea of the types of migrations and the components involved in these migrations, I'll discuss in more detail the process for performing a physical-to-virtual migration to import a physical system into your VMware vSphere environment.

NOTE There is also a standalone version of VMware Converter that does not integrate with vCenter Server or vSphere Client. The standalone version of VMware Converter must be downloaded and installed separately but has the advantage of being independent of vSphere Client.

Perform a Physical-to-Virtual Migration

Importing physical systems into VMware vSphere is a core task that is fundamental to almost every VMware vSphere environment. Unless you are a vSphere administrator who is building the entire IT infrastructure from scratch, you will have physical systems that need to be imported into the virtualization solution. Performing a physical-to-virtual migration is how you will go about bringing those physical systems into your VMware vSphere installation.

A physical-to-virtual migration might be a *hot migration*, in which the source system is running while the migration is occurring, or a *cold migration*, in which the source system is unavailable while the migration is occurring. While the two types of migrations do share some similarities, I'll discuss each of them separately in the following sections.

Perform a Hot Migration

A hot migration, as explained earlier, is a migration that occurs while the source system is running. Hot migrations are supported for systems running Windows 2000 or later, several versions of Red Hat Enterprise Linux, several versions of SUSE Linux Enterprise Server, and several versions of Ubuntu.

vCenter Converter accomplishes a hot migration by installing an agent, the vCenter Converter Agent, onto the source system. This agent enables the physical-to-virtual migration by allowing vCenter Converter to read data out of the source system while it is still running. Without the agent, a hot migration would not be possible.

To perform a hot migration of a system running Windows Server 2003 R2, follow these steps:

1. Launch vSphere Client and connect to an instance of vCenter Server.

2. Right-click a cluster, host, or resource pool and select Import Machine.

3. Click Next to select a source for the import.

4. Choose Physical Computer, then click Next.

5. Supply the IP address or fully qualified domain name (FQDN) of the source system and administrative credentials for the source

system. Be sure to use the DOMAIN\username format if a domain is present. Click Next to continue.

6. When prompted about installing the vCenter Converter Agent on the source system, select Automatically Uninstall The Files When Import Succeeds, then click Yes.

7. If you would like to resize volumes during the import process, you can do so here (Figure 9.1). Specify a new size for each of the volumes or, to maintain the size, leave the size the same as the current size. Click Next when you are ready to continue.

Figure 9.1: When importing volumes, vCenter Converter offers options to selectively import certain volumes, to change the size of volumes, and to ignore the page file.

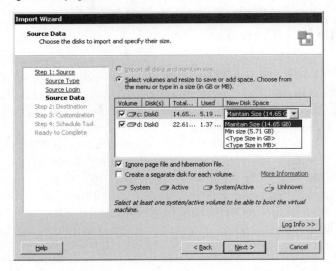

8. Click Next to select a destination for the source system.

9. Specify a name for the new virtual machine and pick a location in the virtual machine inventory where you want to store the new virtual machine. Click Next.

10. If you selected a cluster or a resource pool in a cluster when you initiated the import process, the Import Wizard will prompt you to select a specific host on which the new virtual machine should run. After selecting a specific host, click Next.

11. Select the datastore where you would like the virtual machine's virtual hard disks created and stored. Use the Advanced button to place the virtual machine hard disk files in separate datastores. Click Next to continue.

12. Check the boxes marked Remove All System Restore Checkpoints (Recommended) and Install VMware Tools. Generally, you will not want to customize the system, since the destination virtual machine should be an exact copy of the source system. Click Next.

13. To start the physical-to-virtual migration immediately, click Next. Otherwise, select the Schedule Later radio button and specify a schedule for the migration.

14. Review the settings for the migration. If everything is correct click Finish; otherwise, click Back as necessary to make changes.

vCenter Converter will create an active task for the conversion; you can use the Tasks pane in vSphere Client to track the progress of the physical-to-virtual migration. When the migration is complete, you can start using the new virtual machine.

Configuring Your vSphere Environment

PART II

NOTE   Since the newly created virtual machine is an exact copy of the physical source system, you must first shut down the physical source system before powering on the destination virtual machine. This will result in a small amount of downtime when the applications on that system will not be available. Be sure to plan for this downtime when conducting physical-to-virtual migrations in your environment.

I do recommend some post-conversion clean-up tasks once the physical-to-virtual migration is complete. Refer to the section titled "Clean Up After a Migration" for more information.

Perform a Cold Migration

In the event you can't perform a hot migration, you can instead use a cold migration. With a cold migration, you use a boot CD to boot up the source system. The boot CD communicates with vCenter Converter and reads the data from the source system.

There are a number of reasons why you might want to perform a cold migration instead of a hot migration:

- The source system may have applications installed on it that might not be compatible with a hot migration. Microsoft Windows Active Directory domain controllers are one example.

- You might not want users or other systems to be able to access the source system while it is being converted.

- You don't want the vCenter Converter Agent installed into the source operating system for change control or other organizational reasons.

VMware provides an .iso file that contains the boot CD image. Before starting a cold migration of a physical system, you will need to burn that .iso image to a physical CD.

To perform a cold migration of a physical source system, follow these steps:

1. Boot the source system from the CD you created with the vCenter Converter cold clone .iso file. You may need to modify the system so that it boots from the CD instead of from any local hard drives.

2. Press any key to boot the system from the CD.

3. When prompted, select the radio button labeled I Accept The Terms In The License Agreement and click OK.

4. If you are not using Dynamic Host Configuration Protocol (DHCP) or if you need to manually adjust the network configuration, click Yes when asked if you want to update the network parameters.

5. If you chose to update network parameters, click OK after you have updated the network configuration as necessary.

6. When the VMware vCenter Converter window opens, click the Import Machine button in the toolbar. This launches the Import Wizard.

7. At the Source screen of the Import Wizard, click Next.

8. If you want to maintain the size of the disks on the source system, select Import All Disks and Maintain Size. Otherwise, select Select Volumes and Resize To Save Or Add Space and specify a new size for the volume listed. Click Next when you are ready to proceed.

9. Select vSphere Virtual Machine as the destination, then click Next.

10. Provide the name or IP address of the vCenter Server and appropriate authentication information for that instance of vCenter Server. Click Next to continue.

11. Specify a name for the virtual machine and select a location in the virtual machine inventory where you would like to place the destination virtual machine. Click Next.

12. Select the host, cluster, or resource pool where you want the destination virtual machine to run. If you select a cluster or a resource pool within a cluster, you must also select a destination host on which to run the virtual machine.

13. Select the datastore where you would like to place the virtual machine disk files for the destination virtual machine. Use the Advanced button to place files in separate datastores. Click Next to proceed.

14. Specify the number of network interfaces for the destination virtual machine and the networks to which those interfaces should connect, then click Next.

15. Select Install VMware Tools and Remove All System Checkpoints (Recommended), then click Next. Because you will typically want the destination virtual machine to be an exact copy of the source system, you won't select the check box to customize the system.

16. Review the settings for the migration. If everything is correct, click Finish. Otherwise, use the Back button to go back and change settings as necessary.

A task appears in the VMware vCenter Converter window that shows the progress of the cold migration. After the migration completes, you can shut down the source system and power on the destination virtual machine. I do recommend performing a few post-migration clean-up tasks after the migration is complete; I describe some of these configuration changes in the next section.

Clean Up After a Migration

After you have completed a physical-to-virtual migration and the physical source system has been imported and re-created as a virtual machine on VMware vSphere, there are some additional clean-up tasks you should perform. These tasks are necessary because the migration process, by its very nature, creates an identical copy of the operating system instance in a VM as it was on the source physical system. However, the virtual machine is not the same as the source physical system—it has different hardware than the source physical system. To help optimize the performance of the operating system instance after the import has completed, you should remove unnecessary and missing hardware entries.

On a Windows-based system, you'll first need to tell Windows to show you missing hardware entries in Device Manager. Follow these steps to configure Windows to show missing hardware entries:

1. Log on to the new Windows-based virtual machine with an account that has administrative privileges.

2. Right-click on My Computer and select Properties. If My Computer is not showing on the Desktop, use the Start Menu to open Control Panel, then double-click the System icon.

3. Click the Advanced tab.

4. Click the Environment Variables button.

5. At the bottom of the Environment Variables dialog box in the section marked System Variables, click the New button.

6. For Variable Name, specify DEVMGR_SHOW_NONPRESENT_DEVICES.

7. For Variable Value, specify 1.

8. Click OK to create the new system environment variable and return to the Environment Variables dialog box. The new system environment variable will be listed at the bottom of the dialog box.

9. Click OK to return to the System Properties dialog box.

10. Click OK to return to the Windows desktop.

Once you've completed these steps, you can use Device Manager to remove drivers and entries for hardware that is no longer present in the virtual machine after the physical-to-virtual conversion.

To remove references to missing hardware using Device Manager, follow these steps:

1. Log on to the new Windows-based virtual machine with an account that has administrative privileges.

2. Right-click on My Computer and select Properties. If My Computer is not showing on the Desktop, use the Start Menu to open Control Panel, then double-click the System icon.

3. Click the Hardware tab.

4. Click the Device Manager button.

5. Within the Device Manager console, select View > Show Hidden Devices.

6. Navigate the Device Manager tree to remove missing hardware entries. These are noted with a dimmed icon in the list, as shown in Figure 9.2.

Figure 9.2: This screenshot shows the dimmed icon for the VMware PVSCSI controller, indicating that the hardware is no longer present in the virtual machine.

In addition, you will want to ensure that you have properly "right-sized" the new virtual machine for its needs. The physical-to-virtual migration process simply re-creates an identical virtual machine. You might need to adjust the memory configuration or the number of virtual CPUs to ensure that the new virtual machine is optimally configured.

Of course, not all physical-to-virtual migrations go perfectly smoothly, and there might be migrations that fail. In the next section I'll provide some information on troubleshooting physical-to-virtual migrations.

Troubleshoot Physical-to-Virtual Migrations

A number of factors can contribute to problems with physical-to-virtual migrations. Insufficient memory on the source system, lack of free disk space on the source system, unrecognized hardware, missing or damaged drivers on the source system, and file system errors are all possible candidates as the root cause for a failed physical-to-virtual migration.

To help ensure successful migrations, use some of the following guidelines:

- Perform file system maintenance on the source system. Clean up files, free up disk space, defrag, and run Chkdsk (or fsck) to ensure the file system is consistent. You'll want to confirm that the source has at least 200MB free on the system volume.

- When performing a hot migration, shut down all unnecessary services.

- Avoid converting diagnostic or utility partitions.

- Ensure that you have the proper network connectivity between the source system and the destination vCenter Server system or ESX/ESXi hosts. TCP ports 443 and 902 should be open.

Perform a Virtual-to-Virtual Migration

Unlike physical-to-virtual migrations—which, by their very nature, involve importing systems into a VMware vSphere environment—virtual-to-virtual migrations might involve either importing or exporting virtual machines. Also unlike physical-to-virtual migrations, almost all virtual-to-virtual migrations are cold migrations; the source virtual machine will have to be powered off in order to perform the migration.

TIP In the event you can't afford the downtime of a virtual machine in order to perform a virtual-to-virtual migration, just treat the source virtual machine like a physical system. Install the vCenter Converter Agent on the source virtual machine and perform the equivalent of a physical-to-virtual hot migration.

Virtual-to-virtual migrations are typically used in a few different instances:

- To export a virtual machine from VMware vSphere to run on a different VMware platform, like VMware Workstation or VMware Fusion

- To import a virtual machine currently running on another VMware platform, such as VMware Workstation or VMware Server, into VMware vSphere

- To reconfigure an existing VMware vSphere virtual machine by resizing its virtual machine disks

- To import a virtual machine currently configured for a competing virtualization solution, such as Microsoft Virtual Server

Try not to let the term "virtual-to-virtual" confuse you too much; you can use vCenter Converter in this sort of mode to do quite a few things. In the next few sections, I'll look at the most common uses of vCenter Converter for manipulating virtual machines.

Migrate to or from a Different VMware Platform

VMware vSphere is not VMware's only virtualization platform. VMware has a number of other virtualization platforms, like VMware Workstation, VMware Server, or VMware Fusion. While these products share a great deal of commonality with VMware vSphere, there are enough differences that VMs created on one platform might not run on another platform without modification. For example, VMware vSphere VMs can use virtual machine hardware version 7, but VMs on VMware Workstation 6.0 use virtual machine hardware version 6. Without modification to the VM, a virtual machine created on VMware vSphere won't run on VMware Workstation 6.0.

Fortunately, vCenter Converter can perform a virtual-to-virtual migration to resolve this issue. You can use VMware Converter to import VMs created on another VMware virtualization platform and to export VMs created on VMware vSphere so they will run on a different VMware virtualization platform. I describe the process to import and export VMs using vCenter Converter in the next two sections.

Import VMs from a Different VMware Platform

If you have virtual machines created using a different VMware virtualization platform but you want to run those virtual machines on VMware vSphere 4, you can use vCenter Converter to import the virtual machine and perform the necessary reconfiguration to enable it to run in your vSphere environment.

vCenter Converter can import the following types of VMware virtual machines:

- VMware Workstation virtual machine
- VMware Server virtual machine
- VMware Fusion virtual machine

During the import process, vCenter Converter also offers the option of customizing the virtual machine so that the virtual machine you end up with might be very different than the one with which you started.

To import a virtual machine created using VMware Workstation or VMware Server, follow these steps:

1. Launch vSphere Client if it is not already running and log into an instance of vCenter Server.

2. Navigate to either the Hosts And Clusters view or the VMs And Templates view.

3. Right-click on an ESX/ESXi host, a cluster, or a folder and select Import Machine.

4. Click Next to choose a source image to import.

5. Choose Other from the drop-down list and click Next.

6. Specify the Universal Naming Convention (UNC) path to the folder where the virtual machine files are stored. You must also specify a username and password. If an Active Directory domain is present, you should specify the username in the format DOMAIN\username. Click Next to continue.

7. On this screen of the Import Wizard dialog box, you can choose to import the virtual machine's disks "as is," without any modification, or you can choose to resize the virtual machine's disks during the import process.

   To import the disks without any modification, select the Import All Disks And Maintain Size radio button.

   To resize the disks, select the radio button labeled Select Volumes and Resize To Save Or Add Space. Choose from the menu or type in a size (in GB or MB). Then specify the new size of the disks you want resized.

   When you are ready to continue, click Next.

8. Click Next to choose a destination for the virtual machine you are importing.

9. Specify a name for the new virtual machine and choose a location in the virtual machine inventory. Click Next to continue.

10. If you chose a cluster, folder, or resource pool when you initiated the import process, you must select a host on which to run this virtual machine. Select a host and click Next.

11. Select a datastore where you want to store the virtual machine's files, then click Next.

12. Select the network to which you want to attach the virtual machine, then click Next.

13. On the Customization screen of the Import Wizard dialog box, select whether you want to install the VMware Tools, customize the virtual machine, or remove all System Restore checkpoints. It's recommended to remove System Restore checkpoints; the other two options depend upon the particular circumstances surrounding this virtual machine. In most cases, you will want to install the VMware Tools and not perform any customization. Click Next when you ready to continue.

14. Select the radio button to Run This Task Immediately to start the import process right away.

15. Review the settings summary and click Finish to start the import of the virtual machine.

vCenter Server will create an active task in the Tasks pane at the bottom of vSphere Client window where you can monitor the progress of the task. Once the task has completed, you will have a new virtual machine in your inventory.

NOTE The process for importing a virtual machine created in VMware Fusion is fundamentally the same, but with some additional steps in the beginning to get the virtual machine files from the Mac OS X–based computer to a location accessible to vCenter Converter.

As you can see, using vCenter Converter to bring virtual machines into VMware vSphere from other VMware platforms is reasonably straightforward. But what if you want to go the opposite direction?

What if you want to export a virtual machine out of VMware vSphere to run on a different VMware platform? I'll examine that scenario in the next section.

Export VMs to a Different VMware Platform

You can use vCenter Converter not only to import virtual machines from another VMware platform, but also to export virtual machines to another VMware platform.

To export a virtual machine for use with a different VMware platform, like VMware Workstation or VMware Server, follow these steps:

1. Launch vSphere Client if it is not already running and log into an instance of vCenter Server.

2. Navigate to either the Hosts And Clusters view or the VMs And Templates view.

3. Right-click on a virtual machine and select Export. The virtual machine must be shut down in order to perform an export.

4. Click Next on the first screen of the Export Wizard dialog box, as the source virtual machine is already selected.

5. At the Source Data screen, select whether you would like to export the virtual machine's virtual hard disk files without modification, or if you'd like to resize the virtual hard disks during the export process. Click Next when you are ready to proceed.

6. Click Next at the screen prompting the user to select the destination.

7. From the drop-down list, select Other VMware Virtual Machine and click Next.

8. Supply a virtual machine name and a location, in UNC syntax, to store the virtual machine files.

9. Provide a username and password vCenter Converter should use to authenticate to the location specified in the previous step. If a domain is present, use the syntax DOMAIN\username for the user account information.

10. Select the radio button that corresponds to the type of virtual machine you want to create.

11. Click Next.

12. When prompted for disk space allocation, select the radio button labeled Allow Virtual Disk Files To Grow and click Next.

13. Select how many network interface cards (NICs) the exported virtual machine should have, and whether each of those NICs should connect to a Network Address Translation (NAT) network, a bridged network, or a host-only network. Click Next when you are ready to continue. (See Figure 9.3.)

Figure 9.3: The vSphere administrator has several options for network connectivity when exporting VMs out of VMware vSphere.

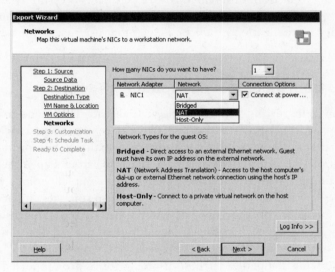

14. Check the box labeled Remove All System Restore Checkpoints (Recommended). Typically, you won't install VMware Tools and you won't customize the identity of the virtual machine, but those options are available here if you need them. Click Next to continue.

15. Select Run This Task Immediately to start the export process right away, or select Schedule Later to schedule this task to run at a later date or time. Click Next to continue.

16. Review the details of the task and click Finish if everything is correct. If you need to make corrections, use the Back button to go back and make any necessary changes.

As with most other import and export processes I've discussed, vCenter Server will create an active task that is visible in the Tasks pane of vSphere Client once the export actually begins. You can monitor the progress of the export using this active task. Please note that you will not be able to use or edit the new virtual machine until the export is complete.

After the export is complete, you will need to add the new virtual machine to the other VMware platform. The procedure for adding the newly exported virtual machine would vary based on the specific platform.

Migrating to or from different VMware platforms is certainly a valid use case, but another very pertinent use case is migrating to or from competitors' virtualization products. I cover that use case in the next section.

Migrate from a Competing Product

In addition to importing and exporting virtual machines to and from VMware platforms besides VMware vSphere, vCenter Converter can import virtual machines from some competing virtualization products. This functionality is invaluable during a migration from some other virtualization product to VMware vSphere. For example, perhaps you initially deployed Microsoft Virtual PC to perform some testing of virtual machine images, but now you want to deploy those images into your VMware vSphere environment for additional testing. You can use vCenter Converter to help with this process.

The following competing virtualization platforms are supported for import by vCenter Server:

- Microsoft Virtual PC 2004 and Virtual PC 2007 (for Windows only)
- Microsoft Virtual Server 2005 and 2005 R2
- Parallels Desktop for Windows and Mac OS X 2.5, 3.0, and 4.0

The process for performing an import of a virtual machine created using a competing virtualization platform is the same as for importing a virtual machine created using a different VMware platform. The instructions provided in the section titled "Import VMs from a Different VMware Platform" are equally applicable to importing virtual machines from a competing virtualization platform.

Virtual-to-virtual migrations sometimes don't involve other virtualization platforms, however: sometimes you might want to perform a virtual-to-virtual migration in order to reconfigure a virtual machine. This topic is covered in the next section.

Use a Virtual-to-Virtual Migration for Reconfiguration

As I mentioned earlier, using a virtual-to-virtual migration is one way to reconfigure an existing VMware vSphere virtual machine. Consider this situation: you have a virtual machine that is running low on available disk space. Using a virtual-to-virtual migration, you could resize the disk volumes during the migration to add disk space to the virtual machine. Conversely, perhaps you have a virtual machine that has been allocated too much disk space, and now you need to reclaim some of that disk space. You can use a virtual-to-virtual migration to accomplish that task.

To resize the disk volumes for a virtual machine using a virtual-to-virtual migration, follow these steps:

1. While connected to a vCenter Server instance using vSphere Client, right-click the virtual machine whose virtual hard disks you want to resize, and select Export.

2. Click Next on the first page of the Export Wizard, as you have already selected the source virtual machine.

3. Because you are specifically performing this virtual-to-virtual migration to resize the virtual machine's hard disks, select the radio button labeled Select Volumes And Resize To Save Or Add Space. For each volume listed, use the drop-down list to choose the minimum size or to specify the size of the volume after the migration. Figure 9.4 shows the drop-down list for a virtual machine. Click Next when you are ready to continue.

4. Click Next to select a destination for the virtual machine.

5. Select vSphere Virtual Machine as the type of machine, then click Next.

6. When prompted for login credentials for ESX or vCenter Server, enter the hostname of the vCenter Server computer and a username and password. Click Next to continue.

Configuring Your vSphere Environment

PART II

Figure 9.4: The drop-down list provides the minimum size possible for a virtual machine's hard disk.

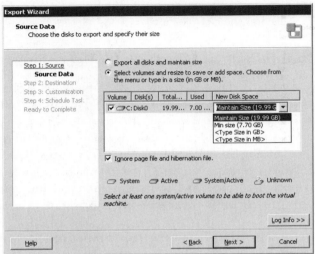

7. Specify a name for the new virtual machine and choose a location within the virtual machine inventory. Click Next when you are ready to continue.

8. Choose the cluster, host, or resource pool where the reconfigured virtual machine should run. Click Next.

9. If you chose a cluster for which Distributed Resource Scheduler (DRS) is not enabled or for which DRS is configured in manual mode, you must select a specific host in the cluster on which the reconfigured virtual machine will run. Select a host and click Next.

10. Select the datastore where the reconfigured virtual machine will reside. If you need to place the virtual machine's disk files separately from the virtual machine configuration file, or if the virtual machine has multiple virtual disks and you need to place those virtual disks on separate datastores, click the Advanced button. Figure 9.5 shows how you can place virtual disks in separate locations. Click Next to continue.

Figure 9.5: The Advanced view show here allows you to specify a different location for virtual disks or the virtual machine configuration file.

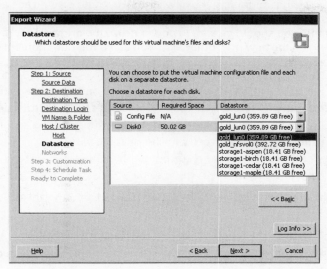

11. Choose the network to which each network interface in the virtual machine should connect, and whether that network interface should be connected when the virtual machine is powered on. Click Next to continue.

12. Select the check box marked Remove All System Restore Checkpoints (Recommended). In most cases, you will want to leave the other two check boxes unselected. Click Next to continue.

13. Select the radio button labeled Run This Task Immediately to start the virtual-to-virtual migration right away. Click Next.

14. Review the settings for the virtual-to-virtual migration. If everything is correct, click Finish to start the migration; otherwise, use the Back button to go back and change settings as needed.

As you have seen in other migrations, vCenter Server will create an active task that is visible in the Tasks pane of vSphere Client. You can use this task to monitor the progress of the virtual-to-virtual migration. When the migration is complete, you can power on the virtual machine and start using it.

> **NOTE** If you did not customize the virtual machine as part of the virtual-to-virtual migration, the new virtual machine created as part of the process is an exact copy of the original virtual machine. This means that you should be sure to power down the original before powering on the new one; otherwise, you could run into problems.

In addition to resizing virtual disks, vCenter Converter can also be used to reconfigure a virtual machine in the event that an error has occurred and it is no longer able to boot. VMware provides a specific option for using vCenter Converter in this specific way.

To use vCenter Converter to reconfigure an unbootable virtual machine so it will boot, perform these steps:

1. Right-click the virtual machine you want to reconfigure and select Reconfigure.

2. Click Next at the Source screen of the Reconfigure Wizard. The source is automatically set to the virtual machine you selected.

3. Select the check box marked Remove All System Restore Checkpoints (Recommended), as in Figure 9.6. In almost all other cases, since you are simply reconfiguring an existing system, you will not want to select either of the other two check boxes. Click Next to continue.

4. Click Finish to perform the reconfiguration.

Figure 9.6: When using vCenter Converter to reconfigure a virtual machine, there's no need to install the VMware Tools or customize the VM.

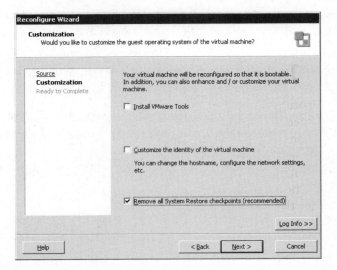

vCenter Converter will reconfigure the virtual machine so that it will boot properly. (Note that this does not fix problems with the guest operating system within the virtual machine. In these cases, the administrator must usually revert to guest OS-specific techniques, like performing a repair installation.) Like other procedures with vCenter Converter, a task is present in the Tasks pane of vSphere Client by which you can monitor the progress of the task.

Troubleshoot Virtual-to-Virtual Migrations

While virtual-to-virtual migrations aren't the same as physical-to-virtual migrations, many of the recommendations for ensuring successful physical-to-virtual migrations also apply here.

In addition, some other considerations for virtual-to-virtual migrations include:

- You don't have the correct files necessary to import a virtual machine from a competing virtualization platform. For example, you might have the .vhd (Virtual Hard Disk) file for a Microsoft Virtual PC virtual machine, but without the .vmc (Virtual Machine Configuration) file vCenter Converter can't import the virtual machine. Similarly, for VMware virtual machines created on other VMware platforms you must have the .vmx (virtual machine configuration) file and not only the .vmdk (virtual hard disk) files.

- If the source is a virtual machine created in Microsoft Virtual PC, remove the Virtual PC Additions prior to importing the virtual machine.

Import an Open Virtualization Format Template

The idea of a virtual appliance—a prepackaged virtual machine that is already installed and configured with the necessary software to perform a specific task—is an idea that VMware has been discussing for quite some time. What VMware needed, among other things, was a standard way of packaging and deploying virtual appliances. The Open Virtualization Format (OVF) is one way of accomplishing that goal. Ratified by the Desktop Management Task Force (DMTF) as a standard, the OVF 1.0 standard is fully supported by VMware vSphere and by several other virtualization products. Additional virtualization vendors have announced support for OVF in their products. Using OVF, creators of virtual appliances have a way of packaging and distributing their products in a format that multiple vendors will understand.

Before I show you how to deploy virtual appliances packaged using OVF, I'd first like to discuss OVF templates in a bit more detail.

Understand OVF Templates

In this context, I'm discussing OVF templates as they relate to VMware vSphere, but it is important to remember that OVF is designed to be a platform-neutral, format-neutral specification. According to the DMTF, OVF was designed to meet the following requirements:

- OVF supports both single-VM and multiple-VM configurations; the latter is key to VMware's vApp functionality.

- OVF is both vendor and platform independent, supporting multiple virtual hard disk formats. In addition, OVF does not depend upon any specific host platform, hypervisor, or operating system.

- OVF is extensible, allowing the specification to accommodate today's requirements as well as tomorrow's requirements.

NOTE I encourage readers interested in more details on OVF to download and review the official OVF Specification from the DMTF at www.dmtf.org/standards/published_documents/ DSP0243_1.0.0.pdf.

An OVF template (sometimes also referred to as an OVF package) will consist of the following components:

- An OVF descriptor with an .ovf extension

- Hard disk images (zero or more)

- Optionally, a manifest (.mf file), certificate (.cert file), and additional resource files (like .iso files)

An OVF template can be distributed as separate files, or the OVF package can be distributed as a single file using the .ova extension. OVF templates distributed as a single file use the standard UNIX TAR format.

This means that you can both assemble and extract OVF packages using standard TAR-compliant tools.

The OVF descriptor is an XML document that contains the definitions for the number of virtual machines in the package, the virtual machine hardware for each of the virtual machines, references to other files (virtual machine disk files, for example), the operating system running within the virtual machines, network and storage configuration, and so on. The complete description of one or more virtual machines is encapsulated in the OVF XML document. It is this document that VMware vSphere and other virtualization solutions use to know how to deploy the OVF template.

Deploy an OVF Template

Now that you have an idea of what an OVF template is, I can show you how to deploy an OVF template into your VMware vSphere environment. As an example, I'll work with the vSphere Management Assistant (vMA), a command-line interface designed for use with VMware vSphere. vMA is distributed as an OVF template.

NOTE   The vSphere Management Assistant is available for download from VMware's web site at www.vmware.com/appliances/directory/178973.

To deploy the vMA using an OVF template, perform the following steps:

1. From within vSphere Client while connected to a vCenter Server instance, select File > Deploy OVF Template.

2. If you have already downloaded the vSphere Management Assistant, select the Deploy From File radio button and use the Browse button to find and select the OVF file you downloaded.

   If you have not already downloaded the vSphere Management Assistant, select the Deploy From URL radio button and enter http://www.vmware.com/go/importvma/vma4.ovf as the source URL to import.

   Click Next when you are ready to continue.

3. Click Next at the OVF details screen.

4. Click Accept, then click Next.

5. Specify a name for the new virtual machine and select a location in the virtual machine inventory. Click Next to continue.

6. Choose a host or cluster on which to deploy this OVF template. When you are ready to continue, click Next.

7. If you selected a cluster that has DRS disabled or configured for manual automation, you must select a specific ESX/ESXi host on which to run the new virtual machine. Click Next to continue.

8. Select a datastore where the virtual machine's virtual hard disks should be stored. Click Next to continue to the next step.

9. Map the vMA's Management Network to an applicable network defined in your VMware vSphere environment. While this virtual appliance has only a single network connection, some virtual appliances may have multiple network connections. Each network connection must be mapped to the appropriate network in the destination VMware vSphere environment. Click Next when you are ready to continue.

10. Review the settings. If everything is correct, click Finish; otherwise, click Back to go back and make any necessary changes.

11. vCenter Server will display a dialog box that shows the progress of deploying the virtual machine from the OVF template. If you chose to deploy from a URL, vCenter Server will download the necessary files from the specified URL. Depending upon the size of the virtual appliance, this may take some time. vCenter Server will also show an active task in the Tasks pane of vSphere Client.

After the new virtual machine has been fully deployed, you can configure the virtual machine in the same fashion as any other virtual machine. Depending upon the software within the virtual machine, there may be additional configuration steps necessary before the virtual appliance is fully functional.

11

Configuring Security

IN THIS CHAPTER, YOU WILL LEARN TO:

▷ **CONFIGURE VCENTER SERVER ACCESS CONTROL (Pages 332–339)**

- Understand vCenter Server's Predefined Roles (Page 332)
- Customize Roles (Page 334)
- Manage Permissions (Page 338)

▷ **SECURE VCENTER SERVER (Pages 339–350)**

- Harden the vCenter Server Computer (Page 339)
- Remove Default Administrative Access to vCenter Server (Page 340)

▷ **SECURE YOUR ESX AND ESXI HOSTS (Pages 342–350)**

- Control Network Access to the Service Console (Page 342)
- Isolate the Management Network (Page 344)
- Authenticate via a Directory Service (Page 346)
- Enforce a Password Policy for Local Accounts (Page 347)
- Delete Unnecessary Local Accounts (Page 348)
- Enable Lockdown Mode (Page 349)

▷ **SECURE YOUR VIRTUAL MACHINES (Pages 349–352)**

- Configure Virtual Machine Isolation (Page 350)
- Harden the Guest Operating System (Page 352)

Configuring Your
vSphere Environment

PART II

There's a saying in the security community: "Security is a pursuit, not a goal." In your VMware vSphere environment, improved security is something for which you should strive. This chapter presents a number of ways to help improve the security of the various components of your VMware vSphere environment.

Configure vCenter Server Access Control

Part of the security of any environment is ensuring that access to resources is controlled properly. Users should have access to only those areas necessary to do their job and should only be able to do the tasks that are applicable to it. For example, a help desk technician might need the ability to change the power state of a virtual machine, but most likely he or she does not need the ability to create new virtual machines.

As a key part of vCenter Server's management functionality, vCenter Server provides role-based access control (RBAC) for the VMware vSphere environment. vCenter Server's RBAC implementation provides granular control over the specific tasks users are allowed to perform on certain types of objects so that organizations can ensure that users are granted the appropriate level of permission on the appropriate subset of objects as determined by the needs of the organization.

To be able to configure access control appropriately, you must first understand the roles that are available with vCenter Server. The next section discusses vCenter Server's predefined roles.

Understand vCenter Server's Predefined Roles

vCenter Server comes with a number of predefined roles. These roles provide a starting point for customers to create the roles that fit their organization's administrative model. Here are the predefined roles that are available with vCenter Server upon installation:

No Access   This role is self-explanatory—it denies access to an object for a user or group. It's primarily used to prevent a user or group that has permissions at some point higher in the hierarchy from having permissions on the object to which this role is assigned. You can use it to create exceptions, where a user or group has access to all the virtual machines in a folder or resource pool except for just a few.

Read-Only   Read-Only allows a user or group to see the vCenter Server inventory. It does not allow the user or group to interact with any of the virtual machines in any way through vSphere Client or the web client except to see the power status.

Administrator   A user or group assigned to an object with the Administrator role will have full administrative capabilities over that object in vCenter Server. A user or group assigned the Administrator role for a virtual machine can change the hardware assigned to the virtual machine, connect and disconnect media, start and stop the virtual machine, and alter its performance parameters.

NOTE   Note that a user or group with the Administrator role does not have any privileges within the guest operating systems installed inside the virtual machines. Those privileges must be assigned within that guest operating system instance.

Virtual Machine Power User (Sample)   The Virtual Machine Power User sample role assigns permissions to allow a user or group to perform most functions on virtual machines. This includes things like configuring CD/DVD and floppy media, changing the power state, taking and deleting snapshots, and modifying the configuration. These permissions apply only to virtual machines. A user or group granted this role would not be able to change settings on objects such as resource pools.

Virtual Machine User (Sample)   The Virtual Machine User role grants a user or group the ability to interact with a virtual machine, but not the ability to change its configuration. Users can operate the virtual machine's power controls and change the media in the virtual CD/DVD drive or floppy drive as long as they also have access to the media they want to change.

NOTE   vCenter Server's permissions are granular. For instance, a user who is assigned the Virtual Machine User role must also be granted the Browse Datastore permission if you want that user to be able to attach an ISO file or a floppy image to a virtual machine. Otherwise, the user will only be able to change the CD or floppy media to his or her own client system's physical CD/DVD or floppy drive.

Configuring Your vSphere Environment

PART II

Resource Pool Administrator (Sample)   The Resource Pool administrator is able to manage and configure resources with a resource pool, including virtual machines, child pools, scheduled tasks, and alarms.

VMware Consolidated Backup User (Sample)   As the role name suggests, the VMware Consolidated Backup user has the privileges required for performing a backup of a virtual machine using VMware Consolidated Backup (VCB).

Datacenter Consumer (Sample)   The Datastore Consumer role is targeted at users who need only a single permission: the permission to allocate space from a datastore. Clearly, this is a very limited role.

Network Consumer (Sample)   Similar to the Datastore Consumer role, the Network Consumer role has only a single permission, and that is the permission to assign networks.

NOTE   For environments not using vCenter Server and instead using vSphere Client to manage ESX/ESXi hosts directly, only three roles are available: No Access, Read-Only, and Administrator. The additional roles are only present when you are using vCenter Server.

These roles can be granted on an object at any level in the hierarchy and the user or group that is assigned the role will have those permissions on that object and—if the inheritance box, marked Propagate To Child Objects, is marked—any child objects beneath it in the hierarchy.

It's likely that these predefined roles won't meet the specific needs of your organization. In that case, you'll need to customize the roles to meet your specific needs, as the next section describes.

Customize Roles

When the predefined roles don't quite fit your specific needs, you can customize the roles to exclude certain privileges or to include additional privileges. Or you might find that none of the predefined roles meet your needs, in which case you'd need to create an entirely new role. vCenter Server provides the functionality to edit the predefined roles, delete roles, clone existing roles, and add new roles.

All of this functionality is found in vSphere Client by navigating to the Roles area by either using the navigation bar or by selecting View ➤ Administration ➤ Roles. The Roles area displays all the currently defined roles. Right-clicking on a role provides commands to clone, edit, or remove the role. An Add Role button is also provided just below the navigation bar to create a new role.

NOTE   The No Access, Read-Only, and Administrator predefined roles cannot be edited and cannot be deleted. To customize one of these roles, you should clone the role and edit the cloned copy of the role.

We'll start by looking at the procedure for creating a new role.

Create a New Role

To create a new role, perform these steps:

1. Connect to a vCenter Server instance with vSphere Client.

2. Select View ➤ Administration ➤ Roles.

3. Click the Add Role button.

4. In the Add New Role dialog box, specify a name for the new role.

5. From the list of privileges, select the privileges you want granted to this role. For example, if you wanted to create a role for managing distributed virtual network settings, you would assign permissions out of the Distributed Virtual Port Group and Distributed Virtual Switch categories, as illustrated in Figure 11.1.

6. Click OK to save the settings and create the new role.

You've now created the new role and can use this role in assigning permissions. If, however, you find that the role is missing some privileges or has privileges that should not be included, you can edit the role and fine-tune the privileges included in the role. The next section describes how to edit a role.

Figure 11.1: The Add New Role dialog box allows you to specify the privileges assigned to a new role on a granular basis.

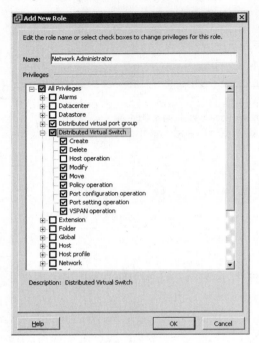

Edit an Existing Role

Editing an existing role is necessary when you find that a role includes privileges that should not be included, or fails to include privileges that should be included. In this case, you can edit the role to add or remove privileges as necessary.

To edit a role, perform these steps:

1. Connect to a vCenter Server instance with vSphere Client.

2. Select View ➢ Administration ➢ Roles.

3. Right-click the role you want to edit and select Edit Role.

4. In the Edit Role dialog box, specify a new name for the role (if desired) and add or remove privileges from the list of privileges.

5. Click OK to save your changes and return to vSphere Client.

> **TIP** Although you can rename the role in the Edit Role dialog box, you can also right-click on a role and select Rename to rename the role.

Sometimes you might find that you need a new role that is very similar to an existing role but with a few privileges added or removed. While you could create a new role and assign all the permissions manually, you will find that cloning the role is quicker, easier, and less error-prone. The next section describes how to clone an existing role.

Clone an Existing Role

To clone an existing role, perform these steps:

1. Connect to a vCenter Server instance with vSphere Client.

2. Select View ➤ Administration ➤ Roles.

3. Right-click the role you want to clone and select Clone. Alternately, select the clone and click the Clone Role button just below the navigation bar.

4. A new role appears in the list of roles. Type a name for the new role, and then press Enter.

The new role is now available for you to customize as needed.

Remove a Role

When a role is no longer needed, you can easily remove it. Simply right-click on the role you want to delete and select Remove.

If the role is currently in use—meaning that a user has been assigned a permission with that role—vCenter Server will prompt you for the correct action to take:

- To remove the permissions, select Remove Role Assignments when prompted.

- To reassign the permissions, select Reassign Affected Users when prompted. You'll have the option to select a different role to assign to the affected users.

Now that you've seen how to create new roles, edit existing roles, clone roles, and remove roles, you're ready to see how to combine users and groups and roles into permissions that you assign to objects in vCenter Server. The next section describes how to manage permissions.

Manage Permissions

After you have created the necessary roles, you must then combine those roles with a user or group to create a *permission*. You'll then assign the permission to an object in order to put it into effect.

You can assign permissions from any of the inventory views: Hosts And Clusters, VMs And Templates, Datastores, and Networking. In all these different views, the process is the same.

To assign a permission to an object, perform these steps:

1. While connected to a vCenter Server instance, navigate in vSphere Client to the inventory view for the type of object on which you want to assign the permission. For example, if you want to assign a permission on a specific ESX/ESXi host, navigate to Hosts And Clusters view.

2. Select the object on which the permission should be assigned.

3. Select the Permissions tab from the content pane on the right.

4. Right-click in a blank area of the Permissions tab and select Add Permission. This opens the Assign Permissions dialog box.

5. Under Users And Groups, select the Add button.

6. Select the specific users or groups to include in the role. When you've added all the users and groups, click OK.

7. From the Assigned Role section, select the role you want to assign to the selected users and groups.

8. If you want the permission to apply to child objects, be sure to leave the Propagate To Child Objects check box selected.

9. If you need to add more users or groups with other roles, repeat steps 5 through 8.

10. When you are finished assigning roles to users and groups, click OK to return to vSphere Client.

The permissions will appear on the Permissions tab for the selected object. If you need to remove a permission, simply right-click the permission and select Delete. To change the role assigned in the permission, right-click on the permission and select Properties. vCenter Server will display the Change Access Rule dialog box to allow you to change the role assigned in the permission for the selected user or group.

With vCenter Server's role-based access control, organizations can properly secure access to the objects and resources in their VMware vSphere environment. This is an important part of every organization's security efforts, but not the only part. In the next section, we'll examine some other ways to help secure vCenter Server.

Secure vCenter Server

By now you are well aware of the central role that vCenter Server plays in the management of your VMware vSphere environment. In addition to securing access to objects and resources within vCenter Server using the access controls we've already described, it's also important to secure vCenter Server and the computer on which vCenter Server runs. In addition, you will want to lock down the default administrative access to vCenter Server, which unnecessarily exposes access to vCenter Server to users who may not need access to the virtualization environment.

First, we'll look at securing the vCenter Server computer.

Harden the vCenter Server Computer

A discussion of hardening the vCenter Server computer is really more of a discussion on hardening Windows Server. Some general guidelines to keep in mind include:

- Be sure to keep the vCenter Server computer properly patched and up-to-date on all security updates.

- Follow published best practices from Microsoft with regard to securing Windows Server.

- Be sure to harden not only the vCenter Server computer, but also the computer running the vCenter Server database (if it is on a separate computer).

- Follow published best practices from the appropriate database vendor for the database server you are using for vCenter Server.

- In accordance with your organization's security policy, properly install and configure antivirus agents, intrusion detection systems, and other security software.

- If possible, control network access to the vCenter Server computer using a firewall or access control lists (ACLs).

WARNING   Using a firewall with Network Address Translation (NAT) enabled between the vCenter Server and the ESX/ESXi hosts might cause problems. Avoid the use of NAT between the vCenter Server computer and the ESX/ESXi hosts.

- If you are using Windows authentication with SQL Server, use a dedicated service account for vCenter Server. Don't share an account with other services or applications.

- Replace the default self-signed SSL certificates with valid SSL certificates from a trusted root authority.

- Restrict physical access to the vCenter Server computer to authorized personnel only.

These are just a few guidelines to get you started; there are many, many more hardening guidelines available for securing Windows Server 2003 or Windows Server 2008. Although many different security guidelines and benchmarks exist to help you harden Windows Server, the best place to start is with Microsoft's website at www.microsoft.com. From there, you will find documentation and references to other useful resources.

In addition to securing the operating system underneath vCenter Server, there are also some steps you can take to secure vCenter Server itself. One of these steps is removing the default administrative access to vCenter Server, as described in the next section.

Remove Default Administrative Access to vCenter Server

By default, when vCenter Server is installed, the local Administrators group on the vCenter Server computer is granted the Administrator role at the datacenter object within vCenter Server. Effectively, this means that the local Administrators group is given full permission on all objects within the vCenter Server hierarchy. When the vCenter Server computer is part of an Active Directory domain, this also means that the Domain Admins group—which is, by default, a member of the local Administrators group on every member server in the domain—also has full permission on all objects within the vCenter Server hierarchy. This default administrative access exposes vCenter Server to personnel that may have no need for access within the VMware vSphere environment.

To remove the default administrative access in vCenter Server, perform these steps:

1. On the vCenter Server computer, use the Computer Management console to create a new local group. You could call the group vCenter Administrators or something similar.

2. Create a new user and place this user into the group created in step 1. Be sure not to place this user in the local Administrators group.

3. Log on to the vCenter Server computer using an account with administrative permissions.

4. Launch vSphere Client and connect to a vCenter Server instance.

5. Assign the Administrator role to the new group created in step 1 to the vCenter Server object at the top of the hierarchy. Be sure to leave Propagate To Child Objects selected.

6. Log off and log back on as the user created in step 2.

7. Log into vCenter Server using vSphere Client and ensure that you are able to perform all tasks available for a vCenter Server administrator.

8. Remove the permission on the vCenter Server object for the local Administrators group.

9. If you are using Active Directory, create a group in Active Directory and add it to the local group created in step 1. Add domain users to the domain group as necessary.

After making this change, only the users that are members of the local group (or the Active Directory domain group, where applicable) will have administrative permissions within vCenter Server.

So far, you've seen two aspects of security within your virtual environment: access control for securing access to resources and objects within vCenter Server, and securing vCenter Server itself. The next section provides information on improving the security of the third aspect of your virtual environment: your ESX/ESXi hosts.

Configuring Your
vSphere Environment

PART II

Secure Your ESX and ESXi Hosts

In addition to securing access to the objects within vCenter Server and securing the vCenter Server computer, you need to appropriately secure your VMware ESX and VMware ESXi hosts. Although these two products are identical with regard to feature support, they are architecturally very different—and therefore end up requiring very different steps to properly secure. Most of the security recommendations for VMware ESX focus on securing the Linux-based Service Console. Because ESXi does not have a Linux-based Service Console, these recommendations don't apply.

In each of the following sections, we'll identify whether this configuration step applies to ESX, ESXi, or both. This will make it easier to know which security configuration recommendations apply to each product.

Control Network Access to the Service Console

To help control network access to the VMware ESX Service Console, VMware supplies a firewall for the Service Console and a command to configure the firewall. You can configure the Service Console firewall via vSphere Client or via the command line. If you choose to use the command line, esxcfg-firewall is the command you will use to enable or disable network services through the Service Console firewall.

NOTE This applies only to VMware ESX.

To view or configure the Service Console firewall from vSphere Client, perform these steps:

1. Connect to an instance of vCenter Server with vSphere Client. If there are multiple vCenter Server instances in your environment, be sure to connect to the instance that is managing the host you wish to configure.

2. Navigate to Hosts And Clusters inventory view using the View menu, the navigation bar, or the Ctrl+Shift+H keyboard shortcut.

3. Select an ESX host from the inventory on the left.

4. Select the Configuration tab from the content pane on the right.

5. Select the Security Profile link under Software.

6. The current incoming and outgoing connections allowed through the firewall are listed in the content pane. If you need to make changes, click the Properties link.

7. In the Firewall Properties dialog box, check or uncheck the services whose state you need to modify. Check a service to allow it through the firewall; uncheck a service to deny it through the firewall. Figure 11.2 shows the Firewall Properties dialog box with some services enabled and other services disabled.

Figure 11.2: Unchecked services, like the Software iSCSI Client, are not permitted through the Service Console firewall.

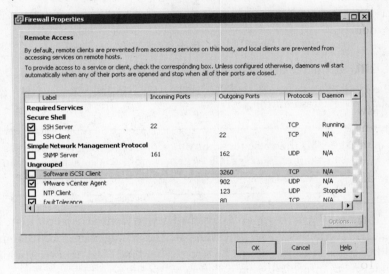

8. Click OK to return to vSphere Client.

To view or configure the Service Console firewall from the command line, perform these steps:

1. Using PuTTY.exe (Windows), a terminal window (Linux or Mac OS X), a remote console technology like HP iLO (Integrated Lights Out), or the physical console, log in to an ESX host and enter the su – command to establish root privileges.

Configuring Your vSphere Environment

PART II

2. Use the `esxcfg-firewall` command to view the current firewall settings:

   ```
   esxcfg-firewall --query
   ```

3. List the defined services that are understood by the Service Console firewall with this command:

   ```
   esxcfg-firewall --services
   ```

4. Enable a service through the firewall with this command:

   ```
   esxcfg-firewall -e <service name>
   ```

5. Disable a currently enabled service using this command:

   ```
   esxcfg-firewall -d <service name>
   ```

Changes made using `esxcfg-firewall` take effect immediately, but may not be reflected in vSphere Client for a few minutes, or when you click the Refresh button.

NOTE You can also leverage other Linux-based network access control features, such as TCP Wrappers, for additional flexibility in controlling network access to the VMware ESX Service Console.

Controlling network access to the Service Console is important, but we also recommend that you segregate the management traffic from other types of traffic on the ESX (or ESXi) host. The next section provides more information on isolating management traffic.

Isolate the Management Network

The VMware ESX Service Console needs its own network connectivity to communicate with other VMware ESX servers and with vCenter Server. Likewise, VMware ESXi needs to be able to communicate with vCenter Server as well via the management network. For both ESX and ESXi, this network connectivity does not need to be shared with VMkernel traffic (used for VMotion, Fault Tolerance logging, or IP-based storage) or virtual machine traffic, so we highly recommended that you isolate the management network using either VLANs or a physically separate network. Redundancy of the management network is important, however, so be sure to include redundant network connections for the Service Console or management network where possible.

NOTE This recommendation applies to both VMware ESX and VMware ESXi.

Figure 11.3 shows a sample network configuration for a VMware ESX host that places the management traffic onto a separate set of NICs. These NICs might connect to switches on a physically segregated network, or just to ports in a different VLAN on the same physical switches.

Figure 11.3: This network configuration allows for the VMware ESX management traffic to be segregated onto a physically separate network.

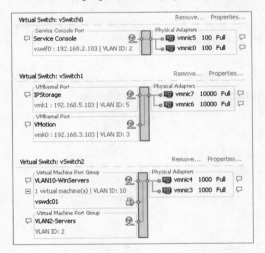

Where it isn't possible to use separate ports in a different VLAN or a physically separate switch, you can at least run the Service Console or management network on a different VLAN than VMkernel or virtual machine traffic. Refer to Chapter 6 for more information on how to configure VLANs.

Configuring Your
vSphere Environment

PART II

Authenticate via a Directory Service

The Linux-based Service Console (alternately referred to as the Console OS, or COS) used with VMware ESX does provide support for using an external directory service for user account authentication. NIS, LDAP, and Active Directory are supported for user authentication. LDAP is supported for both user management as well as user authentication; Active Directory, on the other hand, is only supported for user authentication.

NOTE   This section applies only to VMware ESX.

To configure ESX to use a directory service for authentication, you'll use the esxcfg-auth command. You'll use this command for other tasks as well, as you'll see in the next section, "Enforce a Password Policy for Local Accounts."

To use esxcfg-auth to configure VMware ESX to authenticate against an Active Directory domain, perform these steps:

1. Using a remote console technology such as HP iLO or the physical console, log into an ESX host and enter the su – command to establish root privileges. Because you are modifying authentication behaviors, we don't recommend using a remote connection such as SSH for this task.

2. Enter the following command to enable Active Directory authentication:

   ```
   esxcfg-auth --enablead --addomain <domain name>
   --addc <domain name>
   ```

3. Create local ESX accounts with usernames that match the Active Directory accounts that will be allowed to log into the ESX host. There is no need to set a password on the local account.

4. While still logged in as root, check the ability to log into the ESX host with an Active Directory account using SSH. When prompted for a password, specify the password stored in Active Directory.

5. If the login fails, review the /var/log/secure log file for any errors. Otherwise, if the login is successful, you have completed the configuration.

Because Active Directory is only supported for user authentication, you will still need to create and maintain local user accounts on each ESX host.

In addition to using esxcfg-auth to configure authentication with an external directory service, you can use esxcfg-auth to control the local password policy. The next section describes this functionality.

NOTE   When you have VMware ESX configured to use a directory service, you can enforce local authentication using the esxcfg-auth --enforce-local-auth=<username> command.

Enforce a Password Policy for Local Accounts

In the event that some accounts continue to use local authentication, you should enforce a password policy for those local accounts. Using the esxcfg-auth command, you can configure the password policy for local accounts on each ESX host.

NOTE   This section applies only to VMware ESX.

To configure the password policy on a VMware ESX host, perform these steps:

1. Using PuTTY.exe (Windows), a terminal window (Linux or Mac OS X), a remote console technology like HP iLO, or the physical console, log into an ESX host and enter the su – command to establish root privileges.

2. Use the esxcfg-auth command to set the maximum password age to 90 days:

   ```
   esxcfg-auth --passmaxdays=90
   ```

3. Set the number of days a warning is given before a password expires to 14 days:

   ```
   esxcfg-auth --passwarnage=14
   ```

You can see the current password policy settings by running esxcfg-auth --probe from the Service Console. This will display the current settings to the screen.

You will need to repeat these commands on each ESX host where these settings should be applied.

Another area of concern for security is ensuring that only necessary accounts are present on the ESX/ESXi hosts, as described in the next section.

Delete Unnecessary Local Accounts

In addition to using a directory service for authentication and enforcing a password policy for local accounts, you should be sure to disable and/or remove all unnecessary local accounts.

NOTE This step applies to both VMware ESX and VMware ESXi.

In many environments, especially those environments using vCenter Server, the individual ESX/ESXi hosts will not have many, if any, unnecessary local accounts. In other environments, though, many local accounts might have been created on the ESX/ESXi hosts. When these accounts are no longer necessary, they should be disabled and removed to prevent possible unauthorized access to the hosts.

NOTE vCenter Server acts as an authentication proxy between the end users and the ESX/ESXi hosts. Rather than passing credentials through to the ESX/ESXi hosts, vCenter Server proxies all connections using a special account named *vpxuser*. Do not modify or delete this account on your ESX/ESXi hosts or you will break vCenter Server's management functionality.

On a VMware ESX host, you can delete unnecessary local accounts either using vSphere Client connected directly to the host, or via the Service Console with the userdel <username> command. If you prefer to keep the account but just lock it so that it can't be used for logins, use the passwd -l <username> command (that's a lowercase *L* in the command). The passwd -u <username> command will unlock the account.

On a VMware ESXi host, you must use vSphere Client to delete local accounts that are no longer needed.

To use vSphere Client to remove local accounts on an ESX/ESXi host, perform these steps:

1. Log into the ESX/ESXi host using vSphere Client.

2. From the right-hand content pane, select the Users And Groups tab.

3. Click Users.

4. Right-click the user you want to remove and select Remove.

The next section looks at Lockdown Mode, a special feature that is only available for VMware ESXi and is intended to provide stricter access control to your ESXi hosts.

Enable Lockdown Mode

NOTE This section applies only to VMware ESXi.

While ESXi lacks many of the security controls described earlier—in large part due to the absence of a Linux-based Service Console—ESXi does have *Lockdown Mode*.

Lockdown Mode, when enabled, prevents management of the ESXi host outside of vCenter Server. Direct connections to the ESXi host using vSphere Client are denied—all management requests must go through vCenter Server. This ensures that vCenter Server's role-based access controls come into play and are not circumvented by connecting directly to the ESXi host. Limited administrative functions can also be performed at the local ESXi console; if a root password has been specified, it will be required before these administrative functions can be performed.

NOTE Be sure to specify a root password on all ESXi hosts.

Only a single component remains in our discussion of the security of your virtual environment. The next section describes some security recommendations for the virtual machines in your VMware vSphere environment.

Secure Your Virtual Machines

The fourth major component of a VMware vSphere environment that you need to secure is the virtual machines themselves.

Not only do you need to secure the guest operating systems installed within these virtual machines, but you must also secure the virtual machines themselves. The fact that these are virtual machines, as opposed to physical machines, does introduce new security issues that must be taken into account in an overall effort to improve the security of the environment.

One specific area that is unique to virtual machines is virtual machine isolation—how and when a virtual machine is allowed to interact with the virtualization layer. We'll take a look at this area first.

Configure Virtual Machine Isolation

Isolation is a key benefit of virtualization. It is the isolation of one guest operating system instance from other guest operating system instances that allows you to run multiple operating systems on the same hardware. It is the isolation of the guest operating system from the underlying hardware that gives virtual machines their hardware independence.

Some of this isolation is removed to simplify things for administrators. For example, administrators expect the ability to use copy-and-paste between their local computer and the console of a remote virtual machine. Enabling this greater interaction between virtual machines and the rest of the physical environment has to be weighed with a careful eye toward security.

The next few sections describe some of these isolation settings.

NOTE   Many of the virtual machine security recommendations found here are also found in *ESX Configuration Guide*, available from VMware's website at http://www.vmware.com/pdf/vsphere4/ r40/vsp_40_esx_vc_installation_guide.pdf.

Disable Copy and Paste

By default, the remote console of vSphere Client provides the ability to use copy and paste to move data to and from a virtual machine to the local workstation. To prevent this functionality, disable copy and paste by adding the following lines to the virtual machine's configuration file:

```
isolation.tools.copy.disable = "true"
isolation.tools.paste.disable = "true"
```

You can either edit the virtual machine configuration (.vmx) file directly, or you can add these entries using vSphere Client.

To add entries to a virtual machine configuration file using vSphere Client, perform these steps:

1. Launch vSphere Client, if it is not already running, and connect to a vCenter Server instance.

2. Navigate to an inventory view that displays the virtual machine you wish to modify. The virtual machine must be powered off to make the changes; if necessary, shut down the virtual machine first.

3. Right-click the virtual machine and select Edit Settings.

4. Select the Options tab, click Advanced, and then click General.

5. Click the Configuration Parameters button.

6. Select the Add Row button at the bottom of the Configuration Parameters dialog box.

7. Specify the name of the parameter (like isolation.tools.copy. disable) and a value (like true).

8. Click OK to return to the virtual machine's Properties dialog box.

9. Click OK again to return to vSphere Client.

10. Power on the virtual machine.

You can also edit the virtual machine configuration file directly, but this is more error-prone than using vSphere Client to modify the virtual machine configuration.

Don't Allow a Virtual Machine User or Process to Disconnect Devices

You'll also want to prevent a user or process inside a virtual machine from being able to connect or disconnect devices such as the floppy, CD/DVD drive, or network adapter. Otherwise, the potential exists for an unprivileged guest OS user or process to connect or disconnect these devices. Keep in mind that we are not talking about preventing a properly authorized user, using vSphere Client, from connecting or disconnecting devices. Instead, we are talking about preventing the connecting or disconnecting of devices *from within the virtual machine and the guest operating system.*

To make this change, add this configuration parameter to the virtual machine configuration file:

```
<device_name>.allowGuestConnectionControl = "false"
```

You can add this parameter to the VM configuration file using the procedure described in the previous section. You'll want to replace <device_name> with the name of the device, such as ethernet0 or floppy0.

Making this change ensures that only users granted the appropriate access within vCenter Server are able to connect or disconnect devices like the floppy drive, CD/DVD drive, or network adapter. Again, this change only affects the ability of users and processes within the virtual machine or guest operating system; it does not affect users operating upon the virtual machine using vSphere Client.

NOTE Along the same lines as preventing a user or process from connecting or disconnecting devices, you should also remove any unnecessary hardware components from the virtual machine. For example, if the virtual machine doesn't need a floppy drive, you should remove the floppy drive from the virtual machine configuration.

Harden the Guest Operating System

It should go without saying, but it's also important to be sure to manage the security of the guest operating system within the virtual machine. Controls placed at the virtualization layer—such as access controls within vCenter Server—don't translate into the appropriate security controls within the guest operating systems. So you should be sure to follow established best practices with regard to securing the guest operating systems found within the virtual machines. This includes applying all applicable security patches and updates, using firewalls where applicable, enforcing access controls within the guest OS, and exercising the principle of least privilege. There are extensive resources available from the guest operating system vendors that provide detailed recommendations on how to secure their specific products; we suggest that you refer to the recommendations from your guest OS vendors to secure the guest operating systems appropriately.

12

Managing Resources and Performance

IN THIS CHAPTER, YOU WILL LEARN TO:

Configuring Your
vSphere Environment

PART II

I n a VMware vSphere environment, managing resources and managing performance go hand in hand. Performance will suffer if resources are over- or underallocated. To avoid this situation, you need to understand how to assign resources, control allocation during times of resource contention, and identify when resource contention is occurring.

Understand Resource Allocation

Resource allocation is an area that is often misunderstood by VMware vSphere administrators, yet it is an area that is critical to the effective use of virtualization. Administrators who do not understand resource allocation are more likely to incorrectly configure virtual machines and be able to support fewer virtual machines than those who understand resource allocation and know how to use it effectively.

So what is resource allocation? Resource allocation is the division of a physical server's finite resources—namely, compute power, memory, network bandwidth, and storage capacity—among multiple virtual machines. This division of resources by the administrator might be static, as in the maximum amount of RAM assigned to a virtual machine, or it might be dynamic, as in controlling what percentage of CPU cycles a virtual machine might get during times of CPU contention. You must know how VMware ESX/ESXi allocates resources to virtual machines and how to modify that default behavior to achieve the desired results.

Understanding resource allocation starts with understanding the three ways in which resources are assigned to a virtual machine. First, resources such as CPU, RAM, network, and storage are assigned to a virtual machine via the virtual machine configuration itself. For example, when you create a virtual machine, you must decide how many virtual CPUs (vCPUs) should be assigned to that VM, or how much memory should be assigned to the VM. These resource assignments are fairly static.

Second, you can apply certain controls to dynamically modify the behavior of the assigned resources by guaranteeing certain resource levels or by constraining resource usage. Specifically, you will use *reservations* to guarantee resource levels and *limits* to constrain resource usage.

Third, and finally, you can adjust the behavior of how ESX/ESXi grants resource access during times of resource contention. Using a mechanism called *shares*, administrators can fine-tune how resources are granted when those resources are in scarce supply. When an ESX/ESXi host has plenty of memory, there is no need to control how that memory is granted—there is enough to go around, so every VM gets whatever it needs. When that ESX/ESXi host runs out of memory, though, you need a way to control which VMs get memory and how much memory those VMs get. This is where shares come into play. Shares are only active when there is resource contention; reservations and limits are always active.

The next section discusses these controls in more detail and provides specific information on how to use these tools to control resource allocation for individual virtual machines. In the vast majority of situations, you are primarily going to be concerned with how CPU and memory are allocated, so the content in this section and throughout the chapter will focus heavily on controlling CPU and RAM allocation.

Allocate Resources to Virtual Machines

Efficiently allocating resources to virtual machines is a key skill that every VMware vSphere administrator needs to master. If you allocate too many or too few resources, performance is negatively impacted. VMware vSphere provides a number of ways to help you make sure that resources are allocated and used efficiently, as you'll see in this section.

Allocate Resources in the VM Configuration

The first way in which you control resource allocation is by assigning resources in the configuration of the virtual machine. When you create a virtual machine, you assign certain levels of resources to that virtual machine. For example, Figure 12.1 shows the memory configuration for a virtual machine.

In the same way that the configuration of a physical machine establishes a limit on how many resources are available to that physical machine, the configuration of a virtual machine controls how resources are allocated to that virtual machine and the guest operating system running inside that virtual machine. If a virtual machine is configured for 1GB of RAM, that virtual machine has only 1GB of RAM visible to it, and any guest operating system installed in that virtual machine will not see or use more than 1GB of RAM. The same is true for CPU resources as well.

Figure 12.1: This virtual machine is configured with 1GB of RAM, so any guest operating system installed here will never see or use more than 1GB of RAM.

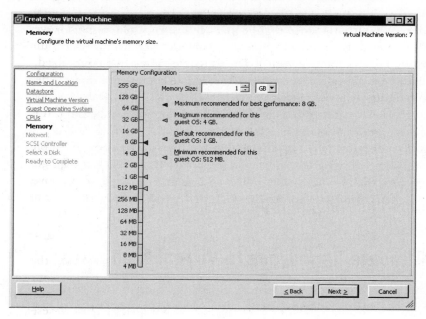

Of course, one key difference between a physical machine and a virtual machine is the ease of adding resources to a virtual machine. If the 1GB of RAM assigned to the virtual machine in Figure 12.1 proves insufficient, it is very easy for you to add more RAM to the system by modifying the configuration. In some cases, you can make this change while the virtual machine is running using the hot-add feature. Hardware hot-add is discussed in more detail in Chapter 9.

If, on the other hand, the guest operating system in that virtual machine is not fully utilizing the RAM that has been assigned to it in the VM configuration, it's also very easy for you to reduce the RAM assigned to the VM.

NOTE   VMware ESX/ESXi utilizes some advanced memory-management technologies that lessen, or perhaps even eliminate, the impact of assigning too much memory to a virtual machine. The same cannot be said for virtual CPUs; assigning multiple vCPUs when the workload can't effectively use multiple vCPUs can negatively impact performance. This fact underscores the importance of "right sizing" virtual machines to give them only the resources they actually need.

This ease of modification—which allows you to quickly and easily add or remove resources assigned to a virtual machine—means that you should be sure to right size virtual machines instead of continuing to provision virtual machines the same way that physical machines were provisioned. Physical machines were provisioned with the maximum amount of resources administrators thought the system might need, because adding more resources was more difficult. Virtual machines should be provisioned for only what they need; should the guest operating system and application prove to need more or less than what is assigned, you can easily change it.

In summary, one way of controlling resource allocation is by controlling how resources are assigned to virtual machines in their configuration. In some cases, though, you need more fine-grained control over resource allocation. One solution is a reservation, which we cover next.

Guarantee Resources with Reservations

Just because you have assigned resources to a virtual machine in the virtual machine's configuration doesn't necessarily guarantee resource availability. If you need to guarantee that certain levels of resources are available to a particular virtual machine, you will need to use a reservation. A *reservation* is a guarantee of a certain amount of a certain type of resource, so a virtual machine is assured of having at least that amount of the resource available to it.

The Resources tab of a virtual machine's properties, shown in Figure 12.2, is where you will set a reservation for a virtual machine. For CPU, the reservation is specified in megahertz (MHz); for memory, the reservation is set in megabytes (MB). You cannot set a reservation on storage (disks) or network activity.

So how do reservations work?

- When you set a CPU reservation, that amount of CPU time is guaranteed to the virtual machine *when needed*. If the virtual machine uses less than its CPU reservation, the excess clock cycles are assigned to other virtual machines. For example, if a virtual machine with a 1GHz reservation is using only 500MHz of CPU time, the remaining 500MHz in the reservation is used by other virtual machines.

- When you set a memory reservation, that memory is set aside for that virtual machine. ESX/ESXi allocates memory on-demand; that is, memory is not granted to a virtual machine until it accesses the memory. In this case, memory guaranteed by a reservation cannot be used by any other virtual machine once it has been accessed (and allocated) to the assigned virtual machine. Furthermore, VMware's advanced memory technologies, like idle page reclamation, do not reclaim idle pages that are part of a reservation. The memory is available for use only by the virtual machine to which it was assigned and reserved.

Figure 12.2: You can set reservations on CPU or memory on the Resources tab of the Virtual Machine Properties window.

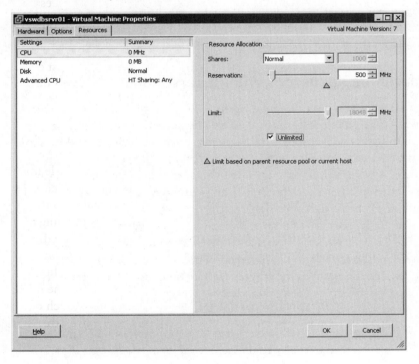

As you can see, CPU reservations and memory reservations work very differently. Given the different nature of these resources, however, these behaviors make sense. When you are setting reservations on virtual machines, be sure to reserve only enough resources to guarantee a minimum level of performance. Otherwise, you run the risk of preventing other virtual machines from starting up or operating properly due to a lack of unreserved capacity.

NOTE   When you power on a virtual machine, that virtual machine will only power on if there are enough unreserved resources—both CPU and memory—available to satisfy the reservations on that virtual machine.

To assign a CPU or memory reservation to a virtual machine, follow these steps:

1. In vSphere Client, right-click on the virtual machine to which you wish to add the reservation and select Edit Settings.

2. In the Virtual Machine Properties window, select the Resources tab.

3. To assign a CPU reservation, select CPU from the list of resources on the left and specify a reservation, in MHz, on the right.

    To assign a memory reservation, select Memory from the list of resources on the left, and then specify a reservation (in MB) on the right.

4. Click OK to save the settings and close the Virtual Machine Properties window.

Looking back at Figure 12.2, you'll note a small orange triangle that indicates the maximum amount of a resource that may be specified in a reservation. This limit is derived from the resources available to that virtual machine based on the ESX/ESXi host on which it is running or the resource pool in which it has been placed. Resource pools are discussed in the "Use Resource Pools" section later in this chapter.

While reservations are useful, you need more than just the ability to guarantee minimum levels of resources to virtual machines. At the other end of the spectrum, you also need to be able to control how much of a certain resource can be consumed by a virtual machine. VMware vSphere provides limits to accomplish this task.

Constrain Resource Usage with Limits

There might be situations in which you need to constrain, or limit, the amount of a particular resource that is consumed by the virtual machine. For example, you might want to limit how much CPU time a virtual machine uses, or limit how much memory a virtual machine is allowed to use. The *limits* functionality within VMware vSphere provides this ability. By default, VMware vSphere sets the limits for CPU and memory to Unlimited; that is, there is no artificial limit.

> **NOTE**   Clearly, a virtual machine does have limits to its computing power or memory. These limits are specified by the configuration of the virtual machine itself. For example, a virtual machine specified with 1 virtual CPU (vCPU) can never use more than 1 logical CPU (core or thread) at a time. Similarly, a virtual machine configured with 1GB of RAM can never address more than 1GB of RAM at a time. Because a virtual machine already has "built-in" limits, many vSphere administrators do not use the limits functionality to constrain resource usage.

As with reservations, limits are specified on the Resources tab of the Virtual Machine Properties window. Figure 12.3 shows a virtual machine with a CPU limit of 1200MHz assigned.

Figure 12.3: Assigning a limit prevents the virtual machine from ever using more of that resource than is specified in the limit.

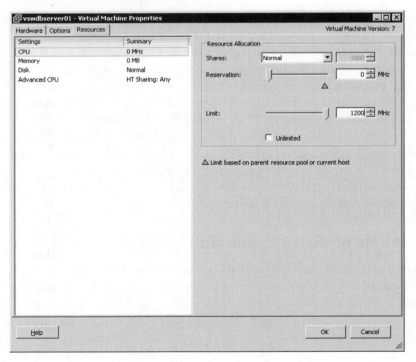

As with reservations, CPU limits and memory limits behave differently:

- With a CPU limit, the ESX/ESXi hypervisor simply does not allow the VM to use more CPU cycles than specified in the limit. Because the hypervisor controls the scheduling of VMs onto logical CPU cores, it is easy to enforce a CPU limit by simply not scheduling the VM onto an available logical CPU core.

- With a memory limit, the hypervisor uses the balloon driver—a guest OS–specific driver installed with the VMware Tools—to control guest OS memory usage. As the guest OS memory usage approaches the limit, the balloon driver starts to "inflate," or request memory from the guest OS. The balloon driver takes the memory assigned to it by the guest OS and passes that memory back to the hypervisor for use by other virtual machines or the hypervisor itself. As guest OS memory usage decreases and falls below the limit, the balloon will "deflate," or return memory to the guest operating system. In this manner, the memory usage of the guest OS within the virtual machine is kept below the specified limit.

NOTE   If the VMware Tools are not installed, VMware vSphere can still enforce the memory limit. Instead of using the balloon driver to control guest OS memory usage, the hypervisor will forcefully swap virtual machine memory pages out to the VMkernel swap file when the memory limit is reached. Because this has a dramatic impact on performance—disk access is many thousands of times slower than memory access—use limits carefully on VMs that do not have VMware Tools installed, or ensure that you have the VMware Tools installed on all VMs.

It's important to understand that you should use limits carefully. VMware ESX/ESXi will not allow access to resources controlled by limits, even when those resources are underutilized. Improper use of limits can significantly impair the performance of the virtual machines and the operating systems and applications running in them.

To specify a CPU or memory limit for a virtual machine, follow these steps:

1. In vSphere Client, right-click on the virtual machine to which you wish to assign a CPU or memory limit.

Configuring Your
vSphere Environment

PART II

2. Select Edit Settings from the context menu.

3. In the Virtual Machine Properties dialog box, click the Resources tab.

4. If you wish to set a CPU limit, select CPU from the list of resources on the left. Then deselect the Unlimited check box and specify a CPU limit in MHz.

   To set a memory limit, select Memory from the list of resources on the left. Deselect the Unlimited check box and specify a memory limit in MB.

5. Click OK to save the changes and return to vSphere Client.

Once the limit is set, the limit is enforced as we described earlier, depending on whether it is a CPU limit or a memory limit.

As you've seen so far, both reservations and limits are absolute values—you can guarantee at least 2400MHz of CPU capacity or limit memory usage to 512MB of RAM, for example. These controls are in effect at all times, whether the ESX/ESXi host on which the virtual machine is running has plenty of resources to allocate or is running low on resources. There is another control to modify resource allocation that takes effect only during times of resource contention. Shares are a way for you to adjust resource allocation behavior only when resources are constrained.

Control Resource Allocation Using Shares

The previous three sections discussed how to use the VM configuration, reservations, and limits to control resource allocation for individual virtual machines. In all three instances, these controls are effective when the ESX/ESXi host has plenty of resources as well as when the ESX/ESXi host is running low on one or more of these resources (i.e., is resource constrained). The last way of affecting resource allocation is through the use of *shares*. This control, unlike the other three controls, is only effective during times of resource constraint. Shares do not impact the resource allocation behaviors of a host when the host is not running low on a particular resource!

Shares allow you to control the proportions of resources that are allocated to virtual machines when those resources are in contention. These proportions are calculated by comparing the number of shares assigned to the specific virtual machine to the total number of shares assigned overall. Consider an ESX/ESXi host with five virtual machines and the following shares assigned:

- RedVM, 2,000 shares

- GreenVM, 2,000 shares

- BlueVM, 2,000 shares

- YellowVM, 3,000 shares

- OrangeVM, 1,000 shares

The total number of shares assigned among all these VMs is 10,000 shares. That total is compared to the number of shares assigned to each VM to determine the proportion of resources that will be granted to each VM during periods of resource contention. Table 12.1 shows the results of this example.

Table 12.1: Using Shares to Allocate Resources Proportionally

VM Name	Shares Assigned	Total Shares	Proportion of Shares
RedVM	2,000	10,000	20%
GreenVM	2,000	10,000	20%
BlueVM	2,000	10,000	20%
YellowVM	3,000	10,000	30%
OrangeVM	1,000	10,000	10%

As you can see in Table 12.1, ESX/ESXi uses the shares to determine the proportion of resources allocated to each virtual machine. Keep in mind, however, that these proportions only apply when the resources are under contention. If these shares were applied to memory and the host server was running out of memory, these shares would affect how the hypervisor allocated RAM to each of the virtual machines. If these shares were applied to memory but the ESX/ESXi host had plenty of RAM to give all the virtual machines all the memory they requested, there would be no need for shares.

Because shares work only when a resource is under contention, they are a valuable addition to the use of reservations and limits.

Reservations and limits are absolute; they don't change as the availability of resources changes, and they don't provide a way to determine how limited resources should be allocated among a group of virtual machines. Shares give vSphere administrators that flexibility.

You can assign shares on CPU, memory, and storage. When assigning shares, you can choose from three predefined selections—Low, Normal, or High—or choose Custom, which allows you to specify a custom number of shares to assign to the VM. For CPU and storage, the default setting is Normal; this translates into 1,000 shares. For memory, the default setting is also Normal, but in this case this setting is equal to ten times the assigned memory value. For a VM that is assigned 1,024MB of memory, the default number of shares for memory is 10,240.

NOTE The predefined High setting doubles the default number of CPU and memory shares; the predefined Low setting halves the default number of CPU and memory shares.

To change the number of shares assigned to a virtual machine for a particular resource, follow these steps:

1. Within vSphere Client, right-click on the virtual machine you'd like to modify and select Edit Settings.

2. Click the Resources tab.

3. From the list on the left, select the resource for which you'd like to change the number of shares assigned to the VM.

4. Change the assigned shares value to Low, Normal, or High. To set a custom value, select Custom and then specify the number of shares to be assigned for that resource to that virtual machine. Figure 12.4 shows the number of shares for CPU being set to a custom value.

5. Click OK to save the changes and return to vSphere Client.

For a quick review of the shares assigned to a virtual machine, select the virtual machine from the inventory and click the Resource Allocation tab. This tab will show you the reservation, limit, and number of shares assigned.

Figure 12.4: The Custom setting allows you to assign the number of shares for a particular resource.

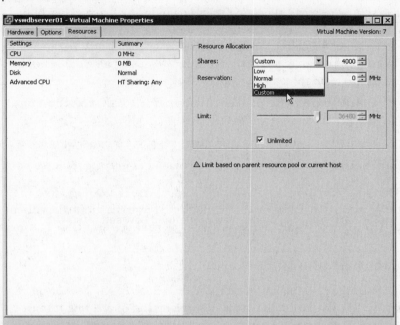

The processes and procedures discussed in this section are great for controlling resource allocation for specific virtual machines, but sometimes resource allocation needs to be controlled for groups of virtual machines. Fortunately, VMware provides the ability to perform this task using an object known as a *resource pool*. The next section discusses how to use resource pools to control resource allocation.

Use Resource Pools

The ability to fine-tune resource allocation settings within a VMware vSphere environment on a per-VM basis is useful, but what about when you want to control resource allocation for an entire group of virtual machines? Surely there has to be a better way. There is, and it's called a resource pool.

Configuring Your
vSphere Environment

PART II

Resource pools allow administrators to set resource allocation settings for CPU and memory for multiple virtual machines at the same time. Unlike setting resource allocation values on individual virtual machines, using resource allocation settings with resource pools only allows you to adjust CPU and memory; you cannot set storage shares on a resource pool.

To control resource usage for multiple VMs using a resource pool, you must perform three basic steps:

1. Create the resource pool on the appropriate ESX/ESXi host or cluster.

2. Assign the desired CPU or memory resource usage settings.

3. Use drag-and-drop to put virtual machines into the resource pool.

The last step, using drag-and-drop to put virtual machines into the resource pool, is straightforward enough that it needs no further discussion. The other two steps are covered in the next few sections.

Create a Resource Pool

You can create resource pools on individual ESX/ESXi hosts or on clusters of ESX/ESXi hosts. You also have the option of creating resource pools inside other resource pools. Resource pools created within a cluster are also called *parent resource pools*; when created inside another resource pool, they are called *child resource pools*. In any case, the process for creating a resource pool is the same.

To create a resource pool, follow these steps:

1. In the Hosts And Clusters inventory view of vSphere Client, right-click on a host, cluster, or existing resource pool and select New Resource Pool.

2. Specify a name for the resource pool.

3. In the CPU Resources section, specify the settings for how CPU resources should be handled for virtual machines within this pool. More details on how these settings work is provided in the next section, "Control CPU Allocation with a Resource Pool."

4. In the Memory Resources section, specify the settings for how memory resources should be allocated for virtual machines in this pool. The next section also provides more information on how these controls work.

5. Click OK to create the resource pool and return to vSphere Client.

Now that the resource pool has been created, you can adjust the settings of the resource pool to modify how ESX/ESXi will allocate resources to virtual machines located in that resource pool.

The next two sections provide more details on the specific settings for controlling CPU and memory usage with resource pools.

Control CPU Allocation with a Resource Pool

By using a combination of reservations, limits, and shares on a resource pool, you can control CPU allocation for all the virtual machines within a resource pool.

Use CPU Reservations with a Resource Pool

To guarantee a minimum amount of CPU resources for a resource pool, specify a CPU reservation. The amount of the reservation, specified in megahertz (MHz) as with individual virtual machines, is guaranteed for use by *all* the virtual machines in the resource pool. This is not a reservation for each VM in the resource pool, but rather a reservation for all the VMs as a group.

Within the resource pool, you might wish to assign CPU reservations to individual virtual machines. This configuration is fully supported, but behaves a bit differently than you might expect. The key to understanding how resource pool reservations and VM reservations interact is found in the Expandable Reservation option, as shown in Figure 12.5.

Figure 12.5: The Expandable Reservation option allows a resource pool to borrow resources from its parent container.

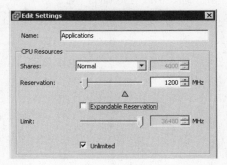

When Expandable Reservation is unchecked, as it is in Figure 12.5, the resource pool has a finite amount of CPU resources that can, in turn, be reserved by virtual machines within the resource pool. In the

Configuring Your
vSphere Environment

PART II

figure, the resource pool has a nonexpandable reservation of 1200MHz. This means that you can assign up to 1200MHz of reservations to individual virtual machines within the resource pool. When you attempt to reserve more than 1200MHz by individual virtual machines in the resource pool, that attempt will fail. Note that this is not a limit on how many CPU cycles the resource pool or its member VMs can *use*, but rather a limit on how many CPU cycles member VMs can *reserve*.

If, on the other hand, the Expandable Reservation option is checked, the resource pool is permitted to "borrow" resources from its parent container. Again, this "borrowing" only pertains to individual VM reservations and does not affect CPU limits. The parent container of the resource pool depends on where it was created:

- The parent of a resource pool created on an individual ESX/ESXi host is the host itself.

- The parent of a resource pool created on a cluster is the cluster.

- The parent of a resource pool created inside another resource pool is the containing resource pool.

Figure 12.6 graphically illustrates the relationships between clusters, ESX/ESXi hosts, and resource pools with regard to how resources might be borrowed from a parent container with expandable reservations.

Figure 12.6: Expandable reservations allow objects to borrow resources from their parent object.

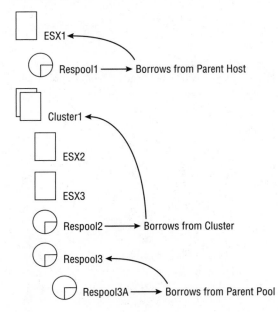

The default setting on a new resource pool is an expandable reservation of 0MHz, which means you will be able to reserve CPU resources borrowed from the parent object, up to the maximum available in the parent host, cluster, or resource pool.

Follow these steps to assign a CPU reservation to a resource pool:

1. Within the Hosts And Clusters inventory view of vSphere Client, right-click on the resource pool to which you want to assign a CPU reservation.

2. Select Edit Settings.

3. Specify a value, in MHz, that you want reserved for the resource pool and its member VMs.

4. Uncheck the Expandable Reservation box if you want to limit the CPU reservations by member VMs to the amount assigned to the resource pool itself.

5. Click OK to save the changes and return to vSphere Client.

Of course, CPU reservations are only one way to adjust resource allocation. You can also use CPU limits with a resource pool to ensure that the resource pool does not consume more than a specified amount of CPU time.

Use CPU Limits with a Resource Pool

In addition to using CPU reservations with resource pools, you have the option of using CPU limits with resource pools. Figure 12.7 shows an example of a resource pool with a limit specified.

Figure 12.7: Setting a CPU limit prevents the resource pool and its member VMs from using more than the specified amount of CPU resources.

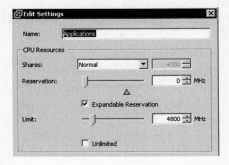

Configuring Your
vSphere Environment

PART II

CPU limits function in much the same way when used on a resource pool as when used on a virtual machine. Of course, the key difference is that the limit applies to all the virtual machines in the resource pool rather than a single virtual machine.

To set a CPU limit for a resource pool, perform these steps:

1. Within the Hosts And Clusters inventory view of vSphere Client, right-click on the resource pool to which you want to assign a CPU limit.

2. Select Edit Settings.

3. Deselect the Unlimited check box.

4. Specify a limit, in megahertz (MHz), to which the resource pool should be constrained.

5. Click OK to return to vSphere Client.

The maximum that you can specify as the limit for a resource pool created on an ESX/ESXi host is the capacity of the host itself. Similarly, the maximum limit that you can specify for a resource pool created on a cluster is the aggregate capacity of the cluster. For a child resource pool—that is, a resource pool created within another resource pool—the maximum amount that can be specified for the limit is whatever limit is applied to the parent. For example, if a resource pool has a limit of 4800MHz, any child pools within that parent pool cannot have a limit set greater than 4800MHz.

In addition to CPU reservations and CPU limits, you can use CPU shares with a resource pool. The next section describes that functionality.

Use CPU Shares with a Resource Pool

Using shares with a resource pool allows you to specify the priority of the resource pool for access to resources. This priority is relative to other resource pools or virtual machines in the same parent container—that is, on the same ESX/ESXi host, in the same cluster, or in the same parent resource pool. Assigning shares to a resource pool does not affect the priority of virtual machines within the resource pool relative to each other; the shares assigned to each individual virtual machine in the resource pool determine that priority.

Figure 12.8 helps to illustrate this point. In the illustration, there are two resource pools—Green and Blue. Green has 2,000 shares assigned, and Blue has 1,000 shares assigned. When resources are allocated between the two resource pools, Green will receive approximately two-thirds of the resources and Blue will receive approximately one-third of the resources. Thus, the shares assigned to the resource pools only establish priority relative to each other. Within the Green resource pool, the VMs have equal priority relative to each other, but within the Blue resource pool VM3 has double the priority relative to VM4. The shares assigned to the pools have no impact on determining the priority of the VMs.

Figure 12.8: Shares only establish priority relative to other objects at the same level in the hierarchy.

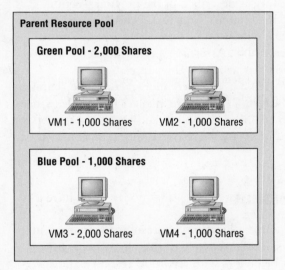

To assign shares to a resource pool to control CPU usage relative to other peer resource pools, follow these steps:

1. In the Hosts And Clusters inventory view of vSphere Client, right click on the resource pool you want to modify.

2. Select Edit Settings.

3. From the Shares drop-down list, select Low, Normal, High, or Custom.

4. If you selected Custom, specify a custom number of shares to assign to the selected resource pool.

5. Click OK to return to vSphere Client.

You must be careful to understand the cascading effect of using shares on both the resource pools and the virtual machines within them. Otherwise, virtual machines could end up getting drastically lower priority to resources than expected. This is true not only for CPU resources, but also for memory resources, as described in the next section.

Control Memory Allocation with a Resource Pool

In all cases, using a reservation, limit, or shares on a resource pool to control memory allocation for the virtual machines in this resource pool behaves the same way as it does for CPU resources. You will assign these controls in the same way as described in the previous section. Refer to the procedures in the section "Control CPU Allocation with a Resource Pool" for specific details on how to assign a reservation, limit, or shares on a resource pool. Assigning any of these controls for memory is done in the same way as for CPU resources.

Controlling resource allocation using reservations, limits, and shares is only part of the picture. The rest of the picture involves being able to identify when hosts or virtual machines are resource constrained so that, as an administrator, you know when to use the resource allocation controls.

Monitor Performance

There's another side to resource allocation and resource management, and that's the monitoring side. It's not enough for you to know how to adjust vSphere's default behaviors with regard to resource allocation; you also need to know how to identify when virtual machines aren't getting the resources they need. Once you've identified a virtual machine that isn't getting enough resources, you can use the settings outlined earlier in this chapter to adjust how resources are allocated to that virtual machine.

Although other resources exist that could become bottlenecks—consider storage, for example—this section focuses on only two major resources: CPU and RAM.

Identify a Resource-Constrained ESX/ESXi Host

So how do you identify when an ESX/ESXi host is CPU- or memory-constrained? In this case, making the identification is reasonably simple.

Rectifying the problem, however, might be a bit more complicated, depending on the environment.

vSphere Client provides a Performance tab when an ESX/ESXi host is selected in the Hosts And Clusters inventory view. This Performance tab provides performance graphs and statistics on the ESX/ESXi host. These performance graphs and statistics make it easy to identify when an ESX/ESXi host is resource constrained.

Figure 12.9 shows the default view on the Performance tab for an ESX/ESXi host. In this particular example, the host is quite clearly not CPU constrained. The memory graphs aren't visible in this example, so it's not possible to tell whether the host is RAM constrained.

Figure 12.9: The Performance tab provides enough information to identify whether an ESX/ESXi host is resource constrained.

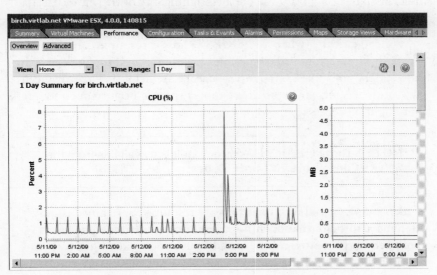

The Performance tab within vCenter Server provides the majority of the information you need to identify when an ESX/ESXi host is resource constrained. Table 12.2 provides more information on where you should look in vSphere Client to find information on ESX/ESXi host resource constraints.

Table 12.2: Identifying Resource Constraints in vCenter Server

To Identify ESX/ESXi Constraints for This Resource...	...Look in This Area of vCenter Server
CPU	Summary Tab > Resources Pane > CPU Usage Performance Tab > Overview > CPU (%) Performance Tab > Overview > CPU (MHz)
Memory	Summary Tab > Resources Pane > Memory Usage Performance Tab > Overview > Memory (MB) Performance Tab > Overview > Memory (MBps) Performance Tab > Overview > Memory (%)
Disk	Performance Tab > Overview > Disk (KBps) Performance Tab > Overview > Disk (Millisecond)
Network	Performance Tab > Overview > Network (MBps)

While identifying when an ESX/ESXi host is resource constrained is usually straightforward, sometimes you might need to dig deeper. In those cases, tools like esxtop or vm-support are helpful. The Advanced view of the Performance tab also exposes specific performance counters that might be necessary as well.

> **NOTE** The esxtop and vm-support tools are available from the Service Console of a VMware ESX host.

Identifying virtual machines that are resource constrained is quite often more difficult than identifying resource-constrained hosts, as explained in the next section.

Identify a Resource-Constrained Virtual Machine

All too often, administrators trying to diagnose a performance problem within a guest operating system running in a virtual machine on VMware ESX/ESXi make the mistake of using guest OS–native tools to determine resource utilization. For example, a Windows administrator might use Performance Monitor or Task Manager to observe memory or CPU utilization of a Windows Server–based virtual machine, or a Linux administrator might use top to observe resource usage on a Linux-based virtual machine. Unfortunately, while these tools are familiar, they don't provide the whole picture. Can you guess why these tools won't provide the right information?

Guest OS–native tools are only able to report on the usage of what the ESX/ESXi hypervisor *allocates to the guest*, not what is *actually available on the host*. This is a key distinction that's important for all vSphere administrators to understand. The resources that the guest OS sees are only those resources allocated to it, not the full resources actually available on the host. So, when a guest OS reports 100 percent CPU usage, that doesn't mean the host is CPU constrained. It only means that the guest OS is using 100 percent of the cycles given to it by the hypervisor. What if the hypervisor is only giving that VM 10 percent of its available cycles because of limits or shares? Using only guest OS–native tools would provide only part of the picture. To effectively diagnose resource-related issues with a virtual machine, you must use tools both inside and outside the virtual machine.

The next two sections describe how to use tools both inside and outside the guest OS to help identify when a virtual machine might be CPU- or RAM-constrained.

Identify a CPU-Constrained VM

As mentioned earlier, vSphere administrators attempting to identify whether a VM is CPU constrained should start by looking both *inside* and *outside* the guest operating system. From inside the guest operating system, use guest OS–native tools to determine current CPU usage. From outside the guest operating system, use vCenter Server's performance-monitoring tools to determine both how much the VM is being granted as well as how much the VM is actually using.

> **NOTE** The performance graphs within vSphere Client are available in environments that are not using vCenter Server. Just connect vSphere Client directly to an ESX/ESXi host to view performance information.

Here are two common scenarios that arise when evaluating CPU usage in a VMware vSphere environment:

The guest OS shows high CPU usage, but the ESX/ESXi host has plenty of spare CPU capacity. In this situation, the guest OS in the virtual machine is using all the CPU cycles granted to it by the hypervisor. If application performance within the virtual machine is not at acceptable levels, then ensure that no limits have been placed on the virtual machine or the resource pool(s) in which this virtual machine resides. Adding a second CPU might help performance, if the applications within the virtual machine are sufficiently multi-threaded to take advantage of the extra processing power. If not, migrating the virtual machine to an ESX/ESXi host with faster CPU cores might help improve performance.

The guest OS shows high CPU usage, and the ESX/ESXi host's CPU utilization is also very high. In this case, the VM needs lots of CPU cycles, but the ESX/ESXi host is already heavily loaded. If application performance is acceptable, no further changes are needed; otherwise, you should also check the CPU Ready counter (available in esxtop or the Advanced view of the Performance tab in vSphere Client) to determine if the guest OS is using all the cycles it can get or if it is waiting on cycles from the host. A high CPU Ready counter would indicate that the guest OS in the virtual machine would use more CPU cycles if they were made available. In this case, using shares to grant this virtual machine higher-priority access to CPU resources might correct the performance issue. Adding a second virtual CPU might not help, as the ESX/ESXi host still might not have enough cycles to provide, and the application has to be sufficiently multithreaded as to be able to take advantage of the additional CPU core. Migrating this VM to a less heavily loaded host might also help. Alternately, you can migrate other workloads to other hosts in order to free up resources for this virtual machine. If VMware DRS is enabled and configured for fully automatic operation, this process would be handled without administrator intervention.

Many of these same techniques apply when diagnosing a virtual machine that is thought to be RAM (memory) constrained, as you'll learn next.

Identify a RAM-Constrained VM

Much in the same way as you would look both inside and outside the virtual machine to determine CPU contention, counters and information from both sides are necessary to help identify a RAM-constrained virtual machine.

Here are two common scenarios that you will encounter when dealing with memory contention issues:

The guest OS reports high memory usage, but the ESX/ESXi host shows plenty of memory capacity. In this instance, the guest operating system is using all the memory given to it by the hypervisor. If the hypervisor is not showing signs of memory pressure, adding memory to the virtual machine might resolve the issue. Also be sure that no memory limits have been applied to the virtual machine or the resource pool(s) in which the virtual machine resides. If limits have been applied, removing them might help resolve the issue and relieve memory pressure within the guest operating system.

The guest OS reports high memory usage, and the ESX/ESXi host's memory utilization is also high. When both the guest OS and the ESX/ESXi host are reporting high memory usage, identifying the real source of the problem is a bit more difficult. Adding memory won't fix the problem, as the host is also running low on memory. In this case, review reservations to ensure that memory has not been needlessly allocated in memory reservations. Recall that with memory reservations, once the guest OS has accessed reserved memory, that reserved memory is never reclaimed by the hypervisor for other purposes. This could lead to a high memory usage situation where some machines are being starved for memory. The Memory Swap Used (Average) counter, available in the Advanced view of the Performance tab, will provide a reasonably good idea of whether the ESX/ESXi host is actually under memory pressure. If the host is indeed under memory pressure and all other measures have been taken, you must migrate VMs to other hosts and/or add memory to the host in order to alleviate the problem.

Configuring Your
vSphere Environment

PART II

APPENDIX

Fundamentals of the Command-Line Interface

IN THIS APPENDIX, YOU WILL LEARN TO:

B eing able to use the command-line interface (CLI) provided by VMware ESX and the vSphere Management Assistant (vMA) is an important skill for all VMware vSphere administrators. The fundamental, frequently used commands described in this appendix focus on basic proficiency, such as navigating around the VMware ESX Service Console; using the esxcfg-* and vicfg-* commands; and managing files and directories.

Navigate and Gather Information Through the Service Console

First and foremost, getting around the ESX Service Console is a critical skill for troubleshooting and managing ESX hosts when the traditional graphical tools are not available. The following commands are some of the common and basic commands for moving around a Linux-based operating system and gathering fundamental bits of information. In all the examples listed here, the hash sign (#) represents the shell prompt.

cd

Used to change directories.

Example: # cd /vmfs/volumes

ifconfig

Used to obtain information about network interfaces. Use the –a parameter to show all network interfaces.

logout

Used to log out the current user.

ls

Used to list files and folders in the current directory.

Example: # ls

ls -l

Used to list files and folders in a long format with rights and owners.

ls -R

Used to list files and folders with the ability to scroll.

ls -s

Used to list files and folders in a short format.

passwd

Used to update a user account password.

Example: # passwd newaccount

pwd

Used to show the full path of the current directory.

Example: # pwd

reboot

Used to reboot a system.

useradd

Used to add a new user.

Example 1: # useradd newaccount

Example 2: # ifconfig -a

whoami

Used to identify the effective user.

who am i

Used to identify the currently logged-on user.

Manage Directories, Files, and Disks in the Service Console

Without a graphical interface available, you will have to use the ESX CLI to create, manage, and delete files and directories. The following commands provide basic instruction on moving, copying, creating, and deleting files and directories. In all these examples, the hash sign (#) represents the shell prompt.

cp

Used to copy directories or files. You can rename a file during the copy process. Use the -f parameter to force the copy, the -p parameter to preserve the permissions, and the -R parameter to recursively copy all subdirectories. The cp command defaults to interactive mode (equal to cp -i), which confirms each operation.

Example 1: # cp file1 /newdocs/file1

Example 2: # cp file1 /newdocs/file2

fdisk

Used to manage disk partitions.

mount

Used to mount CD-ROM or floppy drives.

Example: # mount /mnt/cdrom

mv

Used to move or rename files. By default, mv defaults to an interactive setting (equal to mv -i), which confirms each operation.

Example 1: # mv oldfile newfile

Example 2: # mv file1 /newfolder/file1

rm

Used to remove files and directories. Use the -f parameter to force the removal, and the -R parameter to recursively delete. As with cp and mv, rm defaults to an interactive mode (equal to using rm -i).

Example: # rm -f /olddirectory

rmdir

Used to remove empty directories.

Example: # `rmdir`

touch

Used to create a new file or change file access and modification time.

Example: # `touch mynewfile.txt`

Use the *esxcfg* Commands

In addition to the standard Linux commands we've covered so far, VMware has implemented a specific set of commands directed toward ESX-specific tasks. The following list of commands shows how to manage various components of the ESX host configuration. Again, the hash sign (#) represents the shell prompt.

esxcfg-auth

Used to configure an ESX Server host to support network-based authentication methods. One such authentication method is Active Directory. When used to configure Active Directory authentication, this command uses the following parameters:

`--enablead` to configure the Service Console for AD authentication

`--addomain` to set the domain the Service Console will authenticate against

`--addc` to set the domain controller to authenticate against for AD authentication

`--usecrack` to enable the `pam_cracklib` library for managing password complexity

Example: # `esxcfg-auth --enablead --addomain vmwarelab.net --addc vmwarelab.net`

esxcfg-firewall

Used to query, enable, and disable services on the Service Console firewall. The following parameters are commonly used:

-q to query the current firewall settings

-q servicename to query the status of a specific service

-q incoming/outgoing to query the status of incoming and outgoing ports

--blockIncoming to block all incoming connections on ports not required for system function

--blockOutgoing to block all outgoing connections on ports not required for system function

--allowIncoming to allow incoming connections on all ports

--allowOutgoing to allow outgoing connections on all ports

--e servicename to enable a specific service

--d servicename to disable a specific service

Example: # esxcfg-firewall -e swISCSIClient

esxcfg-info

Used to review the hardware information for the Service Console and VMkernel. Some of the supported parameters include:

-w to print hardware information

-s to print storage and disk information

-n to print network information

Example: # esxcfg-info -s

esxcfg-mpath

Used to view and configure the multipathing settings for an ESX host's Fibre Channel or iSCSI storage devices. Some frequently used parameters include:

-l to list all paths with their detailed information

-L to list all paths in compact form

-b to list all devices with their paths

-P to define a path to operate on

-s with active or off to enable or disable a specific path

Example: # esxcfg-mpath -L

esxcfg-nas

Used to configure network-attached storage (NAS) file systems on an ESX host.

-l to list all NAS

-a to add a new NAS datastore on a specified host

-o to provide the name of the NAS host

-s to provide the name of the NAS share

-d to delete a NAS datastore

Example: # esxcfg-nas –a –o 192.168.31.10 –s /vol/isoimages DatastoreName

esxcfg-nics

Used to obtain information about and configure the physical network adapters installed in an ESX host.

-l to list all the installed NICs and their settings

-s to set the speed of a card to 10, 100, 1000, or 10000

-d to set the duplex to half or full

Example: # esxcfg-nics –s 1000 vmnic5

esxcfg-route

Used to configure the VMkernel routing table.

-a to add a route to the VMkernel

-d to delete a route from the VMkernel

-l to list routes configured in the VMkernel

Example: # esxcfg-route –a 192.168.31.0/24 192.168.31.254

esxcfg-swiscsi

Used to configure the software iSCSI initiator in an ESX host.

-e to enable software iSCSI

-d to disable software iSCSI

-q to query if software iSCSI is enabled

-s to scan for new LUNs using software iSCSI

Example: # `esxcfg-swiscsi -q`

esxcfg-vmknic

Used to configure the VMkernel NIC. You must already have a port group created to which the VMkernel NIC is attached or will be attached.

-a to add a VMkernel port group

-d to delete a VMkernel

-e to enable the VMkernel NIC

-D to disable the VMkernel port

-i to set the IP address of the VMkernel NIC

-n to set the network mask for the IP of the call

Example: # `esxcfg-vmknic -a -i 192.168.28.105 -n 255.255.255.0 PortGroupName`

esxcfg-volume

Used to work with Virtual Machine File System (VMFS) volumes.

-l to list volumes detected as snapshots/replicas

-m to mount a snapshot/replica volume if the original copy is not online

-r to resignature a snapshot/replica volume

Example: # `esxcfg-volume -l`

esxcfg-vswif

Used to set the parameters of the Service Console network interface. You must already have a port group created to which the Service Console interface is attached or will be attached.

-a to add a Service Console NIC (this option is predicated on having IP information and port group names)

-d to delete the Service Console NIC

-e to enable the Service Console NIC

-D to disable the Service Console NIC

-p to set the port group name for the Service Console NIC

-i to set the IP address to be used for the Service Console NIC

-n to set the network mask for the Service Console NIC

Example: # esxcfg-vswif -a -i 192.168.29.150 -n 255.255.255.0 -p ServiceConsole2 vswif1

esxcfg-vswitch

Used to add, remove, or modify a virtual switch. Limited operations are available for vNetwork Distributed Switches.

-a to add a new virtual switch

-d to delete a new virtual switch

-l to list all existing virtual switches

-L to link a physical network adapter as an uplink

-U to unlink a network adapter currently connected as an uplink

-v to set the VLAN ID for a port group

-A to add a new port group

-D to delete a port group

-C to query for the existence of a port group name

Example: # esxcfg-vswitch -v 2 -p VLAN2-Production vSwitch1

Use the *vicfg* Commands

The lack of a Service Console in ESXi has driven the development of a set of remote command-line utilities. In VMware vSphere, the vMA provides a set of commands similar to the esxcfg commands but designed to work remotely with ESXi hosts. These commands are the vicfg commands.

vicfg-mpath

Used to manipulate multipathing.

--help to display help text

-d or --device to filter list commands to display only a specific device

-l or --list to list all paths with their detailed information

-L or --list-compact to list all paths in compact form

-b or --list-paths to list all devices with their paths

-P or --path to define a path to operate on

-s or --state with active or off to enable or disable a specific path. Requires a path with --path.

Example: # vicfg-mpath --list-compact --vihost esx01.vmwarelab.net

vicfg-nas

Used to manipulate NAS/NFS datastores.

--add or -a to add a new NAS file system

--delete or -d to delete a NAS file system

--help to display help text

--nasserver or -o followed by <*n_host*> to add the hostname of the new NAS file system

--share or -s used with -a to provide the name of the directory that is exported on the NAS device

--vihost or -h followed by <*host*> to direct the command to a particular ESX/ESXi host

Example: # vicfg-nas --delete nfsvolume --vihost esx01.vmwarelab.net

vicfg-nics

Used to report on and manage physical network adapters.

`--help` to display help text

`--auto` or `-a` to set the given adapter to autonegotiate the speed and duplex settings

`--duplex` or `-d` followed by [`full` | `half`] `<nic>` to set the duplex value for a given NIC

`--speed` or `-s` followed by `<speed>` `<nic>` to set the speed value for a given NIC

`--list` or `-l` to list the physical adapters in the system

`--vihost` or `-h` followed by `<host>` to direct the command to a particular ESX/ESXi host

Example: # `vicfg-nics --speed 1000 vmnic0 --vihost esx01 .vmwarelab.net`

vicfg-ntp

Used to configure NTP settings.

`--help` to display help text

`--add` or `-a` followed by `<server>` to add an NTP server

`--delete` or `-d` followed by `<server>` to delete an NTP server

`--list` or `-l` to list the configured NTP servers

`--vihost` or `-h` followed by `<host>` to direct the command to a particular ESX Server host

Example: # `vicfg-ntp --add 0.us.pool.ntp.org --vihost esx01. vmwarelab.net`

vicfg-rescan

Used to perform a rescan for discovering new LUNs.

`--help` to display help text

`--vihost` or `-h` followed by `<host>` to direct the command to a particular ESX/ESXi host

`<VMkernel_SCSI_adapter_name>` to provide the name of the adapter to rescan (i.e., vmhba1)

Example: # `vicfg-rescan --vihost esx01.vmwarelab.net vmhba1`

vicfg-route

Used to configure the routing table for the VMkernel.

--help to display help text

-add or -a to add a route to the VMkernel

-del or -d to delete a route from the VMkernel

-list or -l to list routes configured in the VMkernel

--vihost or -h followed by *<host>* to direct the command to a particular ESX/ESXi host

Example: # vicfg-route --add 192.168.31.0/24 192.168.31.254 --vihost esx01.vmwarelab.net

vicfg-vmknic

Used to configure virtual network adapters.

--help to display help text

--add or -a to add a virtual network adapter to the system (an IP address and port group name must be specified)

--delete or -d followed by *<port_group>* to delete the virtual network adapter on the specified port group

--enable-vmotion or -e to enable VMotion on this VMkernel port

--ip or -i followed by [*<IP address>*| DHCP] to set the virtual network adapter to a given IP address or to obtain an address from a DHCP server

--list or -l to list virtual network adapters on the system

--netmask or -n followed by *<netmask>* to set the network mask for the assigned IP address

--vihost or -h followed by *<host>* to direct the command to a particular ESX/ESXi host

Example: # vicfg-vmknic --add --ip 192.168.69.100 --netmask 255.255.255.0 --portgroup VMotion --vihost esx01.vmwarelab.net

vicfg-vswitch

Used to configure virtual switches.

--help to display help text

--add or -a followed by *<vswitch_name>* to add a new virtual switch

--add-pg or -A followed by *<portgroup> <switch>* to add a port group to the specified switch

--check or -c followed by *<virtual_switch>* to check for the existence of a virtual switch

--check-pg or -C followed by *<port_group>* to check for the existence of a port group

--delete or -d followed by *<vswitch_name>* to delete the specified virtual switch (this command will not work if any of the virtual switch ports are in use)

--del-pg or -D followed by *<portgroup>* to delete the specified port group (this command will not work if the port group is in use)

--link or -L followed by *<pnic>* to add a physical adapter to a virtual switch

--list or -l to list all virtual switches and port groups

--mtu or -m to set the maximum transmission unit (MTU) of the virtual switch

--pg or -p followed by *<port_group>* to provide the name of a port group when using the --vlan option (use the *ALL* parameter to set VLAN IDs on all port groups of a virtual switch)

--vlan or -v to set the VLAN ID for a specific port group (using the parameter 0 disables all VLAN IDs; using --vlan requires the --pg option)

--vihost or -h followed by *<host>* to direct the command to a particular ESX/ESXi host

Example: # `vicfg-vswitch -A VLAN31-Finance vSwitch2 --vihost esx01.vmwarelab.net`

vifp

Used to manipulate servers in FastPass. FastPass streamlines the authentication process when using vMA and remote commands.

addserver followed by *<host>* to add a server to FastPass

listservers to list the servers current in FastPass

removeserver followed by *<host>* to remove a server from FastPass

Example: # `vifp addserver esx01.vmwarelab.net`

vifpinit

Used to initialize FastPass.

Example: # `vifpinit esx01.vmwarelab.net`

Index

W